SYNDICATE
Abroad

SYNDICATE
Abroad

Hank Messick

COMMONWEALTH BOOK COMPANY
St. Martin, Ohio

COMMONWEALTH BOOK COMPANY
St. Martin, Ohio

To Bob (the Needle) Peloquin
Who Reaps as Well as Sews

HANK MESSICK (1922-1999) was born in Happy Valley, NC, and educated at the University of North Carolina and the University of Iowa. He began his investigative journalism career in western North Carolina and in 1956 began working at the *Louisville Courier-Journal*, Kentucky's largest newspaper. For the next several years Hank investigated and reported on the Newport, Kentucky, vice industry. He later worked for the *Miami Herald* and the *Boston Traveler*, also investigating organized crime and corruption in those communities. After 1967 he wrote full time, authoring 19 books, mostly about organized crime and its influences in American life.

Hank Messick with wife Faye celebrating their 14th wedding anniversary at the Beverly Hills Country Club, Southgate, KY, June 9, 1961.

Contents

At one stage we began to wonder whether the name of Meyer Lansky was not some vast journalistic piece of fiction, so ghostly and mythical a figure did he appear.

ROYAL COMMISSION OF INQUIRY, 1967

Prologue:
Command Decision

NEW YEAR'S EVE in Havana and two "high rollers" prepared to quit the game.

General Fulgencio Batista y Zaldívar and Maier Suchowljansky —better known as Meyer Lansky—possessed an active sense of realism. International gangsters of long standing, both had surrendered power before only to rebuild as the vagaries of man's ignorance created new opportunities.

It was a warm night as 1958 died, and cloudless. Business boomed in a hundred brothels where virgins—real and alleged— asked top prices. Experience was a commodity also concealed in the plush casinos where syndicate technicians cleaned the suckers as they had done for decades in scores of stateside joints. In the ballrooms of plush hotels subsidized by the casinos, tourist and Cuban bureaucrat danced the old year away.

Reporters, their stories filed, joined the fun and games. *The New York Times* would be scooped by no newspaper next day for reporting:

GOVERNMENT TROOPS SUPPORTED BY TANKS AND AVIATION HAVE FORCED THE REBELS TO WITHDRAW FROM SANTA CLARA, ACCORDING TO REPORTS REACHING HAVANA TODAY.

Perhaps reporters who never learned of the relation of crime to politics back home should not be expected to recognize a similar combination in a foreign country.

For behind the official blandness things were happening. As bands in nightclubs across Havana broke into "Auld Lang Syne," President Batista began a series of telephone calls. The message to crook and crony was the same. Only those who had proven their value in the past received the warning. Presumably they might be useful in the future.

To Camp Columbia, the military fortress in the suburbs of Havana, the chosen were directed. A ten-foot-high Christmas tree still stood in the lobby of the Air Force building, and it attracted the wonder of sleepy children who might otherwise have asked why Santa Claus was fleeing by plane.

The short, stocky Batista, escorted by seven carloads of armed men, arrived about 2:30 A.M. Once again the hopeless military situation was reviewed. Contrary to the reporters' stories, the rebels were advancing, and resistance had collapsed. The decision to run was ratified. Farewells were short. Most of the men had prepared for this day by stashing their loot in Swiss banks. Within the hour planes began taking off with the world's latest—and richest—crop of refugees.

The Dominican Republic was Batista's immediate destination. His home in Daytona Beach, Florida, occupied for four years during a previous exile, was not politically practical. Since regaining power, Batista's public image had suffered. Perhaps later, when the excitement died, and new villains caught the public fancy, it would be possible to return to Florida and from that base plot a new coup in Cuba. Meanwhile, Generalissimo Rafael Trujillo offered temporary haven at a price Batista was well able to pay. Within two years El Benefactor would be dead, shot down like a dog while returning from a visit to his mistress. Unlike Batista, he proved unable to adapt to the realities of a changing situation. Long before that happened, however, Batista moved to the Madeira Islands off the northwest coast of Africa. Portuguese officials were happy to welcome the wealthy visitor.

At least one effort would be made to get Batista into Florida. Leonard Bursten of Miami Beach, a man with important friends, conceived a scheme to have Representative Abraham J. Multer (D-NY) invite the ousted dictator to testify in Washington before the House Banking and Currency Committee. The FBI investigated, and the plan was dropped. Later the Department of Justice found "no sufficient predicate for criminal prosecution."

Meanwhile, as rumors swept Havana, and dice continued to roll, some of the new refugees headed straight for Florida. Among them was Meyer Lansky. He had been an international gangster even longer than Batista but, over the years, had learned how to make himself virtually invisible. The Gold Coast, which he had looted ten years before, was still open to him as home and headquarters. It was to Broward County he flew in a chartered plane.

For the short, slender Lansky, the flight marked his second retreat from Havana. In the late Thirties he had begun building a gambling operation around the Hotel Nacional, only to have Pearl Harbor interrupt his plans. Before the war ended, Batista gambled on a free election and lost—making it impossible for his friend to resume the gambling program when peace returned. Only after Batista's second coup had the syndicate been able to pick up the pieces in Havana.

As the plane soared over the Florida Straits, Lansky wasted no time on regrets. Even yet he was not ready to write off Cuba as hopeless. Every man had his price—be it money, women, ideals—and presumably Fidel Castro was no exception. When emotions cooled, when economics became more urgent than glory—an opportunity to retrieve all or part of the situation might develop. Like Batista, Lansky believed in the Law of the Possible.

Over the decades many of Lansky's associates had died, gone to prison, or been stripped of power because they disregarded or failed to understand the Law of the Possible. The list was long: Arnold Rothstein, Dutch Schultz, Legs Diamond, Waxey Gordon, Al Capone, Frank Nitti, Lepke, Bugsy Siegel, Lucky Luciano, Mickey Cohen, Joe Adonis, Frank Costello, Longie Zwillman, and, most recently, Albert Anastasia.

Lansky had survived, and with the help of silent men around the country had built an organization that relied more on moxie than muscle, more on greed than terror. Let the Mafia boys kill each other off and attract headlines—the silent syndicate turned the bribe into a sophisticated tool that opened the doors of board rooms and brokers' offices. Members of the organization were as at home in the secret sanctums of political power as in the casinos and handbooks that supplied motive fuel.

The loss of Cuba, if confirmed by events, was annoying but not serious. Another area of operations could be found. Possibilities ranged from a drive to legalize Florida gambling—an oft-considered project—to penetration and control of existing casinos in Puerto Rico.

Illegal casino operations of any size were no longer practical in the States. Two such centers still operated—in Newport, Kentucky, and Hot Springs, Arkansas—but it was only a matter of time until public opinion forced the politicians to close them. No complicated drive by law enforcement would be necessary. Attacks of virtue on the part of politicians were becoming more frequent as the public in corrupt cities began at last to realize how it had been exploited.[1]

Luckily, opportunity stayed a long stride ahead of public indignation. Even as the old-style sin city became impractical, the jet plane opened new frontiers. The lure of the roulette wheel could be combined for the first time with the romance of white sand beaches and Caribbean sunlight and be within reach of middle-class America.

Looking backward, Lansky could draw a parallel between present potentials and past techniques. Johnny Torrio in Chicago had proved it was cheaper to buy a suburb than a city—and equally efficient. He set up brothels and gambling joints in Cicero, and the suckers came by auto from Chicago in droves. From this politically secure headquarters Capone gangsters later fought the battle of Chicago. The lesson had been applied in other areas:

---

[1] For an account of the cleanup of Newport see *Syndicate Wife*.

Newport-Cincinnati; Gretna-New Orleans; Jeffersonville-Louis-ville; Phenix City-Columbus; and even in Nevada where the "Strip" was outside the city limits of Las Vegas. Cliff Jones, that old partner in the Thunderbird, and more recently the Habana-Hilton, had taken care of that problem.

With the jet taking the place of the auto, it was cheaper and safer to buy control of an island off the continent than to attempt to operate in the States where protection on local, state, and federal levels was necessary. Only briefly during the Harding Administration had the boys hit that jackpot. Of course, as Cuba dramatically illustrated, one chanced a revolution when he went into a Latin nation. If, say, New England or even Georgia could somehow be transplanted to the Caribbean, the right combination of factors would be achieved.

Inevitably, the thought of the Bahamas came to mind. Stability existed there, by God. The Bay Street Boys, those merchant-politicians, kept the black majority under firm control. Moreover, the Bay Street Boys had a proper regard for the dollar—and a tradition of ruthlessness in its pursuit that carried back to Blackbeard.

The Bahamas were no sudden inspiration. Lansky became acquainted with them in Prohibition days when as co-boss of the Bugs and Meyer Mob he guarded booze shipments from Nassau to New York. One of the island's businessmen of that day, Roland Symonette, had come a long way since he operated the *Halcyon S* on the Nassau to Miami run. Rumor had it that when the Bahamas were given a new constitution, he would be its first premier. Even more important than Symonette, however, was Stafford Sands, the portly director of development for the islands.

In 1946, when Lansky was still debating what to do following Batista's first defeat, he had considered the Bahamas. Sands, however, had failed in a bid to get official approval for a casino system, and Lansky decided the islands were not yet ripe for development. A more immediate opportunity offered itself on the west side of the Gulf Stream. Moving into the Colonial Inn just south of Gulfstream Park, he created a plush casino complex with the aid of state and local officials.

Looking back as the plane thundered toward Florida, Lansky could believe he had been shortsighted. Under the Kefauver blight of 1950 his Broward casinos had withered and died. At the time it hadn't seemed a great loss, because Batista was back in Cuba and preparing to return to power. Now, however, he was ready to reconsider. He had watched developments on Grand Bahama Island carefully since 1955, and of late the feeling had grown that a unique opportunity existed there.

Over the busy decades Lansky had achieved wealth and power unmatched in syndicate history. What challenges remained?

Law enforcement officials were still divided in 1959 as to whether such an animal as organized crime existed. La Cosa Nostra, that vastly simplified half-truth, had not yet been invented. While some sociologists warned occasionally of the relation of crooks to politicians, no one wanted to talk of the financier as a third partner in the firm. To do so would sound un-American somehow.

Eisenhower was still President, and the McCarthy era was more than a memory.

In fairness to officials who, at best, see only a small part of the action, it should be said that the truth was so complex as to be beyond belief. Only an expert could understand the real nature of organized crime, and unfortunately the few experts were such men as Meyer Lansky.

With his great intelligence and limited appetite—to quote an official admirer—Lansky understood the importance of the episode in time when circumstances combined to supply young rebels with ample bootleg profits at the very moment bankers and businessmen were desperate for cash. As a leader of those rebels he knew how that unique opportunity had been exploited and how a steady flow of gamblers' money over the years had financed expansion until the National Syndicate controlled much of the national economy.

Long after personal ambitions were satisfied, Lansky found pleasure in operating the machinery he had helped design. It had proved flexible enough, but new tests were becoming scarce. He was fifty-six years old. There was plenty of time for quick adventures in Florida or Las Vegas, but there was only enough time for one significant campaign. Why repeat the easy conquests of the past? Why not, instead, shoot the works and go for a victory that would have meaning for the future?

Cuba had just demonstrated once more how temporary were political coups if unaccompanied by social change. Why not, therefore, utilize the vast resources of organized crime—its skills, its wealth, and if necessary its muscle—to effect the socioeconomic conquest of a nation?

As the lights of the Gold Coast began to glitter below the plane, the chairman of the board reached a decision. Regardless of what Castro might do, the Syndicate International would concentrate upon the Bahamas. Money, time, and infinite patience would be invested. Insulation, indirection, and intrigue would be employed. Man's greed would, as always, be a major ally.

Back in Havana, the news of Batista's flight spread across the sleeping city. The population reacted cautiously next morning. Hours passed before the more reckless began breaking parking meters in search of coins. When no one stopped them, the petty-cash looters turned to slot machines in the more convenient casinos. Reporters who had ignored the gangsters' role in government now tried to compensate by writing of angry mobs sacking hated casinos.

Soon Castro's advance guard restored order, and the city settled back to await the whim of its new master. It proved to be a general strike, which closed the casinos along with everything else. Later they reopened, provoking a cabinet crisis, which Castro resolved by assuming the office of premier. Months passed before Lansky finally wrote off Cuba as a lost cause and ordered his rear guard to withdraw.

Meanwhile the conquest of the Bahamas had begun. Lansky was driving a troika, confident as ever that the more successful the syndicate, the more nearly invisible he became.

To understand the campaign as it developed, it is necessary to go back in time to learn more of the forces that became involved. Very little was held back, and in this, Lansky's last hurrah, much that had been long hidden was revealed.

7

PART I BACKGROUND

1

Rise of the Syndicate

AMERICANS, uneasily sensing that organized crime is but a logical extension of their cherished free enterprise system, have stubbornly avoided learning too much about the subject. Investigators who try to dig are certain to incur the wrath of the John Birch Society, which wants you to *support your local police* regardless of how corrupt your local police may be.

Million of words have been written and spoken about crime, but there has been very little research worthy of the name. Nevertheless, law enforcement agencies on local, state, and federal levels have amassed a tremendous amount of information while investigating individual cases. Many of the answers to the problems of organized crime are buried in dusty file cabinets from coast to coast. Some day, when citizens fear gangsters more than politicians, a central agency will be created to collect and coordinate these millions of isolated facts and permit investigators for the first time to know what is going on and why. When that happens, a war on crime can begin to achieve results.

In the absence of any real understanding of the problem, certain misconceptions have been foisted on an ignorant public by officials more interested in empire-building than crime-busting. Newspapers, while occasionally living up to their traditions, have welcomed the misconceptions, because they made it possible to treat crime on a day to day basis.

Thus it was in the Depression decade following Prohibition, the emphasis was not on syndicate gangsters, who even then were consolidating their power, but upon such "public enemies" as John Dillinger, Ma Barker, and Pretty Boy Floyd. The FBI, aided by a flock of semi-official books, won great renown during this so-called "Gang era" and became so identified with crime fighting as to exclude from public consciousness such other effective federal agencies as the Secret Service or the Intelligence Division of the Internal Revenue Service.

Nevertheless, it was apparent by 1950 that despite the great work of the FBI, a lot of gangsters were operating almost openly. The Kefauver Committee in 1950–1951 dug for the first time into the compost pile of crime and politics and traced the careers of men and organizations back to Prohibition. The committee's work made it plain that crime was not the special province of any one ethnic group, although it did recognize the existence of the Mafia and called it the "cement" that binds together various syndicates.

Despite the fantastic revelations of the Kefauver Committee, and a degree of public indignation it aroused, very little was done to follow through with new legislation or new investigation in the next decade. The McClellan Committee did produce a mass of testimony that more than confirmed the findings of Kefauver, but its preoccupation with the sins of the Teamsters prevented other findings from being put into perspective. As a result, the labor movement got a lot of heat that could better have been applied to the businessmen of organized crime, who had made league with Jimmy Hoffa to exploit the pension funds of honest truckdrivers. Ironically, although Hoffa at last went to prison, many sincere liberals perferred to overlook his crimes and blame a Bobby Kennedy "vendetta" for the pursuit of Hoffa.

Uninformed liberals notwithstanding, Kennedy learned enough about what he called "the enemy within" to launch a Coordinated War on Crime when he became Attorney General in 1961. The big problem was to bring the FBI into the battle. J. Edgar Hoover had long maintained there was no syndicate, no Mafia, no organized crime. Kennedy could and did get laws passed that put the FBI into the areas of gambling and racketeering for the first time, but more was needed to get Hoover off the limb where he had roosted so long above the battle.

La Cosa Nostra was the answer.

Joe Valachi, a minor punk, was arrested and convicted by the Federal Narcotics Bureau, which had been talking about the Mafia for decades. Joe, seeking a break, began squealing. The narcotics bureau dutifully reported the development to the Organized Crime Section set up by Kennedy in the Justice Department to coordinate the work of a dozen agencies. Who had the inspiration remains a classified secret, but it was quickly decided to turn over Valachi and his tales of the old days in New York to the FBI.

Nothing that Valachi said was new except the name he gave the old "Honored Society" of the Sicilians. Yet such was public ignorance, and credulity, that La Cosa Nostra was hailed as a breakthrough in the fight against crime. The McClellan Committee, which had plowed much the same ground in 1957, cooperated in 1963 by giving Joe maximum publicity. The FBI took bows left and right for exposing the New Menace, and everything that conflicted with La Cosa Nostra as expounded by Valachi was ignored.

Five years after Valachi revealed the alleged secrets of La Cosa Nostra, organized crime was a bigger problem than ever—and even more misunderstood. Some law enforcement officials blamed various Supreme Court decisions, and others groaned about the "apathy of the public." Very few of those talking knew anything about the true nature of the problem, but so long as the public knew even less, it didn't seem to matter.

If "public apathy" was indeed a factor, it can be traced back many years. Americans, with their curious tendency to admire something big, have throughout their history found excuses for the robber barons who stole railroads or banks and condemned the small-time punk who occasionally held up the trains or robbed the banks. We dimly recognize that several big fortunes—Ford's, the Rockefellers'—were built by methods that today would be considered not only illegal but immoral. Yet we continue to admire the men who amassed those fortunes.

While admiring them, we overlook the fact that the first "gangs" of this century were, in the main, private armies of the big industrialists. Newspaper circulation wars before World War I brought together many of the toughs who later were to find opportunity in Prohibition. That many of the recruits were newly arrived immigrants from eastern and southern Europe is a fact we have tried to forget. Introduction to Democracy for many of them was a chance to break a strike or drive a newsboy off a choice corner.[1]

Inspired by the example of the Boss, it isn't surprising that many of the newcomers took advantage of every possible shortcut they could find to pursue the fast buck. A strange marriage of the Protestant ethic and hedonistic qualities in the religions of southern and eastern Europe took place. The new citizens ended with a working philosophy that enabled them to get rich quick without worrying about moral values or man-made laws. Exponents of the philosophy call themselves "liberals," but more often than not they are conservative in politics and conventional economics.

A combination of circumstances gave these amoral young men an opportunity to become lords instead of serfs. A reaction to the idealism of the First World War was one factor. The election of Warren Harding as President was another. Harding represented the businessman-in-politics concept, and the businessmen were the type who saw no wrong in maintaining armies of goons to destroy a competitor or a union.

Add to these developments the fact of Prohibition, and the stage is set. A delayed child of the now scorned idealism of the Wilson era, prohibition had no chance in the twenties. It might have been repealed earlier than it was had it not been such a source of graft for the politicians.

Yet the immense wealth amassed by the amoral newcomers to America would not, in itself alone, have been sufficient to create

[1] See *The Silent Syndicate* for details.

the monster that organized crime has become. Certainly, the gangsters had money to burn, but in that wild decade so did everyone who could play the stock market or invest in a land boom such as Florida's. The old rich may even have had more money than the sons of immigrants, but the difference was not as great as Fitzgerald and Hemingway seemed to think.

Many bootleggers, of course, spent their money as fast as they made it—heedless of the American Way. Easy come, easy go, a short life and a merry one was their motto and often their fate. Others, who had learned something of their new country, prepared against the day the stream of liquid gold would cease to flow. They stashed away their profits. Few desposited money in banks or invested in the stock market—both were too risky in those days before insulation. Instead, they built "plants" in their homes, where the cash could be hidden and yet be immediately available in case of need or opportunity.

Opportunity came knocking long before Prohibition ended. Suddenly, respectable money men were jumping out of skyscraper offices as the stock market collapsed and a financial empire built on credit largely evaporated. How many less respectable money men saved themselves by turning to the one group with ready cash —bootleggers—may never be known, but enough did turn to make the gangster-in-business a reality.

And now a greater opportunity loomed: a chance to put all of crime on an organized basis. Before the National Syndicate could be created, however, a bloody process of self-education was required.

Almost all ethnic groups were involved in the gang wars of Prohibition, and one group seldom achieved domination over the others. Ironically, Al Capone became America's most famous gangster only because he found it necessary to kill so many people in his unsuccessful attempt to conquer Chicago. Ultimately, in almost every city, an alliance of the competing factions was accomplished. Usually it was known as the "Combination."

Immigrants from Italy and Sicily had a big advantage over

other ethnic groups in that secret societies were part of the way of life they had always known. Organizations such as the Camorristi and the Mafia—the latter known in Sicily as the Onorata Societa—had existed for centuries. Unfortunately—from the point of view of organization men—the perverted sense of honor and hot temper of the members kept the societies in a constant state of civil war. Betrayal and secret murder were almost mandatory, and a man achieved "Capo" status by killing off his rivals. Vendetta was a favorite occupation of a people more concerned with personal loyalties than allegience to an abstract ideal of brotherhood.

Borgates—meaning "sections" or "families"—were formed in several American cities before Prohibition. In those days, using the symbol of the Black Hand, the *fratellos* preyed largely on their own people in what amounted to a "protection" racket. Bootleg wealth changed things, however, and rival leaders fought bloody battles for control of the corn-sugar business. Later, as imported booze replaced the rotgut manufactured at home, the individual Capos sought to dominate the retail end of the business.

Inevitably, as local families grew more wealthy and the liquor industry less localized, conflicts arose between cities. In an effort to resolve such disputes a "Capo di Capi Re" was elected with authority to act as arbitrator. This produced on a national level the same kind of struggle for power that hitherto had been confined to individual cities. Strong men were replaced by weak ones as local Capos revolted, but a weak Capo di Capi Re was an invitation to the ambitious to attempt to take from him the supreme authority.

The Capo di Capi Re at the beginning of Prohibition was Piddu Morello. He was soon to be murdered and replaced by Toto D'Aquila, who also was murdered. Joe (the Boss) Masseria took command only to be challenged by Salvatore Maranzano.

The excuse of Maranzano's revolt was the murder of Gaspare Milazzo, Capo of Detroit and a native of Castellammare del Golfo. Maranzano, also a native of that city, blamed Masseria for his countryman's death and called for all brothers from the same city to avenge the murder. As his power grew, he appealed to another group of dissidents—men from Palermo whose former leader had been the late Toto D'Aquila. One high-ranking member of the Mafia has described the budding revolt in this fashion: "A lot of youths desiring to avenge their friends put themselves at the disposition of this new head—Maranzano. The group began to enlarge. The outlaws, so-called, began to meet on the farms of friends, taking possession of them. From there they initiated their purging operations, eliminating those that Maranzano disliked and inviting others, with threats, to pass to his side. With this system Maranzano succeeded in penetrating a lot of cities of the United States, planting terror everywhere."

While this civil war was developing within the Mafia, other gangsters had achieved a degree of unity for business purposes. Various bootleg outfits along the East Coast formed a loose alliance known as the "Big Seven," with the aim of ending hijacking and achieving price and quality control. Included among men of Irish and Jewish backgrounds were such "enlightened" young "Italians" as Frank Costello, Joe Adonis, and Charles (Lucky) Luciano—to use the versions of their names that later became famous. These men had nothing but contempt for the "Mustache Petes" of the Mafia and their endless blood feuds. The so-called "Wars of the Sicilian Succession" brought nothing but "heat" and interfered with business.

Largely because so many members of the Mafia were busy fighting each other, the Bugs and Meyer Mob won the job of guarding the booze shipments of the Big Seven, and in general, taking care of any other muscle work that arose in the normal course of business. Cobosses were Benjamin (Bugsy) Siegel and Meyer Lansky, and a crack crew of gunmen obeyed their orders. A close associate was Louis Buchalter, later to be famous as "Lepke," who finally took over the killers of the Bugs and Meyer Mob and made them into the outfit known as Murder, Inc., the enforcement arm of the National Syndicate.

But that development was still some years away, as in December 1930 a "General Assembly of the Mafia" was called to meet in Boston. The session was forced by Luciano and his allies, who wanted an end to the civil war. Top Capos from around the country attended, and Gaspare Messina, Capo of the host city, presided. The assembly, following the pattern of more legitimate politicians, ducked the issue by appointing a special commission to meet with Maranzano and work out a compromise. Giuseppe Traina, an old aide of the dead D'Aquila, was made chairman. Other members included Toto Lo Verde, Capo of Chicago, and Peppina Siracusa, Capo of Pittsburgh.

The commission met at the Hotel Pennsylvania in New York City, shortly after Christmas, and sent word to Maranzano it wanted to see him. The outlaw chief, however, reacted much like the Viet Cong in 1968, and mounted a new offensive. Bodies began to litter the streets, and not all the dead were members of the Mafia. A few innocent citizens got into the line of fire and finally the chief of police felt compelled to intervene. According to one veteran of the war, the chief called in Masseria—the recognized boss—and told him if he didn't stop the killing, the police would arrest the entire Mafia. Masseria ordered his men to stop shooting, but then as now it takes two to make a peace, and Maranzano refused to cooperate.

The commission was beginning to feel frustrated when one day Paul (the Waiter) Ricca appeared at the hotel with a message from Al Capone. Nominally only a *Capo Decina,* head of ten, Capone had put together a combination of his own in Chicago. While not powerful enough to defeat his enemies, he still controlled enough firepower to be respected by Capos of less belligerent cities. The struggle between rival Mafia groups groups was interfering with his battle for Chicago, so he authorized the commission to warn Marazano to cooperate or face an airborne invasion from the Windy City.

Maranzano responded by sending a car for the commission members and taking them to a secret meeting place. After four days of talk, nothing was accomplished. Nothing was accomplished in other meetings over the next few months. Maranzano grew stronger as Joe the Boss sought an honorable peace and refused to fight back. Ultimately, it became apparent to the "third force"—the group of young businessmen led by Luciano—that Masseria was about finished. Since someone was sure to kill him anyway, the Luciano faction decided it might as well do the job and reap the benefits. Vito Genovese was given the assignment.

Joe the Boss was lured to a restaurant in the Coney Island section of Brooklyn. His executioners entered as he waited at a table and shot him six times in the back. One of the plotters, arriving too late for the murder, drove quickly to Lucky's home. Among those present was Vincenzo Troia, an old friend of Maranzano. Lucky turned to Troia and ordered: "Don Vincenzo, tell your *compare* Maranzano we have killed Masseria—not to serve him but for our own personal reasons. Tell him that if he should touch even a hair of even a personal enemy of ours, we will wage war to the end. Tell him that within twenty-four hours he must give us an affirmative answer for a meeting at a locality which we this time will pick out."

Luciano was Italian, but speaking through his lips was not the Mafia but the "Combination"—and the National Syndicate-to-be. In effect, he was telling Maranzano he could be Capo di Capi Re if he desired, but only if he acknowledged a greater power than the Mafia now existed.

At first it appeared that Maranzano would bow to the new reality. He met next day with Luciano's representatives and agreed to call a new General Assembly to plan the future of the Honored Society. The assembly met in Chicago, with Capone footing the bill, and a revolutionary idea was proposed to abolish the Capo di Capi Re system and replace it with a six-man "Grand Council."

Individual members, perhaps influenced by Luciano's modern ideas, argued for an end to dictatorships and civil war. Despite the opposition of Maranzano, they carried the day, and a nominating committee was picked to select candidates for the Grand Council. Charges of misconduct were immediately filed against committee members, and in the confusion Maranzano's men persuaded the assembly to abandon the plan. The election of Maranzano as Capo di Capi Re became only a formality.

Drunk with the power he had so long sought, Maranzano forgot the fate of Joe the Boss and moved to consolidate his position. He installed himself in a plush apartment behind the Hotel Commodore in New York. The apartment flanked Grand Central Station, a busy place swarming with policemen. The new boss reasoned it would be more difficult to kill him in such a location. When he left the apartment, he rode in an armored car. The apartment included a studio, which was used as a guardroom. Two teams of carefully selected men worked 12-hour shifts. The "Grand Sultan," as some disgruntled brothers called him, felt secure.

The Capos of the country, hopeful that peace had come at last, decided they should honor their new leader with a banquet. Maranzano, recognizing in the proposal the same opportunities certain senators later discovered, ordered thousands of tickets printed and sent to the various cities to be sold at $6.00 each. Capone, anxious to maintain the prestige he had acquired within the Honored Society, bought 1,000. Stefano Magaddino of Buffalo coughed up a like amount.

At the banquet the huge extortion racket continued. According to an eye witness: "On a costly and sumptuously decorated table towered a majestic tray in which those who came placed handfuls of dollars. A group of high-spirited boys were provided to receive guests. The boys greeted the guests with 'Long live our Capo' and conducted them to the tray, watching the offering. Many guests, although peasants trying to look like noblemen, did not make offerings of less than $500. On that night Maranzano picked up $100,000."

Not bad for a testimonial dinner.

Following the banquet, Maranzano expressed mixed feelings. He was delighted with the loot, and the prospect of more to come, but he apparently realized he would be lucky to maintain his power. He was overheard to say: "I wish I was going to Germany to be more secure."

Realities made flight impossible, so Maranzano decided to follow Mafia tradition instead. He drew up a list of sixty names—top men in the Mafia and possible rivals—and ordered them executed. Heading the list was Lucky Luciano.

The men of the Combination had no choice. It was now apparent the Mafia was—as one hood put it—"a pimple on the ass of progress." If ever crime was to be organized on a business basis, the Mafia had to be brought under control. A conference was called. Attending were the same men who had plotted the execution of Masseria. The decision to eliminate Maranzano was easy to reach, but execution would be more difficult. The new Capo di Capi Re was not going to be lured into a trap and killed over the dinner table. Much more was involved than the death of one man. There was no point in repeating the mistake of the past by killing one leader only to have a worse one replace him. A purge of all the "Mustache Petes" was deemed necessary.

The execution of Maranzano was turned over to the killers of the Bugs and Meyer Mob. Siegel and Lansky, as partners in the Combination with Luciano, realized the importance of the task assigned. They asked only for the aid of one Italian, who could identify the target for them.

A highly placed Mafia leader has described the action when six members of the Bugs and Meyer mob, accompanied by "a certain Peppino," went to Maranzano's office at 230 Park Avenue. They knocked on the door of the "Eagle Building Corporation" and identified themselves as federal agents when Maranzano's bodyguards opened the door. Then they pulled pistols.

"While the Jews with leveled pistols held the followers of Maranzano motionless, one of the Jews went out into the corridor and called in Peppino, asking the Italian which of these men was Maranzano."

According to the Mafia leader, Maranzano recognized Peppino and told him: "Peppino, you know that I am Maranzano and that I am responsible for this office. They can make any search they want, because there is no contraband here. This office is commercial."

The killers led Maranzano into his private office "and in order to avoid noise tried to strangle him. Thereafter, they tried to finish him off by stabbing him. But the doomed man, by virtue of his desperation, got loose and, because he possessed a certain strength augmented by fear, sought to fight. The others emptied their pistols into him, killing him instantly."

It was September 30, 1931. Maranzano had ruled five days less than five months. With him died the Mafia as a dominating force in organized crime.

Years later, Joe Valachi gave a distorted version of the murder and identified one of the killers as "Red Levine." When a member of the McClellan Committee asked to what Mafia family Levine belonged, Valachi replied: "Meyer Lansky."

Answers like that are inevitable when one can't see the forest for the trees.

The killers found Luciano's men waiting on the street below. Assured the Capo di Capi Re was dead, the young Italians rushed to telephones. Word was passed to all parts of the country. That night the slaughter began. Mustache Petes in high places were purged. Estimates vary as to the number killed. Police in their isolated cities had no way of connecting up the murders or even relating them to the Mafia. No federal agency was aware of what was going on—the FBI didn't believe there was a Mafia.

Some writers have since pictured the purges as simply the inevitable blood bath that followed the rise of another boss—in this case, Luciano. The truth is confirmed by events. The General Assembly of the Mafia—its numbers now much depleted—met in Chicago and voted to abolish the office of Capo di Capi Re in favor of a "Commission" or "Grand Council." Named to the new ruling body were:

Luciano, Capo of the Mafia family formerly bossed by Masseria.
Vincent Mangano, Capo of D'Aquila's former family.
Joe Profaci, Capo of a Brooklyn family.
Peppino (Joe Bananas) Bonnano, Capo of another Brooklyn family.
Ciccio Milano, Capo of Cleveland.
Masi Gagliano, Capo of the family formerly headed by Gaetano Reina.

Alphonso Capone, a Capo Decina in the Mafia but a power
in Chicago.

Note how the Commission was weighed in favor of New York.
Five of the seven members were from that city, and all had been
allied with Luciano and the non-Mafia members of the Combination.

In the decades to come individual members of the Mafia would
obtain wealth and influence within the National Syndicate. The
Honored Society, however, was relegated to a secondary role.
Even so, a loyalty to the tradition of violence made it a dangerous
vehicle on which to ride to power. Occasionally, hot blood had to
find an outlet, and old fashioned civil wars made headlines in such
cities as Youngstown and Brooklyn.

Ironically, it was this ability of the Mafia to make headlines
that proved most valuable to the syndicate. Such men as Lansky
found they could operate in silence while the Mafia got the heat.

It was all very convenient and rather amusing as well.

The third and fourth stages of Prohibition—smuggling and the
manufacture of illicit alcohol in huge distilleries—provided the
economic basis for regional cooperation, which led ultimately to
the National Syndicate.

After bloody battles between ethnic groups, combinations were
formed in such major cities as Boston, New York, Philadelphia,
Cleveland, Detroit, Chicago, Minneapolis-St. Paul, Kansas City,
Denver, and San Francisco. The men in charge found that just
as cooperation was profitable on the local level, it was also of
value on a broader scale.. Thus it was that a speakeasy in New
York might sell booze brought ashore from Canada in Cleveland
or Detroit. Similarly, a Buffalo bar might offer gin bought in the
Bahamas and landed at Galveston, Miami, or New York. Buyers
from individual syndicates went to Nassau and London only to
discover that competition drove up the price. Joint ventures became the order of the day.

Because of its central location and huge population, New York
City became a focal point. Some twelve miles off its coast was the
largest "Rum Row" in existence—a line of ships laden with booze

from Canada and the Bahamas. The Erie Canal provided a physical link with the armored rummies of the Cleveland Syndicate, and much booze came by barge down the canal. A good railroad system north to New Haven and Boston and south to Savannah and Florida made it possible for liquor to land at almost any point along the East Coast and still reach New York quickly and efficiently.

Across the river in New Jersey, Waxey Gordon ruled for a time. Waxey, whose real name was Irving Wexler, came up through the ranks. As early as 1905 he was convicted as a pickpocket, and later for petty and grand larceny. He also operated a brothel and peddled narcotics, before hitting the big time with beer. An old friend of the Bugs and Meyer Mob, Waxey might have had a great future with the syndicate had not the Intelligence Division of the Internal Revenue Service nabbed him on income tax charges in 1933. The jury required forty minutes to deliberate, and the judge gave Gordon 10 years in prison.

Dutch Schultz, who as an independent built a multimillion-dollar empire out of gambling, booze, and assorted rackets, tried to take over in New Jersey. Ultimately, the syndicate bumped Dutch off and divided up his empire. Abner (Longie) Zwillman succeeded him and won in time the title of "Al Capone of New Jersey." More to the point, he won a place at the council table of the syndicate, and he occupied it for many years.

To the south, in Phildelphia, Micky Duffy proved the Irish could be as stubborn as the Sicilians. When he refused to cooperate, he was knocked off in Atlantic City, and his place was taken by Nig Rosen in the City of Brotherly Love. Rosen was a New York boy who served his apprenticeship with the Bugs and Meyer Mob.

To the north, the big boss was Charles (King) Solomon, who had built an organization around the city of Boston. Among his lieutenants were such bootleggers as Joe Linsey, Hyman Abrams, and Louis Fox. All three enjoyed prosperous careers long after Solomon was gunned down in the Cotton Club in south Boston on January 24, 1933. Fox became the boss of Revere, a Boston suburb as notorious as Newport, Kentucky, or Cicero, Illinois.

Abrams turned to casino gambling, and as an associate of Lansky owned pieces of the action in Las Vegas and Havana. Linsey remained in the liquor business but branched out into a variety of ventures including dog tracks, horse tracks, and country clubs.

Lansky, who as a child had lived in Boston after coming to this country from Russia, retained a special fondness for Boston and often visited there.

To the west was Cleveland. Early in Prohibition the smuggling business came under the control of four men: Moe Dalitz, Sam Tucker, Morris Kleinman, and Louis Rothkopf. An alliance with the Mafia—known locally as the Mayfield Road Mob—was established, and such men as Frank and Tony Milano, Al and Chuck Polizzi, became lieutenants. Working relations were established with combinations in such other Midwestern cities as Detroit, where the Purple Gang imported Yonnie and Peter Licavoli, who took over later, when the Purple Gang was forced to scatter. Dalitz, who had lived in Detroit, united the mobsters and made deals with such local Mafia leaders as Joe Massei.

The Cleveland-Detroit combination had close working relations with the Kidd Cann Mob of Minneapolis-St. Paul. Composed of an unusually violent group of hoods, the gang was led by the three brothers whose real name was Blumenfeld but who became famous as Kidd Cann, Yiddy Bloom, and Harry Bloom. Other lieutenants were Abe Brownstein and Ed Berman. Many years passed before the boys tired of flexing their muscles, but eventually they settled down and became part of the complex financial structure that made organized crime possible.

In Chicago, Capone had long demonstrated his willingness to work with men in other cities and had played a vital role in attempting to modernize the Mafia. While unable to capture Chicago, he did become the most powerful gangster there. After the Internal Revenue Service sent him to prison, the combination he had created found it possible to expand, and the Chicago Syndicate became a reality. Nevertheless, there was enough to keep it busy in its home town, and the Chicago Syndicate—with a few blundering exceptions—never played a vital role in the national organization's varied interests. This didn't prevent the unofficial press agents of the Mob from spreading the notion that the Chicago boys were the meanest and smartest in the nation. Enough gang killings continued to keep alive the Capone image, and the hood of Chicago became the bogeyman of organized crime.

Syndicate gangsters from other cities were entirely willing to let the "Capone Syndicate" take the blame. Like the Mafia, it became a convenient legend behind which to hide. This statement is made in full recognition of the fact it will bring howls of protest from Chicago writers and law enforcement officials. A perverse kind of civic pride has developed in connection with Chicago's reputation, and all efforts to put that reputation into perspective are resisted.

Other gangs existed in other cities and volumes could be written about each one. The pattern, however, was very much the same everywhere, for the same economic and social forces were at work. All pointed inevitably toward closer cooperation and ultimate union in a loose alliance.

Several meetings over the years preceeded the final decision. Out of them came what Dixie Davis, the young "mouthpiece" of the late Dutch Schultz, called "the NRA idea."

The National Recovery Administration, known as NRA, was a short-lived New Deal program, but it had a tremendous impact and touched the lives of all—including the gangsters. Industry codes were created under which industry was supposed to regulate itself subject to supervision from the top by an administrator and four boards set up for the purpose.

When "the NRA idea" was applied to crime, few major changes were required. Local autonomy was confirmed and regional divisions ratified. In some areas such as New York further divisions were made according to racket as well as geography.

Using the solution already applied to the Mafia, a Grand Council was appointed with representation based upon the only reality—wealth. With wealth you could hire troops. Not too surprisingly, the New York combination, known in some circles as the "Three L's"—Luciano, Lansky, and Lepke—dominated the

Grand Council. Leaders in other cities who had cooperated most closely in liquor deals with New York were confirmed in power. Thus Dixie Davis was to write in 1939: "Moey Davis became the power in Cleveland and anyone who questioned it would have to deal with Lucky and Meyer and the Bug."

"Moey Davis" was really Moe Dalitz, and with his partners in the Cleveland Syndicate had long enjoyed business relations with New York. Their most spectacular joint venture was the Molaska Corporation, which manufacured illicit alcohol long after Prohibition ended. Lansky's father-in-law, Moses Citron, was an officer of the corporation. The Cleveland partners were represented by nominees.[2]

Perhaps the most significant development in establishing peace and unity were the rules adopted on murder. If anyone was to be "hit" outside a local jurisdiction, approval of the Grand Council was required. To relieve gangs of the necessity of maintaining squad of expensive "enforcers"—or perhaps hiring some unreliable help in an emergency—the Brooklyn outfit later known as Murder, Inc., was set up. The killers, most of them former members of the Bugs and Meyer Mob, were experts, and prices were standard and reasonable. Lepke had over-all control, but Albert Anastasia handled many of the practical details.

In later years, as the bribe supplanted the bullet, the need for such specialists faded. When murder was deemed necessary, there were always enough young toughs to take on the assignment. Mafia members were especially eager, since a willingness to kill still was considered a mark of manhood, but even the Mafia ran out of killers in New England.

By late 1934 the National Syndicate was a reality, and the bright young men who ruled were shoving aside the veterans. Typical is this complaint: "The *papaveri* [important men] cornered the positions that were most profitable. These men had forgotten me, whom they had used to resolve many risky situations. Meanwhile, the fruits of my labors were harvested by these papaveri who

[2] For the fantastic history of Molaska, see *The Silent Syndicate*.

continued to use me—pushing me around from one point in the United States to another. O, ingratitude of humanity!"

The Mafia can become quite emotional at times.

Events were soon to prove how right the young men of the Combination had been to demand a more sophisticated approach to the business of crime. Less than a year after the National Syndicate was formed, public reaction to the corruption of the Prohibition era began at last to assert itself. Early in 1935 a New York grand jury utilized its authority and demanded a special prosecutor. It got Thomas E. Dewey.

The prosecutor—be he known as the district attorney, the state's attorney, or the commonwealth's attorney—is a key official. Not only does he ultimately have the responsibility for prosecuting, but as advisor to the grand jury he can often determine who and what will be investigated. He can protect the guilty by withholding evidence or giving bad legal advice. No criminal conspiracy of any size can long operate without at least the tacit permission of the prosecutor, unless, of course, he is simply incompetent.

Sensing this relationship between crime and politics, the New York grand jury sought freedom of action. Dewey proved that an able and courageous prosecutor can almost become President by doing his duty. Unfortunately, many prosecutors would rather be rich than President.

The "heat" went on in New York City, and two top men in the National Syndicate were burned—one more fatally than the other. Luciano was ultimately sent to prison and then deported, but Lepke went to the "hot seat."

The fall of Lepke illustrates how, in such a massive operative as organized crime, chance often is decisive. Old records of the United State Customs Service tell the story.

Lepke, Lansky, and Bugsy Siegel were partners in a plant at 2919 Seymour Avenue in the Bronx. The plant extracted morphine from an opium base and was the heart of a lucrative narcotics business. On February 25, 1935—before Dewey could get organized—the plant blew up. A fire put it completely out of operation.

Lansky and Siegel, their eyes on the "cleaner" gambling racket, dropped out. Lepke, borrowing some of the men who had once been liquor smugglers, started importing narcotics from the Far East in huge amounts. To get the "stuff" ashore, he bribed some Customs Service men. Soon, however, both Customs and the Federal Narcotics Bureau were investigating, and Lepke was indicted by a federal grand jury. He went into hiding, but eventually surrendered to J. Edgar Hoover—who had nothing else to do with it—and was sentenced to federal prison. Meanwhile, Dewey probed deeply into other aspects of Lepke's rackets and developed an extortion case against him. Conviction followed, and to the fourteen-year sentence Lepke received in federal court was added thirty years in state court. Shortly thereafter, Burton Turkus, an assistant district attorney in Brooklyn, secured an indictment charging Lepke with murder. For the first time the existence of a National Syndicate, complete with Murder, Inc., as an enforcement arm, was documented.

In the early hours of December 1, 1941, a jury found Lepke guilty of murder. Six days later the Japanese bombed Pearl Harbor. Once again the National Syndicate was able to hide behind other gangsters. By the time the war was won, organized crime had completed the transition from the bullet to the bribe.

And the bloody profits made by Lepke, now clean and camouflouged, began paying dividends in Boston.

The "Dewey heat" actually speeded the transformation of the syndicate by forcing its members to take protective measures. Helping also was the fact that, considering New York too hot, some of them began to travel and discovered vast unexploited areas.

Siegel asked for, and was given, the job of developing the West Coast. From the vantage point of Los Angeles he was able to put Nevada with its legalized gambling into perspective. Las Vegas was a direct result.

While Bugsy was enjoying Hollywood, California, his partner, Meyer Lansky, explored the Gold Coast of Florida and settled in Hollywood—a city in Broward County, north of Miami. Ultimately, plush casinos bloomed all along the coast and in the Caribbean as well as a direct result of Lansky's vision.

Frank Costello, an old rum-runner and associate of the Combination, took Luciano's place when Lucky went to prison, and sent Dandy Phil Kastel—who got his start with Arnold Rothstein before Prohibition—to New Orleans. Slot machines were installed, and later the Beverly Club, of which Lansky had a piece, offered casino gambling in comfortable surroundings. Ultimately Kastel moved on to Las Vegas, where the Tropicana Club remains a monument to his memory.

As sometimes happens in America, the reaction to the violence of Prohibition produced individual reform movements in not one but several cities. While the local crusades may have done some immediate good, they also had the effect of forcing gangsters all about the country to expand into other, and safer, areas. The Cleveland Syndicate, for example, operated casinos around Ohio and then expanded into Kentucky and West Virginia. The old happy relationship with Lansky opened the gates of the Magic City—as Miami likes to be called—to the Clevelanders. Later they moved into Las Vegas on a big scale.

Joint ventures were conducted in such states as Arizona by the National Syndicate. It became more and more difficult to find a major operation anywhere that did not include representatives of several cities. This was the Casino Era, in its own way as brazen and as vicious as the takeover of the garment industry by Lepke, or the organized brothels of Luciano. The bribe became more and more important, but strong-arm collectors made sure the suckers coughed up the cash.

Meanwhile, since Depression days, the syndicate had been investing in legitimate businesses. Liquor was a logical one, in view of the practical experience many gangsters had gained, and so-called "unreformed bootleggers" took over multimillion-dollar companies. Service industries supplying the nightclubs, restaurants, and ultimately, the hotels of the syndicate were taken over and expanded to serve the general public. Real estate, especially in such fast-growing states as Florida, became a huge investment item. World War II, with its civilian shortages, provided many black market deals which brought syndicate hoods into new fields, and there they remained after the war ended.

It took some years before the syndicate overcame its distrust of banks and the stock market, but the opportunities for profit in both were too great to overlook. "Hoodlum banks" came into existence in almost every major city and were used in ways that will be illustrated later, to rob the public "legitimately." In the same fashion, the stock market was employed to get control of a prosperous company and milk it dry, or to push up the stock of a worthless company and make a killing just before the bottom fell out. But more of that is yet to come.

As usual, the syndicate as a whole was able to profit by misfortune. The Kefauver Committee in 1950–1951 could have been a near-fatal development for organized crime. Some big shots were hurt—Joe Adonis, Frank Costello, Ed Curd, and the like—but most of the heat evaporated as the public turned to other things. Yet the investigation smoothed away a number of rough spots and reminded everyone of the value of insulation and indirection.

Labor racketeering got the spotlight during the Eisenhower years, and much was exposed that related organized crime to such men as James R. Hoffa. Again it was shown that the basis of power was not muscle—although it still had its uses—but cash. The millions in the Teamsters pension funds made Hoffa a big man with the syndicate, and no doubt made Hoffa wealthy as well. Ultimately, after Robert F. Kennedy became Attorney General, Hoffa went to prison, but "Teamsters loans" remained an important asset of organized crime.

Over the decades there had been a certain attrition among syndicate hoods. Few of the top men who had formed the National Syndicate remained active in 1960, although, of course, hundreds of the lower ranks were still profitably employed. The syndicate, like the economy, while ever-changing was self-renewing.

Lansky had survived to become undisputed chairman of the board. Actually, the Grand Council seldom held formal sessions. They were not only dangerous but unnecessary. Couriers traveling by jet planes provided a communication link as well as a means of distributing cash profits. Occasionally Jerry Catena in New York or Moe Dalitz in Las Vegas would fly to Miami Beach to consult in person with Lansky. Or the chairman might visit his old friend, Hy Abrams, in Boston and, while there, meet with executives of the New England branch. When hot weather made the Gold Coast uncomfortable, Lansky would fly to Europe and, in the words of a federal agent, "visit his money in Switzerland." While there, he could also meet with jet-set gangsters from Los Angeles or Montreal.

One session might concern a new investment opportunity. Top members of the syndicate were always given a chance to invest in anything good a colleague might discover. Typical was New Mylamaque Explorations, Ltd.

Sam Garfield, long an associate of gamblers in business deals, bought 100,000 shares of New Mylamaque in September 1958, through the Toronto Stock Exchange. Of the total, 50,000 shares were transferred to Edward Levinson, a veteran gambler who had operated in Newport, Kentucky; Miami, Florida; Las Vegas, Nevada; and most recently, in Havana. One-fourth of the total, 25,000 shares, went to Moe Dalitz, first among equals of the Cleveland Syndicate, who even then was in the process of turning the Nacional in Havana over to Mike McLaney. The remainder of the stock was transferred to Allard Roen, one of the second generation executives the Cleveland Syndicate had developed.

That was just the beginning. In November Roen transferred his stock. Benjamin Sigelbaum of Miami Beach—a "money man" in many syndicate deals—got 15,000 shares, and Meyer Lansky got 10,000. Soon thereafter, another large hunk of stock was transferred by other purchasers. Dalitz got 10,000 shares; Sigelbaum, 15,000; and Lansky, 25,000.

Chairman of the board of New Mylamaque was Maxwell Golhar, a partner of Louis Chesler in many ventures. "Uncle

Lou," as the curly-headed Chesler was known, was destined to have a big part in the development of gambling in the Bahamas.

"Money men" were vital to Lansky and the sophisticated financial dealings of the syndicate. Many who filled the need were respectable citizens often referred to in their hometown newspaper as "philanthropist" or "sportsman." Usually they were directors of at least one bank and trustees of a university. Often they were asked to head fund drives. That former "tough" bootlegger of Boston, Joe Linsey, raised millions for Brandeis University. Among the contributors he wooed was his old friend Meyer Lansky.

Meanwhile Lansky's second wife lived quietly in a new and modest home in Golden Isle subdivision, just east of Gulfstream Park. The former manicurist at the Embassy Hotel in New York watched her pennies and sold her used clothing. Interested observers noted that Meyer never tipped heavily when his wife was along. Each year he rented two new Chevrolets for family use. Obviously, tales that he had $300 million in a Swiss bank must be exaggerated. At least Thelma thought so.

Stafford Sands wasn't so sure. He told Robert (the Needle) Peloquin, ace troubleshooter for the U.S. Department of Justice, that Lansky visited him one day in 1960 and offered him $1 million in cold cash.

The money, Sands quoted Lansky as saying, would be deposited to Sands's account in a Swiss bank. In return, all Sands had to do was get permission for Lansky to operate a casino in the Bahamas.

Needless to say, said Sands, the offer was rejected.

Some time later, after it had become known that Sands received $1.8 million to arrange for gambling in the Bahamas, Stafford changed his story a bit. Lansky offered him not $1 million but $2 million, he insisted.

The chairman of the board said nothing.

2

Bullies of Bay Street

STAFFORD LOFTHOUSE STREET was not the boss of the Bay Street Boys any more than Lansky was Capo di Capi Re of the syndicate—but he had a bigger appetite.

Big appetites in the Bahamas are a tradition.

It all began with the Caribs who made a habit of eating people. To escape mastication, the Lucayan Arawaks took to their boats and sailed north and west until they came to some low, sandy islands that apparently no one else wanted. They settled there, and their descendants greeted Columbus.

The Spaniards who followed proved just as hungry. When they couldn't find gold, they carried the peace-loving natives off to Cuba to work on plantations. Most of them soon died. By 1513 more than 40,000 Lucayan Arawarks had been kidnapped, and the Bahamas were virtually deserted once more. Some 450 years later a sentimental soul named a hotel-casino after them, as the syndicate discovered there was gold in the islands after all.

When the labor supply was exhausted, the Bahamas were ignored for more than a century. The French took title for awhile and, according to legend, may have tried to settle on Abaco, but when Wallace Groves arrived there some years later to cut timber, he found no trace of them. English Puritans, calling themselves "Eleutherian Adventurers," settled one island and in all logic named it Eleuthera. They almost starved to death in their first winter, but were saved by Puritans from Boston who sent supplies. In gratitude, the new colony later made a gift of braziletto wood to Harvard University.

Progress continued, and in time the island became a way station for New England merchants importing what was sometimes known as "black ivory."

By 1671 the population of the islands had reached one thousand. Many were pirates. The long struggle between England and Spain turned the gin-clear waters of the Caribbean—to quote the Minister of Tourism—red with blood. The objective of the pirates was Spanish treasure ships. The shoal waters around the Bahamas provided a perfect sanctuary for men who could loot and kill and call themselves patriots.

The Spaniards, having had plenty of experience along similar lines, didn't buy the argument. In 1684 they landed at Charles Town—the first name of Nassau—and roasted the English governor on a spit. Next year they returned and kidnapped all the women, children, and slaves who had not fled to Jamaica. Any men who remained behind were murdered.

The lure of easy money was too strong to resist, however, and the survivors ultimately returned and resumed their profitable occupation. Tales of their wild ways eventually got back to London—not for the last time—and the Crown sent out Governor Cadwaller Jones with orders to keep the peace. Jones found it easier to cooperate with the pirates than to fight them—another precedent set—and when members of the local council objected, he arranged to have a pirate ship in the harbor train its guns on the council building. Ignoring the threat, the councilmen jailed the governor. The pirates promptly rescued him and restored him to power.

After all, he had been appointed by the Crown.

Very little changed until George I appointed Woodes Rogers

governor in 1717 and gave him a Great Seal for the Bahamas. It is still used today and bears the slogan: *Expulsis Piratis Resituta Commercia.*

Bahamians today still have a proper regard for seals, slogans, and titles—they're part of the British atmosphere that attracts American tourists—so it isn't surprising that Rogers achieved results. He pardoned many of the pirates and hung a few. Piracy as a respectable way of life declined. So did the population. Hard times came to the Bahamas, as always happened when the islanders went back to fishing and farming.

The next boom began when the descendants of those old friends in Boston got tired of paying taxes and tossed some tea into the harbor. Other colonials found various reasons to agree with them, and what ultimately became the American Revolution was under way. A lot of Tories felt the uprising was illegal, immoral, and perhaps a threat to privilege, so they loaded their slaves and moved to the Bahamas. By 1785 an estimated 7,000 of them had fled the Land of the Free. Soon they dominated the life of the islands and were importing still more slaves to raise still more cotton. Unsatisfied, they gave the matter some thought and created a new and unique industry—wrecking.

The position of the Bahamas off the Straits of Florida, the many small islands and shoals, the strong currents and sudden gusts of wind—all combined to make passage dangerous to ships. The smart boys who had fled the American rebels soon found ways to give nature a hand. It was found that moving lights on some low-lying cay would be mistaken for a vessel under way, and the captain of a heavily laden ship would follow suit and end up on the rocks. Or fixed lights would lure the trusting master of the ship into shoal water.

Quickly, once the possibilities were recognized, the wrecking business was expedited. From 1858 to 1864, 313 wrecks were reported. In 1858 there were 302 wrecking vessels and 2,678 "wreckers" licensed by the Bahamian government.

Profits came, of course, from salvage of the wrecked cargoes. The legislature passed many laws to "regulate" this most profitable business. Not too surprising was the fact that the legislators were owners of the wrecking vessels, and the electors who put them in office were made up of the crews of wrecking vessels.

One wrecker made a comment that well expressed the attitude of the Bay Street Boys—then and later: "I'm not out for humanity. I'm out for wrecking. It pays better."

More than a hundred years later some critics suggested Stafford Sands had been reading history when he devised a license system for gambling casinos.

Eventually, word got back to London, and an honest governor was sent out to build some honest lighthouses. The economy nosedived, as it always did after an attack of virtue—a fact that Meyer Lansky, who also read history, did not fail to note.

Contributing to the decline was the slump in cotton. Slavery was abolished in the entire British Empire in 1834. Without slaves, it was no longer profitable to grow cotton on the thin soil of the Bahamas. But just as things were getting really bad, the Civil War began in the United States, and immediately the economy went from bust to boom. Gun-running replaced wrecking as the major industry of the islands.

Despite the South's best efforts, England remained officially neutral, but the growing industrial revolution in that country had created a growing need for cotton for use in the sweatshops of Liverpool and Manchester. Plenty of cotton was produced in the red clay of Georgia and other states—the problem was how to get it to England and bring back to the Confederacy the manufactured goods so desperately needed there.

The Bay Street Boys recognized the opportunity. Exports soared from a petty £195,000 in 1861 to £5,000,000 by 1864. The colony became so wealthy the government built the Royal Victoria Hotel on the hill overlooking the harbor so the blockade-runners might have a decent place to live—and spend their profits—between voyages. Again it was the members of the legislature who made the most money—the value of the businessman-in-politics was demonstrated once more. Very little of the new wealth trickled down to the population which, by now, consisted largely of former slaves or their children. Life for the blacks continued as usual—hard work, abject poverty, complete ignorance, and submission. Freedom was an empty, meaningless word in their vocabulary.

In a town as small as Nassau there was no room for compassion.

The economic bubble burst with the Lost Cause. The Royal Vic, as it had come to be known, stood half empty for more than a half century. It proved well built, however, surviving a devastating hurricane which played havoc with the homes of natives. The big wind came just as the Civil War ended, and it was not equaled until 1926. A lot of wealthy merchants took their money and went to England. The remainder exported sponges and attempted to grow sisal, a type of hemp. For once the Bay Street Boys missed an opportunity. If they had used the sisal to make cigarettes instead of rope, they might have made another fortune.

In 1898, after Henry Flagler built a railroad through the swamplands to the village of Miami and attracted a trickle of Yankee "snowbirds," an effort to lure them on over to Nassau was made. Flagler became interested enough to buy the Royal Victoria and build the Hotel Colonial, but the program never amounted to much. The Bahamas were too hard to reach unless one had business there.

A lot of people suddenly had business there, and the biggest boom of all—thus far—began in 1920. Still reacting from the emotional binge of World War I, the American people began their "Noble Experiment." It became illegal to manufacture, sell, or transport intoxicating liquors within the United States, or to import it from without. The Bay Street Boys licked their chops.

In the first stage, before the law went into effect, huge quantities of liquor from the United States were shipped to Nassau and stored in the long-empty warehouses that had been built to hold guns for the Lost Cause. When the warehouses were filled, the liquor was stored in homes and finally on the streets. Import duties were gigantic, and suddenly the government was solvent. Instead of schools and hospitals, it built more warehouses. They were needed to make even more money.

As quickly as the Volstead Act went into operation, all the

liquor exported from the United States was smuggled back where it came from, and new supplies were being brought in from England and Scotland. In theory—and trust the Bay Street Boys to find a way—the thousands of cases were never sold or delivered illegally. The Bahamian merchant simply resold the imported booze to foreign buyers in Bahamian waters or on Bahamian soil. What the buyer did with it was, of course, his own business. And the government, which was getting $6.00 a case in import duties, had no desire to impede the traffic.

More than twenty giant liquor concerns sprang up in Nassau, where 5,700 cases of whiskey cost $170,000, after freight, customs, and handling charges had been paid. Sold to rum-runners supplying the "mother ships" off New York and Boston, they brought $342,000. By the time they were taken ashore—and be it noted that not until the liquor was inside the 12-mile limit was the law violated—the price was $684,000. Once on land, and watered down, the gangsters handling the retail end could expect to collect about $2 million, for the original 5,700 cases.

Profit enough for everyone. Yet not all of the Bay Street Boys were satisfied with the wholesale end of the business. Roland T. Symonette—later to be knighted by Queen Elizabeth and to become the first Premier of the Bahamas—laid the basis of his $80 million fortune by running liquor to Florida. He invested in a cargo schooner known as the *Halcyon S,* and began hauling liquor to the almost deserted beaches along what was to become the Gold Coast.

Sands was only seven years old when the men he was later to dominate began getting rich—a fact which helps explain his appetite in future years. His elders made certain they wouldn't have to share the wealth with outsiders—they passed stringent laws regulating the investment of foreign capital.

Meanwhile the gangsters from a hundred cities swarmed into Nassau—the principal port—and into West End on Grand Bahama and to Bimini, closest of all the islands to the mainland. The Lucerne Hotel, a wooden three-story affair on Frederick Street, became their social headquarters. Presiding over the hotel as manager was a kindly old lady, known to all as "Mother." The gangsters professed to respect her, but on occasion they would build a huge fire on the lawn and order native girls to dance naked around it while a steel band played. The native cops had sense enough not to interfere.

The Chief Justice of the Bahamas, who lived in the hotel, didn't interfere either.

The gangsters had absolutely no respect for local authority. Here is how William McCoy—the man whose name became synonymous with good bootleg booze—has described the scene:

"Bay Street, the waterfront chief thoroughfare of the town, no longer was a sun-drenched idle avenue where traffic in sponges and sisal progressed torpidly. It was filled with slit-eyed, hunch-shouldered strangers with the bluster of Manhattan in their voices and a wary truculence of manner. . . . Nothing like these hard guys had ever crossed the trail of the gorgeously uniformed, pompous coons of the Bahamas police force. The invaders had no reverence whatever for red and blue coats and pipe-clayed sun helmets."

Among those "slit-eyed men" with the "bluster of Manhattan in their voices" was Meyer Lansky.

The boom was the largest and longest in history, but the bust that followed was the worst yet. As always, the wealth had gone to a tiny minority. The black majority was no better able to survive a depression than was the population after the Civil War. A considerable portion of the laboring class emigrated to the United States to seek work as migrant farmers in the tomato patches, cane fields, and orange groves of Florida. Conditions there were not far removed from those their slave ancestors had known, but they were better than then obtained in the Bahamas.

Conditions worsened in 1939, when a blight of the sponge fishing beds wiped out the remaining local industry.

World War II brought a measure of economic recovery as naval and air bases were built and staffed to combat the submarine menace. It also added a new and sophisticated element of cynicism to the top levels of Bahamian life. Hundreds of wealthy British families, many of them more concerned still with the Red Menace than with Hitler, arrived and brought their money with them. Outspoken in their pro-Nazi sentiments, they awaited the downfall of the Churchill government with anticipation.

Leading the pack were, of course, the Duke and Duchess of Winsdor. The Duke was given the job of Governor to get him out of reach of Hitler's agents, but in Nassau he found them by the score. Some very weird things happened during the Duke's tour of service, and not all of them have yet been reported. Typical was the murder of Sir Harry Oakes on July 7, 1943. The Duke's mishandling of the investigation became generally known, but the complete story was hushed up by the Bay Street Boys—who had their reasons.

Oakes, a product of New England, struck it rich in Canada as a gold prospector, and moved to the Bahamas to escape taxes. In so doing he set something of a precedent, but he is important to this history only in that the trial of his alleged murderer offered Stafford Sands his first opportunity in the public spotlight.

Years later the late Sir Harry Oakes's daughter advanced a plan to use casino profits to benefit education. Sands helped make that idea as dead as Sir Harry.

On August 5, 1966, lower levels of the United States Department of State, and upper levels of the Department of Justice, were excited about an official report of a party at the Nassau home of Sir Stafford Sands.

The party was held on July 30 and was "small and intimate" with only a dozen guests. Among those present was Frederick Frohbost, special agent in charge of the Miami office of the Federal Bureau of Investigation. Frohbost confided to a fellow countryman that he and his wife had been in town for three days on a "combination social and business" trip.

The special agent also indicated, according to the official report of the incident, that he was "greatly impressed by Sir Stafford Sands and found him to be a very charming and knowledgeable politician." Frohbost revealed "that the FBI was going to become more active in the Bahamas."

Amazement was expressed, by the person making the report, at "the lack of knowledge of the Bahamas problem on the part of Frohbost."

This ignorance on the special agent's part was matched by Bahamian police officials who, as was learned later, knew next to nothing about American gangsters. Not too surprisingly, it developed, the local cops had been getting their information from the FBI in Miami.

But of that more later.

It should be noted that Sands's charm, which so impressed the FBI agent, was a very real part of his personality. A writer, who by no stretch of the imagination could be called an admirer of the portly Sir Stafford, described him in this fashion: "This powerful man of the UBP (United Bahamian Party) resembles in many ways a younger Sydney Greenstreet. It is almost a case of perfect typecasting for his role. He plays the part to perfection. Sometimes he is the heavy, at times the benign despot, often a gracious and worldly host. He is given to the same mannerisms of the late Sydney Greenstreet which made watching that superb actor such a joy.

"Sir Stafford, like all great actors, is never out of character. He is a man of humour, but quick to anger over some slight, or mistake, by a staff member, which never fails to terrify. Unmistakably, he is a giant in every way among the largely group of pick-noses in the government who do his bidding.

"He is fifty-one years old, and born into a family who have been in the Bahamas for more than three hundred years. Because his roots go so deep it might account for what his critics say: 'Sir Stafford looks upon the Bahamas as though it were his own private sand pile.' "

The same sense of ownership was found by a Royal Commission of Inquiry in 1967. The commission's final report contained this statement: "By the mid-fifties he had achieved a position which might be described, colloquially but accurately, as 'the Doyen of the Bay Street Boys.' "

Sands was born in Nassau in 1913. Later he was to boast that his ancestors had been in the islands for 350 years. The history of the islands was family history.

Enough wealth had been acquired to educate him at home and on Long Island, but "Stahfud," as the natives called him, was in too much of a hurry to want or need a lot of schooling, or a Harvard or Oxford degree. As the son of a Bahamian "Brahmin," he was automatically a member of the Bay Street Boys. How far he would rise depended upon how much money he could make for himself and others of the tight-knit "Establishment." The odds were longer as he began his career, for the Prohibition era had enabled many of his older colleagues to throw away the old family purses and buy new ones—all properly filled.

The first step upward was taken on October 16, 1935, when he was admitted—"called"—to the Bahamas Bar. (It is an interesting bit of legal fiction that a young law student in the Bahamas doesn't have to apply for admittance to the legal profession. As with certain members of the clergy, his unique talents and personal worth are recognized by higher authority, and he is asked to take his place among his peers.)

Everything moved at a proper pace. Two years later he was elected to the miniature House of Assembly, and two years after that he became "Legal Adviser to the House." In this capacity he was able to set in motion the series of events that twenty-five years later brought syndicate gambling to Grand Bahama Island. He ramrodded passage of a bill, which became the famous "Subsection 10 of Section 257 of the Penal Code." The subsection consisted of two paragraphs:

> It shall be lawful for the Governor in Council to exempt any person, club or charitable organisation from the provisions of this section and to issue a certificate to any such person, club or charitable organisation certifying that exemption has been granted as aforesaid.
>
> Any such certificate shall be issued for such period and upon such terms and conditions as the Governor in Council shall

deem fit and shall after issue be liable to cancellation by the Governor in Council at any time in the event of breach of any such terms and conditions or otherwise in the discretion of the Governor in Council.

The effect of this subsection was to create a licensing procedure for the operation of lotteries and gaming houses. Excuse for its passage was the discovery by Sands that two small casinos then operating in the islands were—according to the existing law—strictly illegal. The casino on isolated Cat Cay had been running for only a short time, but the Bahamian Club in Nassau had in its very snobbish way been catering to the wealthy since 1920.

The subsection sponsored by Sands made it possible to legalize these operations for the future. It also made possible other operations, if ever political and economic conditions made them practical. Prior to the introduction of the new Constitution on January 7, 1964, control of the essential "Certificates of Exemption" remained with the Governor in Council. The Governor, of course, was appointed by the Crown and was usually some distinguished civil servant in the twilight of his career. The Executive Council, with which the Governor was supposed to confer, included the Colonial Secretary, the Attorney General, and the Treasurer. In addition six "unofficial" members were appointed by the Governor in consultation with the Leader of the government in the House of Assembly. Since almost all officials, with the exception of the Governor, were drawn from the Bay Street Boys, rather tight control could always be exercised. As a matter of law, should a Governor decide to reject the advice of the Executive Council, he was required to make a written report on the matter to the Secretary of State for the Colonies in London. The Royal Commission of Inquiry in 1967 said it could find no evidence that any Governor had rebuffed the Council since Subsection 10 became law in 1939.

Top officials received no pay on the curious grounds that since the colony could not pay them what they were worth, it was better to pay them nothing. The officials, therefore, had every excuse for devoting much of their time to private business—after all, they had to have sufficient income to live in a state appropriate to their official positions.

And if any question of conflict of interest arose, it was resolved in favor of the private person who made the official person possible.

Whether Sands had any private motive in 1939 for creating the legal device that was later to be the means to a huge personal profit, is not known. At the time, however, Meyer Lansky was building in a modest way a gambling complex in Havana, centering around the casino at the Nacional Hotel and Oriental Park—the local race track. Perhaps Sands was inspired by Lansky's example. In any case, his action protected the Bahamian Club—then open only during the winter months—and the almost private club operated by Louis Wasey on Cat Cay. Both were to figure prominently in future developments and offer Sands ample reward for his public service in 1939.

The young attorney, his appetite growing as his weight increased, was briefly in the spotlight in 1943. Newspapers around the world carried the report that he was to defend Count Alfred de Marigny, son-in-law of Sir Harry Oakes and his accused killer.

Oakes had been stabbed and burned in his sprawling home on the night of July 7, while his friend, Harold Christie, allegedly slept peacefully a few feet away. Christie, as one of the Bay Street Boys, made millions selling real estate. Hog Island, in Nassau Bay, became one of his favorite items. Everyone agreed it was a perfect spot for a casino—if only there was a bridge from the main island.

In the trial of de Marigny, Sands took no part. Older attorneys discredited the testimony of Miami police experts brought in by the Duke of Winsdor, and de Marigny went free. However, the Bay Street Boys decided his morals were not only bad but obvious, and ordered him deported. The murder of Oakes remained an official mystery, and at times threatened to become a political issue —people kept charging that the Bay Street Boys were protecting someone. That sound sleeper, Harold Christie, ignored the rumors and kept on reselling Hog Island until finally Sands arranged for a bridge to be built to paradise. Eventually, when Christie got enough money, he became Sir Harold.

For Sands's service in the Oakes–de Marigny case—the newspaper coverage didn't give his withdrawal proper credit—he was rewarded two years later by being appointed to the Executive Council. At the same time he became Leader for the government in the House. At thirty-two years of age, he was facing his first real challenge: Gambling.

Batista fled Cuba in 1944, after losing an election, and Meyer Lansky began looking for a new base of operations. On May 28, 1945, he bought the Colonial Inn just south of Gulfstream Park in Broward County, Florida. If a new offshore location could be found, then fine, but if not, the syndicate Lansky represented would rebuild in Broward, where Lansky had long enjoyed a working relationship with veteran sheriff Walter Clark.

Sands made his move three months after becoming a member of the Executive Council. On February 26, 1946, he made application to the Governor in Council for one of those Certificates of Exemption he had helped make possible seven years before. Certificates had been issued in 1939 to legalize the Cat Cay and Bahamian Club casinos, but no one had since applied for an exemption. Sands made it clear he was applying on behalf of himself and several other Bay Street Boys. There was nothing modest about his proposal—all he wanted was a complete monopoly on casino gambling for twenty-five years. The Bahamian Club and the Cat Cay casino would become sublicensees of Sands's syndicate.

In support of the program, Stafford stated that in the past eighteen months—since Batista had lost at the polls—at least five persons from the United States and Canada had contacted him about obtaining permission to operate gambling in the Bahamas. Exactly why there should be such interest, and why interested parties should contact him, Sands didn't explain. He did say, however, that upon investigating these persons, he discovered that all but one of them were "representatives of syndicates operating gaming houses in Canada or the United States under very unsavory conditions." The applicants had been told, he added, that in his opinion any certificate should be issued to Bahamians.

Sands explained his request for a long-term certificate on the grounds that if a certificate were given for a short time only, the operator might try to protect the money of the gambling house by cheating. By giving the law of averages more time in which to operate, this danger could be avoided. Nevertheless, he proposed an "inspector" be appointed to see that the gaming was fair.

It was all very logical, but Sands had not yet learned how to handle his colleagues. They were willing to allow a fellow Bay Street Boy to make money, make a lot of money, but they wanted their cut. More than a decade later, a wiser Sands applied the lessons he had learned in 1946, and "consultant's fees" became the means to his ends. In 1946, however, after "lengthy discussions" in the Executive Council, a majority decided the subsection to the Penal Code designed by Sands in 1939 was "too narrow" to achieve his purposes in 1946. Additional legislation, the majority decided, would be needed.

Two months later, Sands—still naïvely hunting a less expensive answer—notified the Colonial Secretary he had withdrawn from the group seeking the certificate. He felt, he said, his continued membership might "cause embarrassment to government."

When this failed to work, Sands, on July 16, withdrew the application completely and, on the same day, filed a new one. It was less comprehensive than the former application, seeking only permission to operate a casino in the former officer's mess at Oakes Field. (Oakes Field had been the dream of the late Sir Harry, who had been very annoyed when the Royal Air Force built a new field during World War II, instead of buying the one he had waiting. After Oakes's murder, it had been largely abandoned.)

The new application was in the name of Brigadier General A. C. Critchley, but patriotism had never been an emotional matter in Nassau. The application was denied on August 9.

It was a major defeat for the still-young Sands and, after stewing about it for awhile, he quit as leader for the government and as a member of the Executive Council. His service in those posts had lasted one year and four days—time spent largely in the futile effort to get gambling under way in the Bahamas on a large scale.

However, Sands was by no means abandoning his place in the sun or his ambitions. He remained as member of the House, but hereafter he would devote himself to private business until, once more, a public career seemed advisable to achieve private gain.

Lansky, meanwhile, concentrated on Broward County. Casinos bloomed all around Gulfstream Park and in the cities of Hallandale and Hollywood. Wire-service operations for Gold Coast handbooks were centered in "the Farm," a Lansky-owned property known before and after as the Plantation Club. The numbers racket was left to Sheriff Clark to operate from his office.

It was a wide-open era, and for a couple of years it seemed Lansky had found a permanent home. Unfortunately for his peace of mind, however, the general prosperity attracted the envious eyes of the Chicago Syndicate. As noted before, the Chicago boys kept pretty much to their home town, but the glitter of the Gold Coast proved too strong. An obvious target, in that it was an operation independent of the national organization, was the S & G Syndicate on Miami Beach. Composed of local men, the S & G was wealthy and well run. Almost all handbooks in the beach's plush hotels were controlled by the S & G, which, needless to say, had the police department in its pocket.

To get the muscle needed to cut themselves in, the Chicago boys had to elect themselves a governor. Three men—Louis Wolfson, a Jacksonville financier; C. V. Griffin, a wealthy citrus grower; and William H. Johnson, former operator of Capone-owned dog tracks—agreed to "underwrite" the campaign of Fuller Warren in 1948. Each man gave in excess of $100,000 to the cause, and Warren was elected. Immediately, pressure began on the S & G Syndicate as "special investigators" for Governor Warren began making raids. In an effort to end the battle, the national Syndicate cut off the wire service to the S & G. Surrender followed, and the Chicago boys were given a piece of the local business.

As part of the campaign, the Chicago hoods even established a newspaper on Miami Beach, *The Morning Mail.* Editor was Harry O. Voiler, whose arrest record on everything from suspicion of murder (twice) to armed robbery—he was even accused of robbing Mae West—should have made him an expert on crime as well as Miami Beach society. Voiler wrote one editorial that, by itself, made him famous. Entitled "Who's The Bogeyman?" it defended Frank Costello.

Inevitably, all the heavy-handed activities of the Chicago Mob created heat and resentment. More than any one thing, it brought the Kefauver Committee to Miami for the first of its hearings. Among other things, the committee learned that Martin Accardo, brother of Tony Accardo who then headed the Chicago organization, put up most of the money for Voiler's newspaper. In a desperate effort to establish an iota of respectability, Voiler said he bought his linotype machines with money "borrowed from a friend of mine who is a very prominent man—Max Orovitz."

Some years later Orovitz admitted the casino on Grand Bahama Island was planned in his Miami Beach office by lieutenants of Meyer Lansky. He was listed as an officer of the operating company.

In 1950, however, the Kefauver Committee sank Lansky's Broward empire along with the revamped S & G Syndicate. The trouble with heat, as most gangsters know, is that it isn't selective. Lansky was driven off the coast once more, and a long step closer to Nassau.

Sands, meanwhile, had found a new approach as well—an ex-convict named Wallace Groves.

The career of Wallace Groves is divided neatly into two sections by his conviction in 1941 on mail fraud and conspiracy charges. Prior to going to federal prison, Groves was the prototype of the big-shot, high-living stock market manipulator, similar to the more famous Alexander Guterma or Louis (Uncle Lou) Chesler. After serving his time and retiring to the Bahamas, he became something of a mystery man. His "personality clash" with the high-rolling Chesler became famous.

The future "King of Grand Bahama" began his career as a bond salesman in Baltimore, but abandoned the profession in the early 1930's to study law at Georgetown University. Even as did another bright young man years later—Alvin Malnik of Miami—Groves began to make money in law school. Aided by his sister who had some money, and a brother in the small-loan business, he began collecting small-loan companies in Virginia, Maryland, and the District of Columbia. The pattern was familiar: As soon as his holdings looked big enough on paper, he merged them with a Chicago company and then sold out his interest. The money he received was the war chest he needed with which to invade Wall Street.

The formula that had worked before was again used. Groves acquired a handful of broken-down investment trusts, put them together as Equity Corporation, and sold Equity to—as *Time* magazine put it—"Rockefeller Son-in-Law David M. Milton" at a profit of $750,000.

Groves was on his way. He became buddies with Philip De Ronde, president of Phoenix Securities Corporation, and deals multiplied. One of his biggest plums was General Investment Corporation. Groves used his associates to put over his deals and used one trust to buy another. Some of his directors began to worry, and one undertook to give the young genius some advice. He wrote to Groves: "We may seem [to you] unduly sensitive to public, or rather informed financial opinion. The reason is that those who disregarded this opinion seem, in the end, to be 'unlucky.'"

Groves paid little heed. Life was too full of promise and excitement. There was too much to be mastered and enjoyed. He gave lavish parties, married a beautiful Hollywood movie starlet named Monaei Lindley, bought a yacht, which he appropriately christened the *Regardless,* and took a cruise to the Bahamas.

Three things happened on that cruise. He met Stafford Sands, and the two young and ambitious men found much to discuss. He founded two Bahamians corporations—Nassau Securities, Ltd., and North American, Ltd.—thus pioneering with Sands' help in a field hundreds of crooks would plow in future years. And, finally, he bought an island—Little Whale Cay, some thirty miles northwest of Nassau.

But suddenly Groves became "unlucky," as his colleague had warned might happen. The Securities & Exchange Commission began an investigation. His wife divorced him and sued a brunette for slander. The Internal Revenue Service became interested. And the house of cards Groves had built began to collapse.

On December 1, 1938, Groves, his brother George, De Ronde, and five corporations—including the two in the Bahamas—were indicted on fourteen counts of mail fraud and one of conspiracy. Allegedly, they had milked General Investment Corporation of $750,000, by the simple device of selling the trust some of its own stock at a profit of $300,000, and by charging improper fees and commissions to render this valuable service.

More than two years passed before the case came to trial. Much of the delay was caused by a search for DeRonde. Groves claimed his ex-crony was to blame. Leo Fennelly, special assistant to the United States Attorney General Robert H. Jackson, trailed De Ronde to South America and then to France, where he discovered the defendant had followed the script of the romantic movies of the period by joining the Foreign Legion. Abandoning his effort, Fennelly moved for trial of the available defendants. One of the most effective witnesses against Groves proved to be his former wife.

In February 1941 Groves, his brother, and four of their corporations were found guilty. George Groves's conviction was later overturned, but the Court of Appeals upheld Wallace Groves's sentence of two years and a $22,000 fine. The four corporations were fined $1,000 each.

Little was heard from Groves for eleven years after his release from prison in 1944. From the wreck of his $10 million empire, he had remaining his island in the Bahamas and his friendship with Stafford Sands. He also had a new wife, Georgette, his first wife's hairdresser, a native of Canada. In 1946 his new wife permitted her name to be used as at the age of forty-five Groves began building a new kingdom. The Abaco Lumber Company, Ltd., was put in Georgette's name. Groves wanted obscurity for the moment. The company had originally been formed to cut timber on the island of Abaco, but at the time of purchase it was concentrating on that flat hunk of scrubland known as Grand Bahama Island. Since bootlegging had ceased, the natives on the island had lived in obscure poverty.

The timber company was almost bankrupt, but—at least so goes the legend—Groves soon had it in the black. And while wandering among the whispering pines, he conceived a great dream, which he promptly took up with his "legal advisor," Stafford Sands.

According to Sands, a personal friendship drew the two men together. It became his practice, he once explained, to take the Sands family to Little Whale Cay to have Christmas dinner with the Groves family.

Sands's family was rather small, consisting of his wife, Winnie, and a daughter, Mercedes. Winnie was soon to divorce Sands, and Mercedes—or Teddie as everyone called her—ran away to Miami. Ironically, she found work with The Wackenhut Corporation—a private detective agency—at the very time the company was hired by Florida Governor Claude Kirk to investigate organized crime. President George Wackenhut explained that Sands was his client, and he gave Teddie work as a means of keeping an eye on her for Sir Stafford. Exactly how an agency could fight crime—which in Florida meant Meyer Lansky—with one hand, and work for Sands in the Bahamas with the other, Wackenhut didn't explain. Perhaps as an ex-FBI agent he got advice from the special agent in the Miami FBI office, who had a somewhat similar problem.

Groves's family was also small—just his second wife. Later, they would adopt five children.

After dinner on Little Whale Cay, it became the custom to go fishing. And there, alone with wind and sky and sea, the two men discussed the future of the Bahamas.

So must have been the mood on Elba when Napoleon began planning a return to the imperial throne.

Carefully, the way was prepared. Advised by Groves, who, after all, was something of an expert, Sands concentrated on corporation law. In the Bahamas that came to mean the establishment of "shell" or "suitcase" companies, for use by Americans in a variety of unethical or illegal ways. The front of the building—it was owned by Harold Christie—housing Sands' office became covered in time with scores of small signs, each bearing the name of a Bahamian Company, and each having Sands' office as its home address.

The next big step came on January 1, 1950, when the Bay Street Boys appointed Sands to be Chairman of the Development Board. The agency was supposed to promote the tourist industry, which at this point was largely confined to wealthy sportsmen who found Nassau a warm place to visit during winter months. If Stafford could find a way to make New Providence another Miami Beach—or even a Las Vegas—the Bay Street Boys were willing to help.

The means to that goal was a subject much discussed on those quiet evenings off Little Whale Cay. As the boat rocked gently on the gin-clear waters, Sands and Groves debated the best way to get rich quick. According to Sands, "Mr. Groves was not interested in the tourist trade. He did not consider it stable. I was a tourism man, and he was an industry man."

Groves's desire for stability is understandable after his experience in New York, but it represented quite a change from the days his yacht was called the *Regardless.*

Sands credits Groves for coming up first with the idea of a "free port" on Grand Bahama, with all imports and exports coming through the port duty free. It would be operated by a private company known as the "Port Authority," to which the Colony would give almost complete authority.

In arguing his position, Groves could point to Boston. Back at the height of the rum-running era, the Boston Port Development Company had been created, and got possession of much of East Boston. Not too much happened, however, until 1941, when Bernard Goldfine got control. Since then, much had happened. Suffolk Downs had been developed, among other things, and Goldfine was in a position to make governors and influence Presidents. On Grand Bahama there would be even greater opportunity, because there would be much more freedom.

Sands is on record as saying he objected to the elimination of customs duties. Since the Colony had no income or profit taxes, customs duties represented a large part of its official revenue. Obviously, it would be difficult to sell a "free port" to the Bay Street Boys, unless something concrete could be promised in return.

Ultimately a compromise was devised: All consumer goods brought into the island would be taxed, but building and manufacturing materials would be duty free. All objects manufactured on the island could be exported without taxes as well.

How much this saved the Treasury isn't known, but its value to the competitive position of Bay Street merchants is obvious.

Considerable planning was required to work out all details, but Sands was being well paid to plant the money tree whose fruit he could hope to share. The dream that came to Groves in the piney woods of Grand Bahama was valid—a tax-free haven for men of free enterprise who wanted only a chance to make more money.

The Hawksbill Creek Act was drafted by Sands and rammed through the House. The name came from a creek which meandered through the woodland where Groves planned to build his city of the future. The creek emptied into a cove where lazy hawksbill turtles were wont to lounge in the past. Groves hoped to replace these loungers with turtles of another kind.

The lack of opposition to Sands's proposal reflected his growth in wealth and prestige since the period nine years earlier when his casino program was rejected. Stafford had earned his spurs in a hundred deals and proven to all that he was a worthy son of Bay Street.

Nevertheless, the cynical might also note that the proposal to develop isolated Grand Bahama did not appear to threaten any interest of the Bay Street Boys. In effect, Stafford was preparing to bake an entirely new pie. If he succeeded, there would be ample time to slice it later.

Lord Ranfurly, Governor of the Bahamas, was, according to some reports, a bit disturbed at the prospect of turning over part of the royal domain to an ex-convict, but he didn't interfere. Later, at Freeport, they named a square after him.

Nor is there any evidence that anyone else objected to the deal. In any event, on August 3, 1955, the Governor signed the "Agreement," and Wallace Groves became—legally and officially—King of Grand Bahama. Eleven years before, he had been released from an American prison. Now he had almost life and death powers over the natives of a large island, and the right to deport any visitor he might consider undesirable.

In many respects the Hawksbill Creek Act was similar to the charters given the Hudson Bay Company in the early days of empire. Groves could buy 211 square miles at the give-away price of $2.80 per acre. He was given legal and economic power to get the rest at prices almost that low. For years to come, American suckers who rebought the land from Grove, at prices up to $50,000 an acre, were greeted with gunfire from the natives who still insisted they owned the land where their ancestors had lived for centuries. In a Colony where few natives—especially on the "Out Islands"—could read and write, charges of land fraud were the rule rather than the exception. Indeed, had Groves not had friends in court, so to speak, he might have lost much of his kingdom to other glib operators who scented opportunity when Lansky gave the word.

Other rights and privileges, which made Groves supreme on Grand Bahama, included exemption from virtually all taxes for 99 years.

In return, the Grand Bahama Port Authority—the vehicle Sands set up in Mrs. Groves' name—agreed to dredge a deep water harbor at the mouth of Hawksbill Creek and to construct a wharf there to accommodate cargo vessels. It also promised to promote the development of an industrial area in the Crown land it had purchased, and to develop within the "Port Area" living and office accommodations, schools, medical services, and other facilities.

Years later the Royal Commission of Inquiry noted in its

restrained way that the Hawksbill Creek Act gave "almost feudal powers to the Port Authority." There was ample evidence that ex-convict Groves used those powers in the style of a feudal lord.

On August 8, 1955, *The New York Times* devoted exactly six inches on page 40 to the new company. Describing Groves only as "a United States industrialist," it quoted the tycoon as saying "companies licensed here would employ 3,000 to 4,000 persons. The plants will process or assemble products for the United States, South and Central America, and Caribbean markets."

It was an ambitious program, but perhaps *The Times* was justified in treating it so casually, for little was achieved in the next four years, and the entire project was on the verge of ruin. Industry failed to come to Grand Bahama, and even Groves was ready to admit it. Under the circumstances, the chairman of the Development Board had every reason to turn to tourism. Something had to be done.

Meyer Lansky was ready to do it.

PART II BEACHHEAD

3

Men of Integrity

And so it came to pass that the man who had been thrown in the slammer in the States twenty-five years before for financial hanky-panky, now stood a mere seventy-six miles from Palm Beach like a Moses in the Promised Land.

Wallace Groves could stick his tongue out in a westerly direction and give a loud raspberry to his tormentors. Of course, at sundown he had to face to the east (Nassau), and give up thanks to Stafford Sands for his deliverance. He was King of Grand Bahama.

SO ONCE WROTE an underling in the kingdom of Wallace Groves, and if his words seem sick, they nevertheless cost Groves a small fortune in burial fees. Even then they escaped the grave to haunt him.

The major problem confronting Groves as he gazed westward across the Gulf Stream was money. The National Syndicate had as standard operating procedure a rule to invest the absolute minimum amount of its own money in any deal, and others had followed the example. When Castro closed the casinos in Cuba, the lost investments in resort hotels ran into many millions, yet Lansky lost very little. Most of the money had been put in by corporate suckers.

So it was that Wallace Groves looked for some suckers to provide development capital. He had, after all, promised to do certain
things in return for his power. Equally important, before money
could start rolling in to Groves, certain facilities had to be constructed.

D. K. Ludwig, a rich and shadowy shipping tycoon, was first
to bite at Groves's bare hook. He agreed to dredge the harbor and
build a shipyard on this never-never land of no taxation so close
to the shopping lane of the Gulf Stream. An honorary member
of the Bermuda version of the Bay Street Boys, known affec-
tionately as "The Forty Thieves," Ludwig was no fool. Yet he sank
more than $5,600,000 in the gin-clear waters off Freeport before
abandoning the whole project and returning to his shipyard in
Japan.

Not only did Groves get a harbor for practically nothing, he
also got the necessary advertising to attract other investors. Charles
W. Hayward, an English industrialist, was steered to Freeport in
1957 by the agile Sands. Impressed by all the dredging activity,
and the promises of Groves, Hayward bought 25 percent of the
Port Authority for $2,800,000.

As managing director of the Firth Cleveland Group in England,
a vast holding company, Hayward had tremendous prestige. His
son, Jack Hayward, became administrative vice president of the
Port Authority, and built a $500,000 house next door to Groves'
ocean-front mansion.

Sort of a double vote of confidence.

Impressed by this, Charles Allen of Wall Street gave the ex-
stock manipulator his blessings by arranging for his investment
company to buy another 25 percent of the Port Authority. This
meant more operating capital for Groves, who, as President of the
Port Authority, owned less than 1 percent of the company. The
rest was owned by Mrs. Groves, and her Abaco Lumber Company.

Nevertheless, despite the snowballing of confidence, the effort
"to attract foreign businesses from the tax burdens to which they
are grudgingly wedded"—as the 1960 *Bahamas Handbook* put it
—began to lag. By 1960 only one major enterprise was out of the

talking stage, and it was owned completely by the Port Authority. The Freeport Bunkering Company, Ltd., began fueling ships in the summer of 1959, and proved an instant success. In its first three weeks of operation the company sold 2.5 million gallons of fuel. Yet Groves had planned more than a filling station on the Gulf Stream.

Forty miles of paved road had been built by 1960. Electricity and running water were now available. A few homes for workers, a school, a police station, and a branch bank had been constructed, as well as a medical clinic, a liquor store, and a beauty salon. An eight-unit guest house known as the Caravel Club had been built to serve clients. It boasted a small restaurant.

Groves, by now being referred to by the Bahamas press as a "gentle-voiced visionary," was very unsatisfied. His "oasis for free enterprise" wasn't catching on. Could it be that some business executives really believed in paying taxes to support their country? It was a frightening thought. But then came jolly Lou Chesler, and Groves stopped worrying.

Chesler appeared out of the blue in Nassau, if Sands is to be believed, and Stafford told him to hop to Freeport and look it over.

Instantly Uncle Lou saw the possibilities—roulette wheels, slot machines, and rolling dice.

It was early in 1960. On July 11, 1960, a "Supplemental Agreement" between the government and the Port Authority was signed. It trebled the size of the "Port Area" and authorized the Port Authority to sell for residential purposes land that was originally allotted to it in 1955 for industrial development. In return, the Port Authority agreed to build in Freeport by December 1, 1963, at least one first class hotel of 200 bedrooms. On the hotel, the future would hinge.

Seldom has failure been so well rewarded.

Louis Arthur Chesler was born at Belleville, Ontario, in 1913 —the same year that produced Stafford Sands. Lou grew into a big man, physically and financially. At maturity he topped six feet and weighed around 300 pounds. Close-cropped curls covered his head, and a wide grin made him appear as friendly as a sheep dog. But there the resemblance ended.

Chesler's father was a solid citizen, owner of a shoe store in a city of 40,000, but Lou wanted something more. At age eighteen he departed for the University of Toronto to find it. Like other bright young men—Wallace Groves, Alvin Malnik, and the late John Fox of Boston—he couldn't wait to begin. While still a student, Chesler received a broker's license from the Ontario Securities Commission in 1933.

Even this was insufficient. He developed such a fondness for craps, he neglected his studies and soon dropped out of school, where he had starred at football, baseball, and hockey. His first job was as a messenger for a brokerage firm, and he began learning the business. In 1936 he joined Draper, Dobie & Company, a respected member of the Toronto Stock Exchange, and there he remained for several years. In 1942, feeling he knew enough to gamble, he began playing around with mining stocks, and within a year had struck it rich. By 1946 he had made a million and thought he deserved a vacation.

He picked Miami Beach.

Miami and Miami Beach, as noted earlier, were wide-open towns at the time, which, presumably, is one reason Chesler wanted to come there. Casinos and nightclubs were many and varied—it was a high-roller's heaven.

The visit coincided with developments in Nassau, where Stafford Sands was attempting in vain to get a gambling monopoly. And to the north of Miami, Meyer Lansky was awaiting the outcome before giving the syndicate permission to proceed with big-scale gambling in Broward.

Exactly who introduced Chesler to the syndicate is unknown, but it was inevitable for such a compulsive gambler as Uncle Lou to be introduced to the big boys. His bankroll, while small by some standards, guaranteed him a welcome.

Among the syndicate elite was Michael (Trigger Mike) Coppola, a veteran gangster who had been associated with the Three L's—Lansky, Luciano, and Lepke—in the old days in New York.

Indeed, he drove the "getaway" car after the shooting of Joe (the Boss) Masseria, and had been rewarded with control of the East Harlem numbers racket. As a successful hood he spent more and more time on Miami Beach, and ultimately would buy a home there. Meanwhile, to keep busy, he acted as a super bookie, handling bets too large for the average bookie. Chesler's bets often fell into that category.[1]

Just as Chesler was beginning to feel at home among the hundreds of others whose parents had known bleak poverty in Eastern Europe, the garish lights of Miami Beach were suddenly too expensive. Perhaps his usual good sense was over-flattered, or had also taken a holiday. In any case, Lou plunged heavily on a broker's tip and lost a million dollars when International Paper nosedived.

It was back to the drawing board for Uncle Lou.

His comeback was swift. Talking some of his new-found friends into investing in Canadian mining ventures, Chesler soon had a stake. He used it well, and in 1950 formed Alan H. Investments, Ltd.—named after his first son. Four years later he sold the company for four million dollars and headed, like others before him, for Wall Street, where the real action could be found.

The basic parlay was the same: Get control of a corporate shell with cash, use it to buy into other businesses and use them to buy still others. Three of his biggest companies were Universal Controls, General Development, and Seven Arts. They represented a wide range of interests: racetrack betting machines, land development, and movie production.

The Wall Street Journal, in June 1964, did a profile on Chesler. To illustrate his business technique, it gave this actual example:

> On Valentine's Day 1956, Mr. Chesler and his associates bought 52% of the stock of P.R.M., the Detroit auto parts concern, for $3.9 million and thereby came into control of $7 million. Within the next 99 days, the Chesler group took over the shells of two more U.S. corporations which gave them access to another $25 million in liquid assets.

[1] For details of Coppola's life and death see *Syndicate Wife.*

These rapid thrusts were regarded by some on Wall Street as just a little too dazzling. . . . A stockholder of Ridgeway Corp., one of the shells, was distressed too—sufficiently to file suit against Mr. Chesler and some of his associates. . . . In essence, the stockholder charges the Chesler group with diverting Ridgeway's assets for their own benefit. He says they used Ridgeway's funds to make six loans totaling $22 million to the other two shells they controlled. These loans, he charges, allowed one of the shells to buy the TV rights for the Warner Bros. movies and enabled the other—Universal Controls—to buy a company which made pari-mutuel betting machines. The three shells had identical directors, consisting of Mr. Chesler and four associates. . . .

Morris M. Schwebel, a New York attorney, was an officer and director of each of the three corporate shells which the Chesler group took over in 1956. He served as president of Universal Controls at the same time Mr. Chesler was the chairman.

Schwebel was to play a strange but minor role in the Bahamas. In 1956, however, he helped Chesler acquire a small company called Chemical Research, which became Florida Canada and then General Development Company. Chesler recognized a good thing when he got it and cut in such friends as Trigger Mike Coppola. Mike was forced to sell a block of General Development stock after a 1958 Las Vegas gambling fling with Sleepout Louie Levinson of Newport, Kentucky. Coppola was "between couriers" and a little short of cash.

The value of General Development stock rose from less than $3.00 a share in 1956 to more than $77. Chesler was able to sell 250,000 shares to Gardner Cowles and still remain the largest stockholder. In 1959 his holdings in General Development alone were estimated to be worth $50 million.

Not only did the company make money for Chesler, but it gave him a reputation as a land promoter. General Development built three small cities in Florida by use of a $10-down, $10-a-month installment plan. Here is how one cynic described the action: "It was a free-wheeling, razzamatazz operation, with all the gimmicks that move the lots. He took an idea that had worked successfully in Palm Springs and used it in Florida. Just as soon as the land drained so that you didn't need a scuba diver to see it, he put in a golf course. . . . The electric golf carts brought the game to the cardiac cases and old guys who were limited to the shuffleboard courts of St. Petersburg. Soon senior citizens who had the 'down' and the rest for monthly payments were populating areas that were known only to lost campers and night crawlers.

"Lou Chesler organized a highly skilled public relations department who knew the selling value of 'big names.' Nationally known entertainers, addicted to golf, were flown in to have their pictures taken on the golf course, and the caption always hinted these big names were associated with the development. Arthur Godfrey is one of the biggest examples of this.

"Byline writers wrote articles extolling the virtues of the area and the men associated with it. Then the nice full-page ads appeared with the 'Move up to Country Club Living' bit. With pictures of extra-happy folks just lazin' around a kidney-shaped pool sipping drinks, and Junior sitting on the marina dock hauling in pan-sized fish, and young Mister-Business-Executive canning a long one on the 18th green, while his adoring (and sexy) bride looks on."

The same techniques were later to be used to sell lots on Grand Bahama. But, of course, the pictures could also show a dark, serious-faced man in a tux, accompanied by a blond with a sophisticated hairdo and a low-cut gown, testing his luck at a roulette wheel operated by a very young and good-looking man with a foreign air about him. (Chances are he had been imported from Sicily.)

Overseeing things in General Development was a man who later was to perform somewhat the same function at Freeport. His name was Max Orovitz and he was very respectable in Miami Beach financial circles. After all, he had been part of the "Miami Group" which invested millions in Israel. Chesler picked him up along with Ridgeway Corporation.

It shouldn't be thought that a man with Chesler's zest for the good life would devote all his time to making money. Shortly after coming to Miami he bought the L'Aiglon Dinner Club, 9585 Harding Avenue, Miami Beach. Rumor had it that a lot more than steak was available. Mike McLaney, who managed the club in 1956–1957, has confirmed the restaurant was operated at a loss.

"We gave away food and drink and had a very good time," said McLaney, but he denied there was any gambling. Shortly after quitting L'Aiglon, McLaney appeared in Cuba, where eventually he "bought" the Nacional from the Cleveland Syndicate. Mike kept trying to operate the casino long after Castro took over, but finally abandoned the effort and turned, instead, to the Bahamas.

Of that more later. Where organized crime is concerned, history has a way of repeating itself.

Apparently the supper club was not Chesler's first venture into the entertainment world of Miami Beach. When the Royal Commission of Inquiry in 1967 asked him about the mysterious John Pullman—reputed international courier for Lansky—Uncle Lou cheerfully revealed a relationship of sorts.

For twenty-five years, said Chesler, he was a partner in Florida with Pullman's brother-in-law, A. C. Cowan. The Copa City, a large and lavish nightclub on Miami Beach, was one of their joint ventures. When it closed temporarily, Cowan moved on—Chesler said—to the Riviera.

Whether it was to the Riviera on the New Jersey side of the bridge to New York, or the casino by that name in Havana, Lou neglected to say. The New Jersey Riviera in pre-Kefauver days was the syndicate's most plush casino in the East—the rival of the Beverly Hills Club outside Newport, Kentucky, or the Mounds Club outside Cleveland. The Havana Riviera in the post-Kefauver days was Lansky's personal project.

The Royal Commission didn't need to ask if Cowan later went to Freeport. His role there as a highly paid consultant was a matter of record.

Nightclubs were little more than hobbies for Chesler, however, as he pressed his luck in that happy-go-for-broke period now known as the "Eisenhower Years." Not since the Twenties had the wheeler-dealers had it so good. Here is an example of the comfortable relations that developed.

Seven Arts, Ltd., became one of Chesler's key companies. A director was Maxwell M. Rabb, who happened to be special assistant to Sherman Adams in the White House and also Secretary to the Cabinet. Adams was, of course, a friend of Bernard Goldfine, the wealthy industrialist and philanthropist of Boston who had been violating federal and state laws for years. When Goldfine got into trouble as a result of a newspaper squabble over a TV station in Boston, Tex McCrary tried to help save his image. Tex had done wonders for Richard Nixon, but he could do little for Goldfine. By no coincidence, Tex was making a nifty $36,000 a year a little later, as "vice president of corporate relations" of Seven Arts. McCrary and Rabb gave Chesler a hand when Lou arranged for Seven Arts to invest in the development of Grand Bahama. Some directors didn't think much of the idea, and their opposition later hurt at a critical time. However, aiding also was Rabb's law partner, David Lubart. Dave became secretary of the Grand Bahama Development Company in 1962.

The respectable Maxwell Rabb was in great demand as a corporate officer after he left the White House in 1958. Among his several posts was that of chairman of the board of the International Airport Hotel System, Inc.

Originally incorporated in 1958 as Airway Hotel, Inc., the company had a fascinating history. Its first project was to build a hotel on top of Miami's airport terminal building with the help of a $2 million Teamsters union loan. The hotel became a staging area for the projects on Grand Bahama, but the company went on to build other airport hotels from Boston to Los Angeles.

A vice president of the company was Bryant R. Burton, who, among other things, was a secretary of the Fremont Hotel in Las Vegas and a stockholder of the Sands. Principal stockholder in the Fremont—a downtown casino—was Ed Levinson. Ed was the brother of Sleepout Louie, that pal of General Development stockholder Trigger Mike Coppola. But Ed had his own friends —among them Meyer Lansky, Cliff Jones, and Bobby Gene Baker, who succeeded Sherman Adams as the man to see in Washington when the Democrats took over.

The syndicate plays both sides of every political street and cultivates friends in high places regardless of party affiliation.

Another figure in the hotel corporation, a future business associate of Baker, was former Caribbean gambling figure, Jack Cooper. His wife was a major stockholder and Cooper received $75,000 for "services rendered" in connection with the Miami hotel project. A "sportsman," he was ultimately to be convicted for failing to report income received from a deal involving the sale of warplanes to the Dominican Republic. His defense: The deal was a fraud and therefore not subject to taxation.

Also an officer of the hotel company was Solomon Levine. He was identified in the company's stock prospectus as president of Greater Boston Finance Company and brother-in-law of Henry Garfinkle, another of the hotel company's promoters.

Garfinkle was president of the American News Company. A subsidiary, Union News Company, obtained restaurant and cocktail lounge concessions at several of the company's hotels. Maxwell Rabb was a director of American News Company.

By a strange coincidence, Garfinkle later became a major stockholder in the Herald-Traveller Corporation, which published two newspapers in Boston. Another stockholder in the newspaper company was Joe Linsey, that old bootlegger and friend of Meyer Lansky.

Perhaps that is why Lansky was also a major stockholder in International Airport Hotel System.

Only such a financial wizard as a Meyer Lansky can easily understand the intricate scheming that preceded the formation of The Grand Bahama Development Company, Ltd., or Devco as Bay Street put it.

Chesler turned first to General Development Company only to encounter unexpected opposition. While he was the largest stockholder, his sale to Cowles had cost him control. Cowles and other members of the board of directors couldn't see the wisdom of setting up a land company just 76 miles from Florida to compete with General Development. Chesler, not daring to reveal at this early stage that some things besides real estate would be offered, turned to other sources.

Playing a key role in what followed was a money man with a thousand interests—Serge Semenenko, officially only a vice president of the First National Bank of Boston but, as a Boston newspaper put it, "in a sense, a 'bank within a bank.'" First National gave him a special staff and freedom of action, and he operated on an international scale. According to *The New York Times* he was best known in financial circles as a "financial doctor of the entertainment industry," where he was said to have "played a major behind-the-scenes role."

The National Syndicate has also "played a major behind-the-scenes role" in the entertainment industry since bootleggers bought into nightclubs and backed their favorite actresses in Broadway plays. And syndicate bigwigs were putting money into motion pictures long before Abner (Longie) Zwillman, the so-called Al Capone of New Jersey and old associate of Lansky, helped finance *Guest Wife,* which won an Academy Award nomination for Claudette Colbert.

Among the movie companies in which Semenenko was active were several with which Chesler had dealings, including Warner Brothers and Seven Arts. In fact, some seven years later Semenenko had quite an argument with his bank before agreeing to turn over to the bank a $1 million fee he received for arranging the merger of the two companies.

Popeye the Sailor was featured in Chesler's venture into Seven Arts. Back in 1958, Globe Film Productions, Ltd., a Canadian company, acquired 325,000 shares of Seven Arts stock in exchange for granting Seven Arts Canadian distribution rights on some feature films and Popeye cartoons.

Four months later Chesler, Morris Mac Schwebel, and fifteen others bought the Seven Arts shares from Globe. Louis Chesler "and associates" took 206,250 shares. Schwebel and his wife took 18,750. Schwebel was president of Universal Controls, Inc., and

Chesler was chairman of the board. Now both had their foot in Seven Arts, and before long Uncle Louis was chairman of that too.

In 1960 Chesler looked to Seven Arts as a source of funds and, ultimately, invested $5 million of the company's assets in the Bahamas adventure. Another $5 million came from Lorado Uranium Mines, Ltd., a Canadian company similar to New Mylamaque, in which Chesler was a major stockholder. But $2 million more was needed by Chesler in his own name if he was to meet the terms offered by Groves and Sands.

On April 29, 1960, "pursuant to arrangements made by Louis Chesler," as the company put it later, Seven Arts issued $15 million of 5½ percent convertible subordinated debentures to a group of investors headed by Chesler. Of the total, Chesler personally purchased $2,175,000, and Chesler Operations, Inc., bought $1.5 million. Another $5 million, with Chesler and Chesler Operations, Inc., listed as the beneficial owners, were registered in the name of S. Rosenbloom, Inc.

Four days later the Meadowbrook Bank of West Hempstead, Long Island, made a $3.5-million loan to Louis Chesler, Chesler Investments, and Chesler Operations, Inc. However, it developed later, Seven Arts supplied the money to the bank for the loan to Chesler and ultimately got its money back plus $20,433 in interest.

Chesler later sold back to the company his share of the $15 million of debentures without converting them. Ultimately, however, Schwebel became Seven Arts' largest stockholder, when he converted a large block of the debentures. Carroll Rosenbloom, an associate in several companies with Chesler, and at one time owner of the Baltimore Colts, became the second largest owner.

The result of this and other financial byplay too complicated to mention—even if it could be understood—was a series of events that reached a climax several years later in the piney woods of Duke University. More immediately, it permitted Chesler to proceed with the development of Grand Bahama as a swinger's paradise.

It was an impressive deal on paper that Groves and Chesler put together. The interests represented by Chesler would receive title to 102,000 acres of land in the so-called "Port Area." The land was valued at $12 million. Considering that the Port Authority paid $2.80 an acre for most of it, Groves obviously wasn't risking much. In return, Chesler agreed to a number of things, the most important being the erection of a resort hotel with 250 rooms. Earlier, it will be remembered, the Port Authority had pledged in the "Supplemental Agreement" to have such a hotel built by December 1, 1963. It now passed along the burden to Uncle Lou.

Other requirements included the construction of an 18-hole golf course—a priority item in any Chesler land development—the grading and paving of several miles of road to service the airport, the town of Freeport, and the hotel, and the construction of a marina area.

While these details were being worked out, good old Mac Schwebel was indicted by a federal grand jury in New York on 41 counts of selling unregistered stock of Soil Builders International Corporation to Liechtenstein trusts. The 62-square-mile principality, tucked between Switzerland and Austria, has long been a hiding place for foreign profits made by American companies.

The indictments, early in February 1961, caused Schwebel to take a leave of absence as president of Universal Controls, Inc. Chesler, still keeping the Bahamas deal quiet, resigned as chairman of the board to devote, he said, full time to General Development. Carroll Rosenbloom was elected to succeed him.

Ironically the investigation of Schwebel by United States Attorney Robert Morgenthau continued and ultimately brought new indictments. It also brought trouble for that prominent citizen of Miami Beach, Max Orovitz. Postal authorities in Miami notified Morgenthau that a small package insured for $50,000 had arrived there. It was from the Union Bank of Switzerland, and it was addressed to Schwebel. When asked about it, Schwebel confirmed the package contained $50,000 in cash. But, he said, it didn't belong to him. It was really intended for Orovitz.

Intrigued, Morgenthau began an investigation of Max that

ultimately led to his indictment in connection with some dealings in General Development stock.

With Universal Controls in the capable hands of Rosenbloom, Chesler was free to finalize the new venture in the islands. In less than a month the Grand Bahama Development Company, Ltd., was formed in Nassau, with Stafford Sands getting his usually healthy fee for handling the legal details. Principal purpose of the company was said to be the sale and development of land. Louis A. Chesler was named president.

In return for the 102,000 acres, Devco gave the Port Authority 50 percent of the stock of Devco. Seven Arts Production (Bahamas) Limited and Lorado of Bahamas, Limited, each received 20¾ percent. Chesler got 8½ percent.

Chesler, who loved to gamble, was taking a chance he could continue to control Seven Arts and Lorado. There is nothing to indicate at this point that he was greatly concerned. He appointed his old partner, Al Cowan, executive vice president and prepared to start developing.

At $60,000 a year, the brother-in-law of Courier John Pullman was ready to help.

On October 20, 1961, the Port Authority's accounting firm—Peat, Marwick, Mitchell & Co.—completed an audit of the Grand Bahama Development Company Limited. Assets were listed at $25,465,233.37, of which the biggest item was land and interest in land valued at $12,510,000. Devco had only $200 in cash on hand, but it had $10,521,277.28 in banks, and another million in escrow. Investment in shares of affiliated companies was placed at $798,000. Tied up in an option for additional land was $500,000 more.

Liabilities were estimated at $1,465,233.77. Under "Capital," it was noted that five million shares at $8.40 each had been authorized for a total value of $42 million. Of the total authorized, 2,400,000 shares, having a value of $20,160,000, had been issued.

The accountants noted without comment a rather curious violation of the company's own rules. It quoted the Articles of Incorporation as providing: "No part of the funds of the company shall be employed in the subscription for, or purchase of, or in loans upon, the security of shares in the company. The company shall not directly or indirectly give any financial assistance for the purpose of, or in connection with, a subscription for, or purchase of, such shares, nor make any loan to any of the directors or officers of the company, or enter into any guarantee or provide any security in connection with any such loan."

Despite this rule, the accountants reported: "The directors have passed a resolution ratifying arrangements to provide that the company would keep on deposit with one of its bankers substantially in excess of $5,00,000.00 U.S. for a long period of time, and give said bank ten days prior written notice of commitments for the expenditure of a large sum of money out of such accounts *in consideration of that bank furnishing $5,000,000 U.S. to a shareholder for investment in this company."*

The accountants didn't identify either the bank or the shareholder involved, but they did quote that legal eagle of Bahamian law, Stafford Sands, to ease any fears anyone might have as to the legality of the arrangement.

"Counsel for the company" had ruled: "In my opinion, notwithstanding that the arrangements have been ratified by the company and recorded in its minutes, under Bahamian law the correspondence does not constitute a binding contractual obligation to maintain in the account a balance substantially in excess of 5,000,000 dollars for any period of time. Further, in my opinion, the company would not commit a breach of a legally binding obligation if it withdrew its funds from the bank, at any rate provided it gives at least ten days' notice thereof."

Stafford was beginning to earn the 1.8 million he would receive over the next few years. In his view, no illegal conflict existed, because—in his opinion—the deal with the bank wasn't binding legally under Bahamian law.

And this wasn't just any attorney's opinion—it was the view of the chairman of the Development Board and the most powerful member of the House of Assembly. It was the verdict of the "Doyen" of the Bay Street Boys, the future Minister for Finance and Tourism.

When you could combine such official force with the resources of Serge Semenenko's "bank within a bank" at the First National in Boston, you had quite a parlay going. The possibilities were endless. Of course, where both were concerned, there was always the question of how long they would be on your side. Under the circumstances, however, Chesler could be sure Sands would cooperate for awhile—at least until the casino was a reality.

Sands wanted the casino as intensely as Dick Nixon wanted the Presidency. He had no intentions of operating it. Leave that to the professionals. His reward would come from the exercise of legal control, which, under the circumstances, amounted to powers of life and death over the project.

The fall of Batista and its implications for gambling had not escaped Sands's attention. As in 1946, after the dictator's first flight from Cuba, Stafford moved in 1959 to cash in on the opportunity. On behalf of a "syndicate" composed of three Earls and a Viscount, he asked for a Certificate of Exemption to permit a casino at Delaporte Point on New Providence Island. The request promised an annual "licence" fee of £12,000 for twenty years.

The Governor in Council routinely rejected the application on the grounds that one casino on New Providence was enough— the Bahamian Club was still operating in its exclusive way—and that the law sponsored by Sands in 1939 wasn't intended to permit exemptions for lengthy periods. Not for the first time did Sands wish he had not been so inexperienced when the legislation to legalize the Bahamian Club was drafted. Yet he declined an invitation from the Governor in Council to petition for legislation prescribing a casino licence fee system. He wanted less regulation, not more.

A few months after the application was rejected, Meyer Lansky —according to Sands—approached him with a new proposal for gambling, and shortly thereafter Lou Chesler appeared in Nassau. Chesler and Lansky had been involved in Canadian mining deals in the past, but Sands insisted officially that Chesler's proposal for gambling was unrelated to Lansky's proposition.

Events seem to prove otherwise. The evidence is plain, however, that Sands—while favoring gambling—still wanted it on his own terms in 1961. Like others in the Bahamian government, he had to be won over gradually to the syndicate's way of thinking. The big legal fees he received helped do just that.

A memo from Groves to A. C. Cowan—Chesler's man and Pullman's brother-in-law—in August 1961 put the problem into perspective: Groves wrote:

"The matter of the Casino is so important and so delicate it must not be talked about and must be handled with the greatest care. I have given considerable thought and study to this matter and enclose herewith my present thinking.

"I have not discussed this with Mr. Sands, or anyone for that matter. Although Mr. Sands is greatly in favour of what we are trying to accomplish, he, nevertheless, has some ideas of his own which would not suit me and I am sure would not suit you, such as trying to tie the matter down so that it would be in the hands of a European syndicate and limiting the operation to the winter season only. I would, if possible, have legislation authorizing Government to amend our Government Agreement and in this way we would be assured permanency. This may be so difficult, unless coupled with some major contribution to Government which would be acceptable, we may have to be content with a short term permission rather than legislative approval.

"As you know, the Governor in Council has authority to grant short term permission. Whether or not they would do so has always been in my opinion exceedingly doubtful. For that reason we should try and present what we wish in a form that would be acceptable. The strongest independent member of the Executive Council is Mr. Eugene Dupuch who with his brother, Etienne Dupuch, publisher of the Nassau *Tribune,* has always been the strongest opponent of all forms of gambling.

"I would say that if it would be possible that these gentlemen approve, or at least not oppose what we wish, our chances would be greatly enhanced. Both of these gentlemen are friendly, have great confidence in us and I consider them to be men of highest integrity."

If words are judged by their usual meanings, Groves's description of the Dupuches as "men of highest integrity" would seem to conflict with his hopes of persuading them to change their mind on gambling. However, in the underworld, words and phrases sometimes take on special meanings. Thus a "liberal" is not a person favoring left-wing programs of the New Deal or Great Society type, but an individual opposing strict enforcement of antivice laws in a community. In the same way, a "man of integrity" is a man who will keep his part of a bargain once the deal is made—regardless of how distasteful it may be. When considered in these terms, Groves's description was to prove completely accurate.

A few weeks after writing the memo to Cowan, Groves offered Eugene Dupuch $10,000 as a contribution toward his campaign expenses at the next general election. Dupuch, while living in Nassau and serving as a member of the Executive Council, represented a remote district on Crooked Island where campaigning was expensive. Gratefully, Dupuch accepted the offer. In 1962, however, with a crucial election coming up, Dupuch decided his health didn't permit him to face the rigors of an out-island campaign. He decided, instead, to run as an independent for the East Central District of New Providence. Generously acquainting Groves with this decision, Dupuch said he offered to return the money. Generously, Groves refused to accept it and told Dupuch to use the surplus after the campaign for the incidental expenses a man in public life has to meet.

In the election that followed, Dupuch was not opposed by the United Bahamian party—the Bay Street Boys—so after being elected as an independent, he joined the UBP. A "man of integrity" was Eugene Dupuch. So much so that when the new constitution was adopted, Dupuch was appointed Minister of Welfare in Sir Roland Symonette's Cabinet.

Groves also had some dealings with Etienne Dupuch. An agreement was reached which provided the Port Authority would guarantee the newspaper an annual income of £10,000 in return for printing and advertising work. In addition, a check for $10,000 was drawn on January 10, 1962, and made payable to the Nassau *Tribune*. Another $10,000 check was drawn on January 25, 1962, and made payable to Etienne Dupuch.

And suddenly the publisher lost his crusading zeal.

Back on April 29, 1961, Dupuch had commented in a hot editorial: ". . . if anyone is fooling any group into believing that they have a chance to get a licence . . . we can tell them right now they have as much chance to establish a legalised gambling operation here as a snowball would have to survive in hell."

But in April 1963, after the Miami *Herald* had revealed a casino was in the works for Grand Bahama, the publisher asked quietly for more details. When he got them four days later, he commented editorially:

> Our opposition was based on the fear that this kind of operation would most definitely provide an open field for underworld operators from the United States.
>
> It is clear from the conditions contained in the agreement that this danger has been overcome.

An optimistic newspaperman was Etienne Dupuch, but he continued to be valued highly by Groves and Sands. Just after the casino opened in January 1964, Dupuch discovered he was a paid consultant of the Grand Bahama Development Company, Ltd., at £500 a month. He promptly wrote a "Dear Stafford" letter, which said in part: "I am sure you know that I am not happy about having casinos in the islands but since a casino has been established at Grand Bahama I am concerned to see that a high standard is maintained. If you think that my services in this way might be helpful I shall do my best but I want you to feel that it is an arrangement that can be terminated at any time by either side."

Exactly what Sir Etienne—for by now he had been knighted and elected to the Senate—did to maintain high standards isn't quite clear. But he served as a consultant for two full years.

Another man of highest integrity! Wallace Groves was quite a judge of character.

Things were beginning to fall into place quite nicely on Grand Bahama. And there was progress on other fronts as well.

4

Friends Indeed

MEYER LANSKY had not received such applause from top syndicate circles since he persuaded Lucky Luciano to cooperate with Naval Intelligence in "Operation Underworld" during World War II.

Some leaders had grumbled a bit when Lansky began concentrating upon the Bahamas. They cited the fall of Batista as proof that international deals were risky. Better, they argued, to stay in the good old USA where the political rules were known and officals had "integrity."

The grumbling ceased early in January 1961, when Robert F. Kennedy became Attorney General. The appointment sent a collective shiver down the underworld's spine. Foreign ventures seemed suddenly attractive, and Lansky's wisdom in launching the Bahamas Campaign back in 1959 was praised as the work of a true statesman.

Bobby Kennedy at the beginning of 1961 was Bad News, and syndicate executives knew it. Enough of them had done business with Teamsters President Jimmy Hoffa to be worried on that score alone. More, Kennedy announced a "Coordinated War on Crime," and as the brother of the President of the United States he had the muscle to make it work.

Three years before, Attorney General William P. Rogers had set up a "Special Group on Organized Crime" within the Justice Department and put Milton R. Wessel in charge. In its final report, submitted on February 10, 1959, the "Special Group" made several important points:

> Syndicated crime today presents a serious threat to our society. . . . It is a startling fact that nowhere in Government does there exist a permanent force capable of unifying action of the thousands of federal, state, local and special law enforcement units all over the country. . . .
>
> A syndicate itself does not ordinarily act as a cohesive unit in committing crime for profit. It merely supplies a code of conduct protecting its members from detection. . . .
>
> Syndicate crime has undergone great changes in the last thirty years. Indeed, the most startling developments have come only since World War II. . . . While government has created a new socio-economic structure to deal with the modern economy, it has done little to enable criminal law enforcement to deal with modern syndicated crime. . . .
>
> Just as with big business, management of the syndicate acts on a very different level and often miles away from operation. . . . Experience has taught syndicate members to acquire the services of highly qualified attorneys and accountants. Penetration of the cloak of legitimacy created by their efforts is sometimes almost impossible. . . .
>
> The profits of criminal operations are being more and more channeled into legitimate investments in business and industry. The result is that some of the most important syndicate leaders are men of outstanding public reputation with no criminal records, or, at least, none for two or more decades. . . .

Despite the evidence that the Special Group headed by Wessel knew the score, its recommendation that a permanent "Office on Syndicated Crime" be set up within the Justice Department was disregarded. It remained for Kennedy two years later to expand on the idea and begin a concentrated attack.

Ulimately, the syndicate's assumption that the Bahamas operation was out of reach proved erroneous. The agile Lansky, however, actually made use of the covert pressure from Washington to achieve his more subtle goals.

Additional support for Lansky came in April 1961, when the hopes of some Mafia leaders—as well as a lot of average citizens —came to grief in the Bay of Pigs. Santos Trafficante, Mafia leader in the Tampa-Orlando area of Florida, dreamed of succeeding Lansky as gambling czar of Cuba. As Cuban refugees went ashore in the ill-starred invasion, a Trafficante aide was waiting in Nassau with a fortune in gold. Bahamas police in a secret report identified him as Joe Silesi, better known as Joe Rivers, who had worked in Havana in the old days. Joe hoped to follow the victorious troops into Havana and reopen the casinos.

Somewhat annoyed when the plan failed, the Mafia announced it had let a $1 million contract for Castro. It was a futile gesture. The more intelligent sons of the Honored Society began begging for a piece of the action-to-come in the Bahamas. Other non-Mafia tycoons began surveying the Caribbean for additional casino sites.

Pressure for new developments began building in November 1961, when the veteran gambling empire at Newport, Kentucky, fell to local reformers aided by Kennedy's men. Five major casinos and scores of handbooks and bustout joints closed. Literally hundreds of "technicians" were thrown out of work, and the convention business in Cincinnati—just across the Ohio River—nosedived. Las Vegas and Lake Tahoe absorbed some of the unemployed, but many more ended up in Miami looking for "a break" from the elder statesmen of crime who had retired to plush homes there years before.

And this was just the beginning, according to all indications. Federal pressure mounted on such centers as Hot Springs, Arkansas, and Biloxi, Mississippi. New laws sponsored by Kennedy put the FBI into the syndicate-fighting business for the first time. The men of J. Edgar Hoover, forced to start from scratch, started bugging every telephone in sight. They got a lot of information, but they didn't always know what it meant.

Nevertheless, the heat was on. The blue-green waters of the Bahamas never seemed more attractive.

Not every one attracted to the developing opportunity on Grand Bahama was a member of the syndicate. While few people knew the true story, many sensed a chance for quick profits. Groves needed all his power as King of Grand Bahama to beat off the vultures.

Looking like anything but a vulture was middle-aged Virginia—that isn't her real name. She was the mistress of a south Florida man who had made millions in real estate along the Gold Coast. It was entirely logical that Virginia, on a visit to the Bahamas, saw a chance to get a bargain and snapped it up. For less than $100 she got an option on Grand Bahama property next door to the site of the future luxury hotel.

Pleased with herself, she talked freely of her bargain. She was sure her "patron" back home would want to invest heavily in a hotel on her land. Swiftly the word spread around Nassau. Early next day Virginia was "arrested" and dragged screaming through the lobby of her hotel. She was questioned for several hours at a secret location. After telling about her rich friend in Fort Lauderdare, she received more respectful treatment but was still held "incommunicado."

The following day her worried millionaire arrived and took charge. Virginia was returned to Fort Lauderdale and lodged in a mental hospital. She stayed there until she was willing to admit it was insane to try to purchase land on Grand Bahama from the *natives*. When this lesson was mastered, she was released to return to the $250,000 home her "lover" had built for her in Hallandale near Lansky's modest ranch house. Shortly thereafter she was robbed, and again, without intending to do so, caused the millionaire considerable embarrassment.[1] Ultimately he bought her a small hotel in Jamaica to get her out of trouble.

A less accidental encounter with King Wallace was had by Joseph Fortman and Sam Krevitt. They had been around Miami long enough to hear the whispers. On a trip to Grand Bahama early in 1961 they bought—or thought they bought—400 acres from the *natives*. Some of it was later to be valued at $2,000 per front foot—located on the beach near the future site of the luxury hotel.

[1] For details, see *Syndicate in the Sun.*

Getting even a dubious title was one thing—getting the money to develop it was another. One man reported to have money was Al Mones of Miami Beach. Mones was a leading layoff bettor of the class of Gil (the Brain) Beckley and Eliott Paul Price. He also operated, for bookies about the country, a check-cashing service known as Metro Mortgage Loan Company, Inc. In 1959, gambling on a deal with Castro going through, he invested heavily in the Capri in Havana. When that failed he put a large amount of money into the Carver House in Las Vegas, a proposed hotel-casino for Negroes. The project went under with the building half completed. But Mones had made profits in various land deals in Brevard County, Florida, close to Cape Kennedy. In Miami and Miami Beach he owned various apartment buildings and vacant parcels of land.

That Mones had money to invest, no one could doubt. What Fortman and Krevitt failed to realize, however, was that in a syndicate deal Mones was not a free agent. Yet he didn't turn down the applicants cold. Had he done so, they might have sought, and found, a more naïve backer. Better, from the syndicate's point of view, that the would-be investors should gradually become discouraged and quit. The direct treatment given Virginia was not appropriate in this situation.

Indicative of this technique is a letter from a Nassau law firm to Miami Beach attorney Lawrence Lazar. Dated May 8, 1961, the letter states that the Port Authority claims most of the land allegedly bought by Fortman and Krevitt. The writer gave as his opinion that the two men did not have title to the land and were still searching for evidence of title.

The attorney in Nassau noted that he had given the same information to "Mr. Malnik" and that Malnik might be able to inspect the title records because he was on "close terms" with Dawson Roberts, an attorney representing the Port Authority.

This seems to be the first mention of the ubiquitous Alvin Ira Malnik in connection with the Bahamas. His role here was a negative one, but in the months ahead he was to be a key figure in a bewildering complex of multimillion-dollar deals that kept him dashing from Paris to Los Angeles to Honolulu and back to Nassau.

Malnik began as a protégé of Mones. While still in law school, he was a partner in a second-mortgage business that caused a flock of citizens, including a Cincinnati rabbi, to complain they had been cheated. Some even demanded that Dade State Attorney Richard Gerstein investigate, but his office reported "your complaint does not reflect sufficient evidence for this office to successfully file and maintain a criminal action in our courts."

Meanwhile, graduating from the University of Miami Law School in 1959, Malnik found office space at Metro Mortgage, the check-cashing service Mones provided for bookies. Later he moved to 605 Lincoln Road, when Mones reorganized Metro Mortgage as Mall Mortgage and relocated it there. Serving as his clerk was a young law student who happened to be Mones' nephew. The student-clerk lived at Mones' home and called himself Daniel Wiselberg—his real name—Daniel Mones, or Daniel Malnik as the occasion indicated.

Lazar was attorney for Louis Ceader at the time he checked out "the Fortman-Krevitt deal." Ceader had been partner with Mones and Charles (the Blade) Tourine in the Capri at Havana. Lazar was also a partner with Jay Weiss in a huge Florida liquor empire. Weiss, who was to become a junior partner of Malnik in many deals, was able to buy land on Grand Bahama from Ceader. Malnik arranged it.

The youthful Malnik once explained his success to a reporter in these words: "Because of friendship people go out of their way."

Weiss, it developed, was a good friend of State Attorney Gerstein, who had been unable to find "sufficient evidence" against Malnik, and Gerstein admittedly made much money in Weiss-Malnik stock deals. Malnik, meanwhile, found an even more powerful friend than Al Mones—an old associate and close personal friend of Meyer Lansky known to the underworld as "Jimmy Blue Eyes."

The nickname was considered the cutest in syndicate social

circles since "Dimples" Wolinsky died suddenly, but it was applied with caution. Vincent Alo, despite the nickname, was a high-ranking Mafia figure and the Honored Society's liaison man with Lansky. Malnik was so proud of Alo's friendship, a well-known hood was heard to crow: "Al's got a new rabbi—Jimmy Blue Eyes."

Malnik was to make good use of Alo in years to come, but at this stage of his career—in 1961—he was still proving himself. His work paid off, however, as Krevitt and Fortman gave up their dream of developing the land they still insisted they had purchased. Eventually they began selling bits and pieces of the disputed land to other speculators who were willing to take a chance on some day making a huge profit. Ironically, for those who had patience, such land investment ultimately paid off. In 1968, after certain events had weakened King Groves' control, the question of title went into court. When evidence was introduced, proving that at least some of the Port Authority's claim was based on forged instruments, Groves made a huge out-of-court settlement to rival claimants. Fortman, who had retained a few acres while selling the rest, got nothing.

The great majority of those who challenged Wallace Groves got nothing. Indeed, some honest citizens who bought building lots from Groves and Chesler were startled to be greeted with gunfire when they tried to visit their future homes. It seems that some of the natives still clung to the notion the land belonged to them.

The natives were in a minority. As late as August 30, 1965, Sam Rice, a Fort Lauderdale real estate broker, received a letter from the president of a realty company at Freeport. It was in reply to a letter from Rice on August 26 in which he solicited the aid of the Freeport firm in establishing title to twenty-five acres in the Dundee Bay area of Grand Bahama.

In his reply, the Freeport dealer made it plain that he considered Wallace Groves to be "the man who has made Grand Bahama what it is today." He added candidly that his firm advised Americans and others not to attempt to get title to land on Grand

Bahama and told the "natives" that if they had land to sell, they should sell to the Port Authority at "a nominal price."

The Freeport operator concluded by inviting Rice to come over to Grand Bahama, but, under the circumstances as outlined, Rice saw little point in accepting the invitation.

The memo was prepared in the Organized Crime Section of the Justice Department and was circulated widely on a "confidential" basis. Entitled "Banking of 'Hot' Money," it began: "Information has been developed through surveys conducted by the Internal Revenue Service that 'shell' banking institutions have been established in the Bahamas by individuals closely connected with gambling interests, international underworld couriers, James Hoffa and the Teamsters Union. The banks are in many instances empty office space with the 'bank's' name on the door, or space retained in the office of the Bahamian lawyer who obtained the charter for the bank.

"The banks are apparently formed for the purpose of concealing the names of the depositors through means of secret numbered account systems. Money is alleged to be transported from the United States mainland by couriers using various methods including private planes and chartered boats. The money is then redeposited by the 'shell' bank into the more substantial English or Canadian banks located in the Bahamas—the accounts being under the name of the depository 'shell' bank. The funds can then be either retained in Nassau or forwarded on a commission basis to Switzerland for redeposit in that country.

"From the background of the individuals in the establishment of these 'shell' banks, it appears that the banks have been set up by underworld interests as repositories for skimmed gambling money from the United States in a location outside the jurisdiction of Internal Revenue Service. The funds can be further used for the financing of gambling casinos in the Bahamas and Caribbean area.

"Information has been received that the more substantial English and Canadian banks in Nassau are conducting an operation whereby an American citizen who wishes to get the use of his 'hot' money will pay a ten per cent fee to such banks in return for the banks executing a note for a principal amount. There will, however, be no transfer of funds. It will be merely a paper transaction ostensibly indicating that the principal amount has been loaned by the Nassau bank, thus enabling unrestricted use of the 'hot' money already held by the American taxpayer.

"Gerald Nelson Capps and Edward Dawson Roberts were originally officers and stockholders in both the Bank of World Commerce, Ltd., and the Bank of the Western Hemisphere, Ltd. Capps is an American attorney who works for Roberts who is a prominent Nassau attorney. Capps has been described by Bahamian police as a member of the 'fringe element' involved in the forming of the Bahamian corporations for questionable purposes. Capps associates with American hoodlums and Teamster officials who have come to the Bahamas to open bank accounts and safety deposit boxes and usually introduces same to the British and Canadian bank officials.

"The September, 1962, annual statement of the Bank of World Commerce, Ltd., lists John Pullman as President; Capps as Secretary and Treasurer. Philip J. Matthews and Alvin I. Malnik are listed as directors. . . ."

The story of the Bank of World Commerce is as complex as sophisticated financial minds could make it. Official investigators have been running hard since 1962 and still are tracing some of the seemingly loose ends. Some understanding was provided shortly before his sudden death by Meyer (Mike) Singer.

Singer first appeared in the Los Angeles area in 1953. He was something of a mystery man but boasted of his friendship with the late Louis Lepke of Murder, Inc. Early in 1964 he became business agent for a Teamsters Union local and began organizing grease peddlers.

The Los Angeles Police Department's intelligence division—the first in the nation and one of the best—developed information that heroin was being smuggled into the United States from Mexico by way of a grease-collection system. Under the direction of Singer, some members of the union were allegedly picking up the drug in Mexico and hauling it across the border buried in 50-gallon barrels of grease.

Investigation disclosed that Singer had helped organized kosher butchers in New York. From New York he went to Las Vegas and joined with Irving (Nig) Devine and Irving Blatt—two half-brothers—in forming the New York Meat and Provisions Company. Devine was a former Newport, Kentucky, gambler who had moved to Miami with Ed Levinson in the late 1940's. Kefauver heat drove them to Las Vegas where they ultimately invested in the Fremont Hotel and Casino.

The police were unable to prove Singer had anything to do with the narcotics traffic, and Mike consolidated his position as Jimmy Hoffa's Man on the West Coast. In August 1958 Singer was sent to Honolulu with orders to "organize everything on wheels." He failed, but he returned with some ideas that later were to be explored. Hoffa, not one to admit failure, ordered a testimonial dinner for Mike. It was held December 19, 1958, at the Ambassador Hotel in Los Angeles, and was attended by meat packers, grease buyers, and union officials. Everyone but the officials was required to donate $100 to buy Singer a $5,700 Oldsmobile. Mike said he was "overwhelmed," but Hoffa said he deserved nothing less for doing such "a great job for the Teamsters in Hawaii."

The long arm of friendship began flexing its muscle a few months after the dinner and, coincidentally, about the time Lansky began making plans for the Bahamas. Mike ran into an old friend Philip Matcovsky, who now called himself Matthews.

Matthews had come a long way since leaving his boyhood home in New York, and like Singer was planning to go still further. From 1954 to 1957 he had worked for the Saving and Loan Commission of California, and had been appointed conservator of Empire Savings and Loan at Van Nuys. The company was purchased by Empire Financial Corporation, a holding company, and Matthews became director.

Shortly after Matthews and Singer had their reunion, Singer was told that Martin Oschin, president of Empire Financial, wanted to acquire a bank outside the United States. It seems, Matthews explained, that it was against the law for any United States holding company to control more than one savings and loan association within the United States.

Making use of those contacts so necessary to businessmen on the fringes of organized crime, Matthews and Singer visited Miami Beach where they were introduced to young Mr. Malnik. Yes, indeed, he could help them. To Grand Bahama they went where a friend of Malnik, a Philip Mero, held a charter for the Bank of the Western Hemisphere, Ltd. Malnik, through his friends in Nassau, could have formed a new bank in a few minutes, but it served his purpose to negotiate with Mero for the purchase of the existing charter. A Canadian, Mero was a friend of Chesler. Later he was to be an officer of a huge stock promotion known as Scopitone, Inc., with which Malnik and his friend Weiss made millions. When that ended, Mero went back to Freeport to sell lots for Chesler.

Mero sold the bank charter to Empire Financial for $25,000, and, according to Singer, Malnik took half the money.

Impressed with the idea, Matthews broke with Empire Financial and combined with Philip Nasser, a motion picture executive who headed a firm called Allied TV. Out of this marriage came Allied Empire, Inc. Named corporate counsel was that bright young attorney Alvin Malnik, who had done such a good job in negotiating for the Bank of the Western Hemisphere.

Singer admitted that he invested heavily in Allied Empire, and was agreeable when Matthews and Malnik decided they needed their own bank in the Bahamas. Malnik was spending much time in Los Angeles and was introduced by Singer to George Raft. A former small-time hood turned successful movie gangster, Raft was impressed by Malnik's talk of Al Mones and Jimmy Blue Eyes. His movie career about finished, Raft was dependent upon gamblers for a living. His name was enough to guarantee him employment as a shill in some Las Vegas casinos. He had worked in that capacity for Lansky in Havana until Castro spoiled things. Later he would be sent to London to front for a casino there, but right now he was out of work and eager to win the friendship of a man with contacts in the Bahamas. After all, the grapevine said big things were planned there.

To consolidate his friendship, Raft gave Malnik a set of expensive cuff links and introduced him to Clifford A. Jones, former lieutenant governor of Nevada. Jones had fronted for Meyer Lansky in early Las Vegas casinos, and as late as 1957 had been exposed as his front in the Thunderbird Hotel. More recently, with Lansky's blessings, he had operated a casino in Haiti, but after falling out of favor with Papa Doc, the local dictator, he sold it. Bad luck had dogged him in Havana too—he won the casino rights at the plush Habana-Hilton just before Castro came out of the hills. However, in conjunction with Ed Levinson, he had formed a new connection with Bobby Gene Baker in Washington, and new plans were being pushed in the Caribbean.

The two men found much to talk about, and when on March 10, 1961, the Bank of World Commerce, Ltd., was formed, Jones was an investor with $56,000 worth of stock.

Singer's former partner in the meat company, Nig Devine, bought $2,800 worth of stock, as did Devine's partner, Ed Levinson. Coming in with $28,000 were Mr. and Mrs. Irving J. Leff. Associated with the New Frontier Casino in Las Vegas, Leff had also been a partner with Al Mones in the ill-fated Carver House venture.

Matthews, with an investment of $231,000, was the largest stockholder. Phillip J. Nasser bought $33,101 of stock. Malnik, organizer of the bank and its general counsel, held only $2,800 worth of stock.

The man who was to replace Gerald Capps as president of the Bank of World Commerce, once the organizational stage was completed, proved to be the mysterious John Pullman.

Formerly an American citizen, Pullman got his start, as did so many of his colleagues, in Prohibition days. Born in Russia in 1901, he came to the United States in 1918, and was convicted in

1931 for violating the liquor laws. In the same federal prison was a man to become famous as Yiddi Bloom, a member of the notorious Kidd Cann Gang of St. Paul-Minneapolis. In later years Pullman was to find a place as an international courier for Lansky, while Yiddi and his brothers fronted for Lansky in the purchase of land under Miami Beach hotels.

In 1943 Pullman became a United States citizen. He married a Miami girl and settled down in south Florida, where his brother was a respectable businessman. But the pressure of syndicate affairs caused him to renounce his citizenship and move to Canada. In 1954 he became a Canadian citizen, but the travels of the restless Russian had just begun. In 1960 he moved his residence to Switzerland, where he established an official relationship with the International Credit Bank. Thereafter he made regular trips to Las Vegas and Nassau, and his reputation as a courier grew into a legend.

Several episodes serve to illustrate his other functions. In 1962, for example, Fat Tony Salerno, New York lieutenant of Trigger Mike Coppola—Chesler's friend—wanted to buy a home in Miami for his mistress. Malnik took care of the transaction and a $75,000 mortgage was recorded at the Dade County courthouse. Shortly thereafter a $75,000 money order was drawn by Pullman on Barclay's Bank in Nassau and made payable to Malnik. The money order was marked, "Salerno loan."

Investigators said it was Fat Tony's cash coming home from Switzerland in the form of a "loan" to Malnik. The mistress, known to the boys as "Peggy," reportedly was pleased with Salerno's generosity. Love was wonderful.

Pullman was helpful even when love failed. The wife of Gil (the Brain) Beckley, at the time leading layoff bettor in the country, divorced her husband after the cleanup of Newport drove him to the Blair House on Miami Beach. A $10,000 check was cashed by Ben Cohen, famous syndicate attorney on Miami Beach. The check was drawn on a Swiss bank by Pullman and made payable to June Beckley. Cohen had represented June in the divorce settlement, just as earlier he had represented Trigger Mike when Ann Coppola got enough of beatings and abortions and divorced him.[2]

Investigators also identifed Pullman as the source of loans made to Sleepout Louie Levinson—Ed's brother—at the Flamingo Club in Newport. Other "loans" went to a Florida corporation controlled by Al Mones.

It was the Syndicate—one big happy family most of the time. Mike Singer disclosed that on one occasion two Las Vegas colleagues got annoyed with Malnik for allegedly not paying off a loan fast enough, and made arrangements for someone to "take care" of their young friend. However, "word came from Florida" to leave Al alone, and the contract was voided.

Singer also revealed that another courier for the International Credit Bank in Switzerland was Sylvain Ferdman. Singer and Ferdman became good friends, and when Ferdman visited Singer in exclusive Palm Desert, California, it was worth a byline story and picture in the *Daily News*. The reporter noted that Ferdman was only thirty years old but was "considered one of the most brilliant bankers on the international scene." He could speak French, German, English, Hebrew, and Italian "fluently," the story added.

Ferdman opened an account for Singer in Switzerland and introduced him to Dr. Tibor Rosenbaum, president of the International Credit Bank. He noted that Dr. Rosenbaum had diplomatic status as consul of Liberia. Shortly thereafter, however, Ferdman opened a branch of the International Credit Bank in the Bahamas, and the process of getting out the cash became simpler. Meanwhile the Bank of World Commerce was available.

Early in 1962, Singer said, he and Malnik left Las Vegas for Nassau. Al carried a small suitcase containing $250,000 in cash. He allegedly asked Mike to handle an envelope with $50,000 in it. The money was taken to Barclay's Bank in Nassau and deposited to the account of the Bank of World Commerce.

BWC, as it was known, then consisted of a mailing address—the office of Edward Dawson Roberts on Bay Street—and bank ac-

[2] See *Syndicate Wife*.

counts in Barclay's Bank and the local branch of the Royal Bank of Canada. In the early days the only known employee of the bank was Charlotte Rudeau. A New York native, Charlotte had worked as a waitress in the Junknoo Club in Nassau before being employed by Singer. Details of her employment became known when she was searched on February 21, 1962, by United States Custom Service officials at the Miami International Airport. The officers were looking for narcotics. They found instead a sheet of paper containing minute instructions as to her duties at BWC. The duties consisted largely of opening the office at a specific time each day and closing it at another time. She was also instructed when to pay the rent and the light bills, and to forward certain types of mail to Malnik in Miami Beach and other types to Singer in Los Angeles. For this she was paid $100 a week.

The twenty-eight-year-old blonde added the information that she took orders only from Malnik and Singer. She was fired by Malnik in May 1962. During the time the office had been open, she added, it had not contained a single file cabinet.

But of money it had millions.

Meanwhile there was a significant shift in Singer's position. In a well-staged little drama designed to impress the public, he broke with Hoffa. On May 22, 1961, Hoffa met Mike in San Francisco and officially fired him. Six members of Local 208 barricaded themselves in the union's office and refused to leave. Ultimately, Singer officially resigned, and the incident ended. Mike opened an office as "labor consultant" in the Gibraltar Building, 9107 Wilshire Boulevard. It was no coincidence that sharing the office was Allied Empire, Inc.

Hoffa's real relationship with Singer is perhaps better illustrated by the fact that on May 31, 1961—nine days after Singer was "fired"—Hoffa and his wife bought 400 shares each of Allied stock. Three days later Hoffa bought another 300 shares.

Since 1959 the Allied market price had fluctuated around $1.00 per share. By the middle of May 1961, it had climbed to $1.50. Suddenly it took off in a typical Malnik-type jump, reaching its historical high of $76 per share on November 24, 1961. By having inside information, Hoffa was able to get in on the killing.

Allied's climb was fueled in part at least by money "borrowed" from the Bank of World Commerce in Nassau. The first "loan" of $250,000 was granted by BWC to Allied on July 10, 1961. A total of $565,000 in 1961 and $375,000 in 1962 was "loaned" to Allied by the Nassau "bank." When the Allied loans were granted, Matthew, Nasser, and Malnik were directors of both organizations. Cliff Jones, a stockholder in BWC, was elected director of Allied as well.

It was a cozy arrangement all around.

Labor Consultant Singer, meanwhile, was picking up retainers from such companies as West Coast Fertilizer & Rendering Co., Huntington Meat Packing Co., and Golden Wool Co. Later he was to add such customers as the Beverly-Rodeo Hotel in Hollywood, California, and the Serv-U Corporation.

Serv-U paid Singer $300 a month. Ed Levinson recommended him for the job. Levinson allegedly also talked Jack Cooper and George M. Simon into investing in Serv-U. Both Cooper and Simon had earlier been involved in the International Airport Hotel System deal along with Lansky, Henry Garfinkle, Bryant R. Burton, and Maxwell Rabb. The two ventures seemed to illustrate the value of having friends in both political camps. Rabb had been Secretary of the Cabinet under Eisenhower, and, of course, the most famous official of Serv-U was Bobby Baker, Secretary of the Senate Majority and close friend of Vice President Lyndon Johnson.

Meanwhile, Matthews, Malnik, and Singer were wheeling and dealing in the savings and loan association field. Investments ranged from Anjon Savings and Loan Association in Baltimore to Citizens Savings and Loan Association in Albuquerque.

According to Singer, Bank of World Commerce funds were used to form the associations. Devine, Levinson, and Jones took part. Account 804 at Anjon was set up to hold funds for the eventual purchase of the Merritt Savings and Loan Association. Among persons paying money into Account 804 were: Irving Blatt, $10,000; Florence G. Baker, $5,000; Cliff Jones, $10,000; Ed Levinson, $12,500; Nig Devine, $25,000; Ben Sigelbaum, $12,500; and John Pullman, $5,000.

The big push came, however, when Matthews and Singer organized the Waikiki Savings and Loan Association in Honolulu on September 1, 1961. The application was approved on September 26 and the list of subscription depositors made public. Matthews was by far the largest with 136,250 shares. Others who had 5,000 shares or less included Irving Blatt, Louis Weiner, Charles Turner, Pullman, Levinson, Jones, Aaron Magidow, Joe Fendel, Sidney Levy, and Nig Devine.

Matthews soon sold 2,500 shares to Bobby Baker and an equal amount to Baker's partner, Fred Black. Singer took 15,000.

Goal in Honolulu was Ewa Plantation, a major sugar-producing company, which owned a lot of surplus land and had considerable cash. Its stock, of which 250,000 shares were outstanding, was selling at below book value. Singer had discovered the opportunity when he visited Honolulu for Hoffa. It seemed exactly the type of situation that delights the heart of stock promoter from Groves to Guterma, but the boys miscalculated.

On December 15, 1961, Matthews acquired an option exercisable only during the week of July 7, 1962, to purchase at $29.50 per share a total of 8,270 shares of Ewa. The unofficial closing quotation for Ewa on that date was 21 bid, 22 asked. Matthews gambled the price would be much higher by July. He promptly assigned the option to Allied Empire.

The role of Waikiki Savings and Loan Association in the campaign was to finance efforts to woo Ewa workers. Singer arranged for Matthews to give 6,000 shares of Waikiki to Teamsters union members in Hawaii as an inducement to open accounts at Waikiki. Plans were made to develop building sites of Ewa's surplus lands, and workers were assured easy credit could be obtained at Waikiki. Implicit in the background, if enough Ewa workers could be won to the Teamsters, was the threat of a general strike against the plantation.

Meanwhile, through the Bank of World Commerce and by means of the several stateside savings and loan associations, syndicate money was pumped into the campaign to buy Ewa stock. Hoffa, not one to miss out on a good thing, quickly got aboard the rocket as it began to soar. So did a lot of other people.

The founders of Ewa fought back. Chief among them was the firm of Castle & Cooke, Inc., one of the so-called "Big Five" of Hawaii. Fearing "manipulation by unscrupulous persons," as a representative of the company delicately put it, Castle & Cooke increased its holdings in Ewa from 40 percent to more than 50. Unlike the Bay Street Boys the Big Five had no intention of giving the National Syndicate a beachhead on one of its tight little islands. Alarm signals began buzzing in the offices of federal agencies ranging from the Securities & Exchange Commission to the Bureau of Labor-Management Reports.

As far as is generally known, Hawaii has continued to resist organized crime's efforts. Even a move to introduce legalized gambling as a "boon" to the tourist industry has been resisted. Much of the success of island leaders in beating off the syndicate can be attributed to Hawaii's isolated role during the Prohibition era. The boys had no opportunity to get entrenched.

In the battle for Ewa, however, Singer, Malnik, Levinson, Matthews, etc., couldn't really lose. Even if they failed to get control of Ewa—as eventually they did—the stock battle drove up the price, and they were able to make a bundle on their initial investment. After some of the intricate financial deals caused an investigation by the Securities & Exchange Commission, the Allied management team was moved out by dissident stockholders. Matthews resigned as Allied Empire president on January 2, 1963. Malnik, Jones, and others resigned as directors. Six days later Malnik was removed as Allied's secretary. On June 6, the reorganization complete, Allied changed its name to Riverside Financial Corporation.

Matthews took off for Israel, where he amused himself by examining 50,000 silver dollars belonging to Singer to see if any had value for coin collectors. Singer originally sent the coins to the International Credit Bank in Switzerland, allegedly intending to use them in the manufacture of money clips. Matthews was able to get them shipped to him in Israel. Singer was too busy building the International Motor Lodge, a $500,000 venture at Palm Desert, to worry about silver dollars.

One final transaction in 1962 illustrates how complicated the relationship between Allied Empire and the Bank of World Commerce had become. It went like this:

Allied needed $150,000 to reduce its indebtedness to BWC. Sidney V. Levy, a stockholder, agreed to lend it. But Levy had to borrow it from his bank, the Trade Bank and Trust Company of New York. Arrangements were made to give Levy 8,270 shares of Ewa stock held by Allied and 2,000 shares of Ewa held by Matthews. Malnik was given power of attorney by Matthews to pledge his stock.

The stock was given by Levy to the New York bank as security for the bank's $150,000 loan. Levy turned the cash over to Allied, who gave it to Malnik, who used the net proceeds to reduce Allied's debt to BWC by $149,081. Allied, in turn, gave Levy a $150,000 note at 6 percent interest. It would fall due in 30 days.

A special meeting of the board of directors was called to ratify the procedure. Malnik promised that, if necessary to repay the loan, he would "prevail upon a client" to lend Allied the $150,000. The client, he added, was John Pullman, president of BWC.

On the day the note to Levy came due, Pullman borrowed $150,000 from the obscure South Dade Farmers Bank of Homestead, Florida. As security, he pledged the Ewa stock, which was already pledged to the New York bank by Levy. Somehow the deal went through. Pullman gave the $150,000 from the Homestead bank to Malnik, who gave it to Levy, who gave it to the New York bank. The Ewa stock then went down the same ladder from New York to Homestead, south of Miami.

Pullman, meanwhile, was protected. Malnik arranged for Allied to give Pullman a $150,000 demand note at 10 percent interest. In March 1963 Pullman's note at the Homestead bank became due. The Ewa stock was at last sold. Allied's block payed off the debt to Pullman, who payed his debt to the Homestead bank. The 2,000 shares belonging to Matthews was sold to the Bank of Hawaii for $60,000—the price of Ewa was falling back to its original level. Of that total, $3,000 was given Pullman for his trouble. Malnik kept $10,000 for his trouble and sent $47,000 to the BWC account at Barclay's Bank in Nassau. Where it went from there was the syndicate's secret—safely hidden in the anonymity of Stafford Sands's treasured banking system.

Singer put it into perspective just before he died. Malnik, he said, was "very close" to Lou Chesler of the Grand Bahama Development Company, and had frequent financial dealings with him.

Malnik explained his success to a reporter: "The formula is one's relationship to other people. They have to have more than a passive interest."

It was a formula well understood by Meyer Lansky.

5

The Big Payoff

A FEDERAL AGENT, in Nassau to investigate the Bank of World Commerce, had an interesting conversation with police early in January 1963. Stanley Moir, superintendent of the Criminal Investigation Branch, revealed that the islands had just experienced a narrow escape from syndicate gangsters who—perish the thought —wanted to introduce big-scale gambling.

When the federal agent expressed concern, Moir explained. Certain American gambling interests, he said, had been displaced from Cuba by Castro. In the recent general election they had supported the Progressive Liberal Party in opposition to the United Bahamian Party. In return, the Negro leaders of the PLP had promised gambling concessions in case of victory. Fortunately, the Bay Street Boys had won an overwhelming decision.

In support of his statement, Superintendent Moir produced this Bahamian Police memorandum:

INFORMATION RE: ELECTION OFFENSES
On Saturday 24 November 1962, shortly before darkness, a DC-6 arrived at George Town, carrying 3 Americans and 2 Bahamian Customs Officers. The information is that the three Americans went to Rolleville and handed M.L.B. Johnson a sum of money

believed to be 2,000 pounds. This was said to be part of a deal made by the P.L.P. with an American gambling syndicate who had been assured by the P.L.P. that in the event of their having a majority in the next House of Assembly they would legalize gambling in the Bahamas. The DC-6 left George Town during the hours of darkness.

(*signed*) E. J. Bryan
Superintendent
of Police

The federal agent did not laugh. The secret deal Stafford Sands, boss of the ruling United Bahamian Party, had made with Groves and Chesler was still a secret and would remain one for two more months. The long delay of two years had been necesary to permit Chesler to get his hotel started and to let the UBP win the 1962 general election. Until the election was safely in the bag, any whisper of gambling could spoil everything.

Meyer Lansky, back in 1959, had taken the Bahamian political climate into account while making his big decision. He had been following developments for years and was well aware of the increasing restlessness of the black majority. He took that restlessness into account in making his long-range plans.

Democracy in the Bahamas was relatively new. Universal use of the secret ballot dated back only to 1949. Property ownership as a requirement for voting was not abolished until 1959. Women did not get to vote until 1962.

The real beginning of the black man's political freedom came in 1956 with the formation of the Progressive Liberal Party, known as the PLP. For the first time the Negro could vote for candidates not selected by the Bay Street Boys. In the general election that year the PLP—despite a system of districting that favored minority white rule—won six seats in the House of Assembly.

Matters became complicated when a PLP member formed the Bahamas Federation of Labour in 1957. Early next year a general strike erupted as the native began to employ his newly discovered muscle. Wealthy guests in Nassau's finest hotels suddenly found themselves without servants. The tourists left immediately, and the hotels closed. Fearing violence, the governor called for troops from Jamaica to keep order—a development greatly resented by the strikers. After nineteen days the strike ended, but the economy was slow to recover. The tourist total for the year decreased for the first time since 1945.

Blaming the PLP for the trouble, the Bay Street Boys formed the United Bahamian Party. Nineteen members of the Assembly declared themselves UBP members, and for the first time the division was officially on a racial basis. Nevertheless, the strike and the resulting publicity achieved constructive results. The Colonial Office in London, which usually ignored the Bahamas, sent over a representative to investigate. Ultimately he made it clear that Her Majesty's Government would support majority opinion despite minority control in the Assembly. To achieve this aim, property qualifications were abolished, and a single voting date was established. In the past, election day had varied throughout the islands, thus making it possible for enterprising individuals to vote several times. Nassau was alloted four additional seats to provide more representation for natives in the "over-the-hill" area. When by-elections were held in 1960, PLP won all four and added another on Grand Bahama, which gave them a more respectable representation than the Republicans achieved in 1964 in the United States.

Symbolizing the development of black power was the action in 1959 of Cyril St. John Stevenson, cofounder of the PLP. He startled Nassau by demanding the reopening of the investigation into the murder sixteen years before of Sir Harry Oakes.

"I could point my finger at the man responsible," Stevenson said. "Oakes was killed by one of his closest friends, a man he had no reason to suspect, and he drank with him several hours before the murder."

This resulted in a demand for a renewed investigation of the Oakes killing and the possible involvement of Harold Christie, who claimed to have slept through the killing. The demand was potentially dynamite, but it was handled in the usual agile way. A resolution was adopted asking Scotland Yard to reopen the case. Months later, when excitement had died, Scotland Yard announced there was insufficient evidence to justify reopening the investigation, and Sir Harry was again forgotten.

As the 1962 general election approached, both parties were demanding a greater measure of internal self-government. Regardless of who won, a constitutional convention was in the works. Nevertheless, the election would determine which party would supply the Premier and Cabinet officers. However, plans for gambling wouldn't wait that long. The necessary Certificate of Exemption would have to be pushed through the existing legislative and executives processes.

A key man was the Governor. As the representative of the Queen, he controlled the police department and presided over the Executive Council—which he appointed. Strict rules of secrecy cloaked council's deliberations, which, perhaps, is one reason the Bay Street Boys made such consistent use of it. Most legislation and all money bills originated there.

The Legislative Council served as an upper house and, when the new constitution was adopted, became the Senate. Its eleven members were also appointed by the Governor, but they could do little other than amend non-money bills. The House of Assembly, consisting of 33 Nassau residents—to represent an Out Island it wasn't necessary or practical to live there—offically handled the money bills dreamed up by the Executive Council. Presiding officer was the Speaker, who followed in an illustrious line. In 1701 Speaker John Warren broke the head of Governor Haskett for attempting to clean up pirates. Another early Speaker was a confederate of Aaron Burr in his conspiracy to overthrow the United States. Later Houses of Assembly passed laws regulating wrecking, accommodating the gun-runners of the Civil War, and the rum-runners of Prohibition.

The question in 1962: Could a House of Assembly be elected that would permit big-time gambling? A lot of syndicate money had been invested in the future of the UBP.

Lansky had not been idle while waiting for the right political climate. Plans for the Lucayan Beach Hotel on Freeport had been drawn. The architect was A. Herbert Mathes, the man who designed lavish International Hotel at the Miami Airport for Lansky and Garfinkle. Mathes had also drawn the plans for the Taj Mahal of Miami Beach, the Fontainebleau, where in the old days Mike Coppola had met with Chesler.

The hotel, when completed, was by far the most expensive ever built in a British colony. Cost per room was estimated at $25,000. The 1964 *Bahamas Handbook* lingered lovingly on details of construction: 40,000 bags of cement and some half-acre of glass from Belgium; 20 miles of electrical wiring and cables from Great Britain; 250 multi-coloured bathtubs and a complete air-conditioning plant from Miami; 850 tons of steel from Luxembourg and the United States; 6,000 square feet of marble from Italy; teakwood from Ceylon; telephone switchboards from Canada; laundry equipment from New York; carpeting from Georgia and Connecticut; silk draperies from the Far East; china, silver, and glassware from Europe.

Outside there was a tropical garden with $250,000 worth of trees and flowers; a 1,000-foot white sand beach; a 6,800-yard championship golf course; swimming pool and tennis courts galore. Inside were a nightclub, two restaurants, and three bars. There was, in short, just about everything but a handball court. And on that omission hangs a tale.

When Mathes drew up the plans, a large section was labeled "Handball Court." Handball is usually confined to men's athletic clubs in the States and is not at all popular in the Bahamas. Furthermore the room was large—76 by 120 feet. It was set just off the main entrance and handy to the nightclub and restaurants as well as to the bar.

Only a handful of people in early 1962 knew "Handball Court" was the name for the casino. The election was still ahead, the Certificate of Exemption had yet to be won, but confidence in Stafford Sands was high. After all, he was getting the pay of a miracle worker. Nevertheless, as the months wore on, the handball court was changed to convention hall in press releases. That made more sense in a hotel ostensibly intended to attract tourists.

No leaks occurred as the election date drew near. The campaign bore more than a superficial resemblance to the Kennedy-Nixon battle in 1960 and the Johnson-Goldwater mismatch in 1964. Conservative was pitted against liberal in both elections. In the Bahamas, however, it was the conservatives who were the incumbents.

The Bay Street Boys who ran the UBP stressed two points at the start of the campaign. They insisted that they alone had capable and experienced leaders. They also maintained that a PLP victory would be disastrous because American investors would refuse to deal with colored officials.

If elected, continued the UBP, the colony's tax structure would be preserved. No personal, corporate, or capital gains taxes would be permitted, and, because of this, capital would continue to flow into the islands. Tourists spending an average of $164 each would continue to come by the hundreds of thousands, and good times would remain.

Such campaign propaganda made sense to Bay Street merchants, perhaps, but it had little meaning for the natives in the "over-the-hill" slums or on the Out Islands. The wealth coming into Bay Street never trickled down. Communication and sanitation facilities were equally nonexistent.

In its reply the PLP argued that American businessmen were tired of doing business with the Bay Street Boys, of making secret payoffs, of seeing foreign capital exploited for the benefit of the few. Leading the attack was Stevenson, the man who had earlier asked that the Oakes case be reopened. As editor of the Nassau *Herald,* in a colony that had no television station and only one radio station, Stevenson was a man of influence.

In eagerly read editorials, Stevenson made fun of the leadership of the UBP with the exception of Stafford Sands. The boss of Bay Street was no laughing matter. Stevenson called Sands "utterly ruthless," and few were ready to argue the point. He blasted class distinction, which, he said, "places the white man automatically in the upper brackets of Bahamian society."

The editor noted that many educated nonwhites were not permitted to engage in political activity because of a Bahamian

"Hatch Act" that prohibited government employees from so doing. Yet civil service was the only area of employment open to such people. On the other hand, only rich white men could afford to hold positions of power that paid no salaries.

Stevenson's editorial thunder was countered and, to a degree, canceled by the Nassau *Tribune*—published and edited by Etienne Dupuch. A "man of color"—his skin is almost white—Dupuch was a highly literate man. He married a white American girl and their six children attended the best American schools. Indeed, one of his daughters obtained a certain pleasure from dating college boys from the Deep South.

The Dupuch family had its roots in the Bahamas for many years. Etienne, like his brother, Eugene, had served on many boards and committees while maintaining—outwardly, at least— an independent attitude. His ambition was to make his newspaper the "Voice of the Bahamas." To do this he needed new presses, and new presses cost money. Stafford Sands understood the problem.

As the campaign waxed hot, Dupuch warned his fellow colored people that they were trying to move too far too fast. They were not yet ready, he said, for the heavy burden of leadership.

Other editorials were devoted to praise of Sands and kind words for pioneers such as that "gentle-voiced visionary," Wallace Groves.

The editorial stand of the *Tribune* raised serious doubts in the minds of many people who did not know about the money Sands had arranged for the Development Company to send the newspaper and its publisher. At this stage, when a casino was unthought of by the public, no one could forsee that Etienne would soon be a paid consultant for a casino. After all, the Dupuches were men of integrity.

As the campaign came down to the wire, the UBP was frightened. Too much was at stake to gamble on the whim of an unstable black majority. Something more was needed to improve the odds.

Exactly who came up with the gimmick isn't known, but it was one familiar to syndicate-associate politicians in a dozen American cities—communism.

Wherever "do-gooders" have challenged entrenched vice in recent years, there has always been a ready reply—the reform crusade is really a communist plot to undermine confidence in local law enforcement. Naïve members of the John Birch Society are quick to rally to battle, and corrupt officials join in the fray to protect that good old American right—as A. B. (Happy) Chandler once put it in Newport—"to have it dirty."

With the specter of Castro looming larger across the Caribbean, the cry of "communism" had an even more immediate appeal. The platform of the PLP, with its demand for economic justice and its criticism of class distinction, lent itself perfectly to distortion and the label of "communism." In a very real sense the PLP was preaching revolution against the status quo, against the Establishment.

So it was that tales of secret landings spread by word of mouth. An American agent might be told the mysterious visitors were representing gamblers run out of Cuba, but the Bahamian people were told they represented Castro himself.

How much harm was done to the PLP cannot be assessed. Some leaders thought the entire smear was wasted—the average Bahamian knew nothing of communism and cared less. Others thought the stories provided the margin of victory for the UBP.

When the votes were counted, the real reason proved to be the unique system of apportionment. Had a "one man, one vote" rule been in effect, the outcome would have been different. The PLP won the popular vote easily, but gained only 9 of 33 seats.

Confidence in Stafford Sands had been justified. Now the supreme test was at hand.

Sands wasted no time in delay. On January 7, 1963, the Leader for the Government, Sir Roland Symonette, recommended Sands be appointed to the powerful Executive Council. Governor Robert Stapledon promptly obliged.

Any student of Bahamian history could have predicted the next move by recalling what happened immediately after Sands's first appointment to the Executive Council on November 14, 1945.

Three months later he applied for a Certificate of Exemption to permit gambling. In 1963, Sands waited only two months.

Appointed to the Executive Council at the same time was C. Trevor Kelly, one of those associated with Sands in the 1946 application. Logically, he could be expected to favor the new attempt. Also appointed was D. E. d'Albenas who had opposed gambling in the past. It was almost as if Symonette wanted to blur the situation just a bit. After all, secrecy still remained absolutely essential.

The next and decisive step came on March 20, 1963. Bahamas Amusements, Ltd., was incorporated with an authorized capital share of 500 £1 Class A shares and 500 £11 Class B shares. Lou Chesler was allotted 498 of the Class A shares and Mrs. Groves—Wallace still believed in keeping things out of his own name—was allotted 498 shares of Class B. The remaining two A shares went to friends of Chesler and the two B shares to friends of Groves.

The Articles of Association provided for three directors to be appointed by Class A stockholders and three by Class B. All stockholders had to be of Canadian or British nationality, as were both Chesler and Mrs. Groves.

On the very same day—March 20—Governor Stapledon received a detailed application for a Certificate of Exemption from the new company. The application was signed by Chesler and Mrs. Groves, but bore the unmistakable style of Sands, who had drafted it. The terms under which it was suggested the certificate be granted were spelled out completely. The efficient Sands also included a draft copy of a proposed agreement between Chesler and Mrs. Groves on the one hand, and the government on the other.

The next step was up to the Governor. Stapledon, a career diplomat on the verge of retirement, showed none of the hesitation displayed by his predecessor in 1955 when the Hawksbill Creek Act was presented for his rubber stamp. The boys had brought Sir Robert to Grand Bahama several months earlier to dedicate the new $112,000 airport terminal building, and an all-out effort to impress him had been so successful, Groves noted in a memo: "Much good was done in my opinion."

With secrecy still being maintained, the Governor put the application on the agenda for the next meeting of the Executive Council, which was set for March 27—just one week later. The Royal Commission of Inquiry noted dryly that consideration of the application was arranged with "unusual expedition."

An intense week of lobbying followed. Sands, with occasional help from Groves, pulled out all the stops in his effort to persuade a majority of the Executive Council.

The six unofficial members of the council—all owing allegience to the United Bahamian party, by no coincidence—included Sands, Kelly and d'Albenas, the recent appointees, and Sir Roland Symonette, Eugene A. P. Dupuch, and Dr. R. W. Sawyer.

Kelly had proved long before that he had no scruples about gambling, but Stafford Sands—who had grown wiser over the years—had sense enough not to rely on past positions. If the other members of the Executive Council were to be rewarded for services rendered, Kelly had to get a cut of the pie as well. A rather unique deal was worked out shortly after Kelly was appointed to the Executive Council on January 7.

Kelly was president of Greenacres, Ltd., a shipping company, which owned what has been described as a "king-sized version of the *African Queen*." It was called the *Betty K III*. Sands proposed the *Betty K III* make two trips weekly for five years from Miami to Freeport with loads of freight. The subsidy proposed, together with the gross freight income of the ship, would amount to $208,-000 each year. For every scheduled trip not actually made, the subsidy was reduced by $2,000.

While the scheme was decided upon, it was not until April 1—the Big Day—that Groves signed the agreement. After all, he wanted to be sure he was getting what he paid for.

As a footnote it might be added here that the *Betty K III* operated for nine months. The actual gross freight income was so far below the guaranteed amount, the Port Authority settled the contract for a flat $100,000.

Not bad for voting one's principles.

The $10,000 paid to Eugene Dupuch for election expenses has already been mentioned. Groves, who had been concerned about the Dupuch brothers, had the satisfaction of seeing the editor support the UBP while brother Eugene joined it. Eugene's appointment to the Executive Council was an added bonus.

A similar $10,000 payment for election expenses was made by Groves to R. H. (Bobby) Symonette, son of Sir Roland and later Speaker of the House. A noted amateur yachtsman, Bobby was also given a consultant's agreement. Investigation disclosed that he, like Kelly, was approached by Sands before the Amusements Company was formed. For a fee of £5,000 a year he was to give advice on how the yachting business might be promoted on Grand Bahama by the Development Company. He received the fee for five years and was never consulted about anything.

Unlike his father, Bobby openly favored gambling and was one of the few Sands confided in before filing the application for a certificate. Bobby suggested some amendments to make the idea palatable. Perhaps Sands considered that consultation enough for one man.

Sir Roland was delegated to Groves. A week after the certificate was signed, the King of Grand Bahama appeared with a draft agreement already signed by Chesler. Only the remuneration to be paid Sir Roland was undecided. His duties as consultant would be to advise "on the planning, construction and layout of roads, airfields, docks and harbours." Symonette agreed that £6,000 per annnum would suffice. After all, the father should get more than the son.

Dr. Sawyer, as a member of the Executive Council, couldn't be overlooked either. On April 5 he signed an agreement to provide consultant services for five years up to a maximum of 100 hours a year in return for an annual retainer of £2,000. His duties were to advise "on medical and dental requirements, services and facilities" needed for the "Port Area" of Grand Bahama.

Testifying before the Royal Commission of Inquiry, Dr. Sawyer raised some eyebrows by declaring he needed between $75,000 and $100,000 a year just "to get by." Thanks to Sands, he received a total of £10,000. Every little bit helps.

Apparently Sands saw no need to waste money on the remaining unofficial member of the Executive Council—d'Albenas. After all, some opposition to the certificate might be useful in stilling possible criticism that the whole affair was rigged.

The three ex-officio members of the Executive Council included Colonial Secretary K. M. Walmsley, Attorney General L. A. W. Orr, and Receiver General and Treasurer W. H. Sweeting. Along with Sir Roland and their respective wives, all had been given a flying tour of two Florida cities built by the General Development Company and credited to the genius of Uncle Lou. The trip had been billed as "Operation Indoctrination" and toward its success much Tex McCrary public relations talent had been devoted. The operation ended in the plush luxury of the Fontainebleau, where, in informal conversations, it was agreed that gambling as an inducement to tourism might be a good thing.

So it was, as the hour of decision—the hour Meyer Lansky had been pointing toward since January 1, 1959—approached, everything seemed as certain as human ingenuity could make it. Sands could also look back to 1959 and realize how naïve he had been in his aproach to getting a Certificate of Exemption. At last, now that arrangements had been made to share the wealth, he could be sure the rules he had drafted in 1939 would be interpreted to mean what he wanted them to mean.

Details of the proposal were circulated to members of the Executive Council. Sands discussed the plan with key members of the Legislative Council and outlined the program at the weekly meeting of the United Bahamian Party's executive committee. The session was held at the office of d'Albenas. Somehow, testifying to the tight control exercised by Sands and the Bay Street Boys, no word of what was pending leaked out.

All members of the Executive Council were present at the meeting on March 27. Proceedings in council were, by convenient law, supposed to be confidential. To disclose how members voted was, in itself, a law violation. So few details of the debate, if debate there was, have been made public. In any event, the Governor in Council approved the application subject to certain modifications. It was agreed that the submitted draft agreements would be revised by the Attorney General and Sands in such a fashion as to incorporate the desired changes.

The decision was officially communicated to the Bahamas Amusement Company in a letter from the Colonial Secretary dated March 29. The letter ended in these words:

"I am also to say that it is the wish of the Governor in Council that publicity of this matter be avoided until such time as all negotiations are completed."

The letter was old news by the time it arrived. Early on the morning' after, Sands called Groves. The King of Grand Bahama, perhaps not wishing to use the notoriously poor telephone service on the island, scribbled a note to Chesler as follows:

28th March, 1963

Dear Lou,

Stafford called me this A.M. The *news* is of course grand and definite. Vote 5/3. I do not know full details but gather RTS voted No.

Stafford is *really* concerned over leaks, rumours, etc. and says the matter can still be defeated. It will take two weeks more or less for certificate of exp. to be signed and in addition he has *promised* no publicity until after return from England. Stafford blames S. Kelly and us (He thinks you). Please, please, be careful.

Elis of Freeport *News* (and one other) says *you* laid at Caravel Bar 50 to 1 bet that there would be gambling at Freeport before end of year and Frank Stream told all over that Wednesday was D.Day—and that you did. We are being flooded with requests for information. Too bad.

Do hope you feel better.

I am now *most concerned* over *money* and think a meeting must be held on that soon.

My best,
Sincerely,
Wallace.

Apparently fearing Chesler would be unable to keep his big mouth shut if lured into a drinking bout, Sands rushed the matter through. On April 1—four days after the Executive Council meeting and only eleven days after the application was made—the Certificate of Exemption was formally granted.

The certificate as revised by Sands and the Attorney General conferred upon Bahamas Amusements, Ltd., the sole right to operate an unlimited number of casinos on Grand Bahama Island for a period of ten years from January 1, 1964.

This right was subject to the condition that every casino opened had to be operated in, or in conjunction with, a hotel having at least 200 bedrooms. Another condition, inserted to make sure the amusement company would not serve as a "front" for "undesirable interests," prohibited the company from surrendering control or management of the casinos.

After all, the joint must *look* respectable.

The certificate was subject to termination by the Governor in Council in the event of any breach of its conditions. It was also terminable three years after the opening of the first casino if, by that time, the total number of bedrooms in luxury hotels within the Port Area had not been increased by at least three hundred over the total available or under construction when the certificate was granted.

Really, old chap, the purpose of the casino was to increase tourism.

The agreement between Mrs. Groves and Chesler on the one hand, and the government on the other, contained several important points, which on paper, at least, made the proposed casino operation seem well regulated.

Prior written approval by Governor in Council was required before there could be any increase in the capital of the company, any change in the Memorandum or Articles of Association, or any change in the company's directors. Mrs. Groves and Chesler agreed to deposit all their share certificates in the company with the Trust Corporation of the Bahamas, Ltd., and to sign a letter of instruction to the Corporation requiring it to hold the shares in custody. If any director desired to sell his or her shares, the government got first chance at them—and at par value.

In the event the Governor in Council suspected someone other than Chesler or Mrs. Groves was in reality running the company, the two shareholders could be required to submit the matter to arbitration. If it was found on arbitration that the suspicions of the Governor in Council were correct, all of the A and B shares would be offered forthwith to the Governor at par.

Sands, by such provisions as these, made sure the boys on Grand Bahama would continue to need his expensive services for a long time to come.

Speaking of money, Sands decided it was time to submit a bill for his help in getting the certificate approved. He again wasted no time. On April 1, the day the Governor signed the exemption, Stafford told Chesler what his fee would be. According to Sands, he asked for £200,000. Deducting the money he had already received on account, he said, this left a balance due him of $515,900. Needless to say, this would be on top of various retainers and consulting fees he would also receive.

Chesler remembered the figure wanted by Sands as $576,000. The disagreement as to the amount caused the Royal Commission of Inquiry many headaches in 1967, when it began its effort to unravel the financial dealings of the Grand Bahama complex of companies. Evidence was found that Sands did receive a check for $515,900. What complicated the matter was not only Chesler's recollection but unsigned minutes of the Development Company board, which recorded that a motion was made and unanimously carried to pay Sands $576,000.

The matter was never settled, raising the possibility that Sands received *both* payments. The needed financial records were not produced.

Chesler later admitted he was quite shocked to hear Sands name his fee, but Groves assured him it was proper, he said. "There wasn't much I could do about it," Uncle Lou added candidly.

"Doing business in the Bahamas is a little different than anywhere else."

Asked, if he had signed a check for $576,000, on what bank it would be drawn, Chesler replied: "The First National Bank of Boston."

As a matter of fact, that is where the mony to pay Sands $515,900 was obtained. There is on record this letter:

April 1, 1963

First National Bank of Boston
Milk Street
Boston, Massachusetts
Gentlemen,

This will confirm our telephone request that you telegraph $515,900 to our account at Irving Trust Company, New York City, this day.

This amount is to be charged to our regular account at your bank.

Very truly yours,

THE GRAND BAHAMA DEVELOPMENT COMPANY, LIMITED

(*Signed*) Louis Chesler
Authorized Signature
(*Signed*) C. Gerald Goldsmith
Authorized Signature

The money was transferred as requested. A letter to Irving Trust arranged for the money to be shifted to the account of Stafford Sands. Why it wouldn't have been simpler to draw a check on the Boston bank in the first place was later explained in a cryptic statement by Development Company Treasurer K. W. Catren, who said: "They [the First National Bank of Boston] were payee and payer."

In a development reminiscent of some of the wheelings and dealings conducted by Malnik and Pullman at about the same time, $500,000 was transferred one week later from Irving Trust to the Boston bank.

It will be remembered that on April 28 Groves concluded his

good news note to Chesler by noting: "I am now *most concerned* over *money* and think a meeting must be held on that soon."

Apparently the immediate crisis was solved with help from Serge Semenenko's "bank within a bank." Stafford Sands got his payoff and the promise of more to come. On April 25, 1963, the man who had drawn up consulting agreements for others signed one he had drawn for himself. If ever there was a case of writing one's own ticket, this was it.

Under the agreement, the chairman of the Development Board of the Bahamas' duties for the Grand Bahama Development Company included: "Advising on advertising, publicising and promoting all phases of the Development Company's development programme and advising on methods of attracting to the Island of Grand Bahama visitors and potential purchasers of building sites in the Development Company's real estate developments in the said Island of Grand Bahama."

Some cynics might suggest that this was allegedly why Lou Chesler was brought to Grand Bahama. Others might wonder if Sands's official duties didn't include such activity. But of course Sands could reply that he was not paid for his official duties, and after all a man has to live.

To help Sands "get by," the contract provided he would be paid $50,000 a year for no more than 200 hours of work. And where other consultants were retained for five years, Sands's contract specified ten years. But there was another important clause. He was to serve for the duration of the Certificate of Exemption as well, and if the certificate were canceled in less than ten years, Sands's contract would also be canceled.

In other words, the employment of Consultant Sands was made contingent on the continuation of casino gambling on Grand Bahama.

Groves, who had once worried about Sands's interest in a seasonal operation in a European style, could now relax. Stafford now needed the gamblers as much as they needed him.

Perhaps this is why—according to Chesler—Sands wasn't satisfied with his $250-an-hour consultant's fee. He wanted it doubled. Once again, Groves assured Chesler it was proper to do so.

Sands was not through, however. Mining every possible lode, he asked Groves and Chesler to make regular political contributions to the United Bahamian Party. The entire package deal to permit gambling depended upon the political health of the UBP, so why—asked Sands—should not the Development Company contribute money? After all, in the absence of principle, money is the lifeblood of a political party. Of course it was assumed there would be no new election for four years, but, naturally, the UBP had expenses all along.

The boys on Grand Bahama were in no mood to argue with Santa Claus. They agreed to pay Sands personally the sum of $10,000 a month. Allegedly, it was to be used on behalf of the UBP, but it went into a private bank account at the Royal Bank of Canada. On the books of the Development Company the payments were listed as legal retainers during 1963.

Although Devco—the development company—incurred the obligation to make the political payments, it was Amco—the amusements company—that ultimately footed the bill. Devco charged Amco with what were called "management fees" of $24,000 per month to meet the political contribution and the consultancy fees. The contributions were paid directly by Devco to Sands during 1963, but payment for 1964 and 1965 was made in a lump sum in March 1966. A total of $182,448.32 was made by Devco to the new company, Paradise Enterprises, Ltd., which, in turn, paid it to Sands. Payments totaling $50,000 for 1966 were made to Sands via Paradise Enterprises, Ltd., but this time the money was transferred directly from Amco.

By 1966 such a corporate maze had been created by Groves that money could flow in any direction and get to its destination by a dozen different routes. However, the ultimate source was the same: The money Amco made at the casino in the Lucayan Beach Hotel.

An interesting aspect of the political payments was the fact that

Sir Roland Symonette, titular head of the UBP, knew nothing about them. Even stranger was the ignorance of H. R. Saunders. Since 1960 he had allegedly been treasurer of the UBP. Saunders was responsible for the party's official bank account and admitted only that he had heard Stafford had "funds available" if needed.

By 1967 there were $207,000 in the special bank account, which Sands said he was holding as trustee for the party. Why there might be a rainy day even in sunny Nassau!

The Royal Commission of Inquiry noted wryly in its final report:

> We find it hard to understand why these monies have been retained by Sir Stafford in his private account for so long. We appreciate that contributors might have preferred to make political payments directly to him in the first place. In this way they were able to conceal the nature of such payment; but it would have involved no breach of confidence on the part of Sir Stafford if he had then made a transfer into the Party's account of the amounts so paid.

Sands—as Groves noted in his March 28 note to Chesler—had promised no publicity on gambling "until after return from England."

The promise wasn't kept. Chesler was unable to keep the secret and blabbed to a friend, who leaked the news to a Canadian reporter. Soon the real estate editor of The Miami *Herald,* Fred Fogarty, picked it up, and within hours the story was all over Nassau.

The PLP was indignant. Some churchmen also protested. But the lack of information made criticism difficult, and the newspaper of Etienne Dupuch—which always had opposed gambling—felt that everything would be all right. No really effective anti-gambling campaign was organized.

Meanwhile, the spotlight of public interest shifted to England, where in May a constitutional convention was convened. Delegates from all political parties in the Bahamas attended, and the constitution of 1729 was scrapped and replaced in a matter of three weeks. Essentially, the old constitution was similar to the thirteen that had been in effect in mainland America at the time of the

American Revolution. The descendants of Loyalists who fled to the Bahamas to escape independence cherished the past, but with the decline of the British Empire and the rise of black nationalism it could no longer serve.

Under the new constitution the House of Assembly remained the seat of basic legislative power. The Legislative Council was reconstituted as the Senate. The Executive Council became the Cabinet, consisting of a Premier and fourteen ministers.

The Premier—following the British system—was that member of the House who, in the judgment of the Governor as the Queen's representative, was best able to command a majority in the House of Assembly. When tapped for the job, the Premier formed his government by asking the Governor to appoint such other ministers as he might suggest. The Governor had no choice but to comply. A vote of no confidence could unseat a Premier at any time.

The most important officer under the Premier, with responsibility for all financial matters was the Minister for Finance and Tourism. Like the Premier, he had to be a member of the lower house.

Under the new constitution, members of the Senate number fifteen. Five are appointed by the Governor on the advice of the Premier, and two on the advice of the Leader for the Opposition. The remaining eight were members in 1964 of the Legislative Council. These were to serve the Senate for the balance of the term for which they were originally appointed to the Legislative Council. As their term expired, they were to be replaced by the Governor after consultation with the Premier.

Administration of government was continued in the hands of a nonpolitical civil service supervised by a Civil Service Commission. This did nothing for the PLP's complaint that qualified Negroes were barred from political careers by the necessity of joining the civil service to make a living.

A Judicial Service Commission had similar control over the courts, with the exception of the Chief Justice and Attorney General, who were to be nonpolitical appointees of the Governor.

The Governor remained the ceremonial head of state, charged with reading each year the "Speech from the Throne." As in England, the speech was written by the majority political party.

Internal security and the police force were left in the hands of the Governor, just as questions of defense and treaty making were reserved to the United Kingdom. Local nationalism took a back seat to economy when it was pointed out that the Bahamas would save much money by having access to British embassies and consulates throughout the world.

This government of the Bahamas was the only government. There was no need for taxes to support a state, county, city, or other municipal body, because no such animal existed. Even the large city of Nassau had no separate governing body. It was bossed by the same people who governed the Out Islands. Of course, on Grand Bahama, Wallace Groves was king and a law unto himself, thanks to Stafford Sands and the Hawksbill Creek Act of 1955.

Since members of the Cabinet and the Legislature were to receive no pay—another factor making politics impractical for the poor—the cost of government was not great. Such taxes as were collected could be used "for the good of the people." Unfortunately, for the good of the people, about the only tax was customs duties.

Stafford Sands, now Sir Stafford, got the job he wanted under the new constitution—Minister for Finance and Tourism. When you had that, the rest was unimportant. He also became deputy Premier, more or less as a precaution.

Premier, as everyone had long expected, was that old rumrunner, Sir Roland Symonette. The 1964 *Bahamas Handbook*—under editor Etienne Dupuch, Jr., not the most objective publication—said this of the new Premier:

> Taciturn in manner, an attitude which is sometimes mistaken for disinterest by those who don't know him, Sir Roland has a steel-trap mind which cuts directly to the core of complicated problems, throwing trivia and legal double-talk to the four winds. His manner may sometimes appear brusque, but that is only because his mind is usually a half-dozen steps ahead of

everyone else's, and there is nothing that delights him more than "getting straight down to the brass tacks" in the shortest possible time. Positioned at the right of the Speaker's chair —in a seat he has occupied both as Leader of the Government and now as Premier—Sir Roland often sits with his eyes half closed, his head bobbing now and then with apparent drowsiness, as the pros and cons of debate drone on and on. But when it comes his turn to speak, you'd be safe to bet your last shilling that he hadn't slept a wink. For when he speaks, it is immediately apparent that he has grasped every detail. His sheer logic and sound reasoning often makes a shambles of the fancy words of those who have had the misfortune to precede him.

Shortly after becoming Premier in 1964, Sir Roland applied that "steel-trap mind" to the deal with Sands. Throwing "trivia and legal double-talk to the four winds," he wrote to Groves that he was terminating his consultant's contract. The Royal Commission of Inquiry commented on this action in 1967: "We should like to think that there was perhaps more than a twinge of conscience in his surrendering his consultancy after only ten months of its enjoyment and a total payment of £5,000."

PART III BUILDUP

6

Wheelers-Dealers

SHORTLY AFTER the Certificate of Exemption was signed in Nassau on April 1, 1963, an interesting collection of men gathered in the plush Miami Beach office of Max Orovitz.

On the wall were trophies that marked Orovitz's varied career as sportsman, philanthropist, businessman, and civic leader. Animal heads alternated with plaques. Like Joe Linsey in Boston, Orovitz had held many posts and given much money to charity. A bank director, a university trustee, an economic developer of Israel—Orovitz was wealthy in more ways than one.

To his office at 1 Lincoln Road came A. Herbert Mathes, the architect who had designed the Lucayan Beach Hotel, with its famous "handball court"; Lou Chesler, with whom Orovitz was associated in General Development and Universal Controls; and Meyer and Jake Lansky.

In admitting the meeting to federal agents years later, Orovitz claimed to have taken little part in the discussion. He was "in and out" of the room during the entire session, he said, and really didn't know what decisions were made.

A small man physically, Orovitz had gray hair, a thin mustache, and a penchant for bow ties. He also had a very well-developed respect for men of wealth and big ideas, and he was certainly aware that Meyer Lansky was chairman of the board. Therefore, his modest disclaimers notwithstanding, it is safe to assume he missed very little of the discussion.

Business at hand was to convert the "handball court" into a casino. It was no simple task and required expert knowledge. Architect Mathes did not have such knowledge, and neither did Chesler—casino patron though he was. Meyer Lansky and his brother, hump-shouldered Jake, had been designing casinos for years and were tops in the field.

Thus much of the discussion was technical—how many roulette wheels and where should they be located. Roulette is largely a woman's game, as contrasted to craps, so there were several factors to be considered. And where do you put the blackjack or "21" tables? Where do the "birdcages" go? How many crap tables?

A million other points had to be settled. How about the "eyes in the sky"—the concealed peepholes where silent watchers stare through the ceiling at both the players and the dealers? How about the cashier's cage, the money room, the counting room? Where should the casino bar be located? What about the guards, the sliding steel doors, the one-way glass? Etc., and etc.

The Lansky boys knew all the answers, and the business with the architect was soon completed. Now the discussion turned to the human equipment so essential to success—the casino personnel. Here Chesler's experience and understanding of human nature had meaning, but he found nothing in Lansky's suggestions with which to disagree.

Five men were named to serve as a nucleus: Frank Ritter, also known as Red Reed; Max Courtney, whose real name was Morris Schmertzler; Charles Brudner, also known as Charles Brud; Dino Cellini; and George Sadlo.

All were veteran gamblers. All had long been associated with the varied interests of Meyer Lansky.

Shortly thereafter a second meeting was held at Orovitz's office. Brudner and Sadlo couldn't attend, but Ritter, Courtney, and Cellini were present, as were Chesler and the Lansky brothers. Gaming equipment was ordered from Las Vegas, and plans were made to open a school in London for dealers. The school was made necessary by Clause 7 of the Certificate of Exemption. It provided:

> The Company shall not employ any croupiers or dealers or (except as hereinafter provided) any other staff in a Casino on the said island of Grand Bahama except persons who shall have been born in, and during at least Three (3) years before their first employment in the Colony by the Company shall have resided in, the United Kingdom of Great Britain and Northern Ireland, the Republic of Ireland or a country or countries in Western Europe, Provided Always that the provisions of this paragraph of this Certificate shall not apply (*i*) to the employment of one credit manager for each such Casino, (*ii*) to the employment for a period of Three (3) years from the date of the opening of the first Casino on the said Island of Grand Bahama by the Company of supervisors for the dice or "Craps" tables operated in each such Casino, and (*iii*) to the employment in any such Casino of persons solely in connection with the provision of entertainment and music in, the preparation and service of food and drink in, the maintenance and cleaning of the premises occupied by, and the driving and maintenance of vehicles used for and in connection with, any such Casino.

The purpose of Clause 7 was to reassure the innocent that no American mobster would be permitted to muscle in. Exceptions were permitted for credit managers and dice supervisors for reasons that seemed logical to the Bahamian mind. After all, the bulk of the players would come from the United States. Obviously a credit manager should be someone acquainted with what is sometimes politely called the "sporting fraternity." Craps, being an almost exclusively American pastime, would also require experts from the States.

The joker in the deck was the international nature of the syndicate. Lansky's boys operated far beyond the powder-blue waters of the Caribbean. Just opening at the time of the conference was a new casino on the Isle of Man in the Irish Sea. Scores of bright young men had been recruited in Sicily—it was thought the Mafia influence would keep them in line—and brought to the Isle of Man as dealers. This met the requirement of birth and residency made by the certificate. A quick course in the ways of American gamblers would equip them for duty on the pinelands of Grand Bahamas, and their presence would add a certain "foreign" glamour sure to appeal to naïve American tourists. As the transplanted Sicilians moved across the Atlantic, still others could take their places in the Irish Sea.

So the plans were made in Orovitz's office. Lansky was in evidence now—but briefly. Chesler had little to say. Four years later, when the Royal Commision of Inquiry asked him if he had consulted Lansky, Chesler gave a somewhat different version. The meeting, he said, occurred at the Fontainebleau, and only Ritter, Meyer, and Jake were present.

"I was told Lansky was the Dean of gambling and the most knowledgeable man, and that's why I requested the meeting," Chesler said. Lansky supplied advice, he added, but was "pessimistic" about the casino's success.

Chesler was not asked about the meeting in Orovitz's office. He identified Ritter, Courtney, and Brudner as his bookies for many years. He had bet with Ritter on that first trip to Florida in 1946, he added. "We offered the position of being head man of this casino to many bankers," Uncle Lou continued blandly. "We would have liked to get Eisenhower or maybe a man of the clergy, but they won't take such a position."

So he was forced to fall back on his bookmakers. They weren't a bad lot, he explained—just misunderstood. Why, a magazine wrote an article mentioning "a fellow in the casino" as being a member of Murder, Inc. The truth was, he, Chesler, went into the casino one day, and a mouse ran across the floor, and the man fingered by the magazine jumped up on a table and said, "God help me."

Following the same line, Max Courtney told the Royal Commission of Inquiry how he happened to adopt his name. At age seventeen, he said, he became a professional boxer, and, of course, Schmertzler wasn't quite the right name. There was a vaudeville act, known as the Courtney Sisters, which he liked, so he borrowed the girls' name.

When his boxing days ended "I was probably the youngest

bookmaker that ever booked on a New York racetrack." It was during these years that he became associated with Ritter, and the association continued after on-track booking became illegal in 1938 with the introduction of pari-mutuel betting.

The old fondness for boxing led to a relationship with the International Boxing Club, which—as all television viewers of the early 1950's knew—was headed by James D. Norris, president. The friendship with Norris was obviously of value to such a bookie as Courtney and—with help from such men as Frankie Carbo and Fat Tony Salerno—boxing became a national scandal.

Norris was to prove of value in the early days of the casino on Grand Bahama. Telephone service to the mainland was still unreliable, and Courtney often used the radio-telephone on Norris's boat to check out a sucker's credit rating back in the states.

Courtney gave this version of why he was hired by Chesler: "He knew of the following we have from the Vice President, the ex-Vice President, on down. I could say that great statesmen, without mentioning names, were customers of mine through the years. There hasn't been a big actor of any account in the United States that ever reached New York that was a player, who was not my customer. Same goes for songwriters, big businessmen, bankers. In forty years you get to know these people, and they get to know you. When you get their confidence, you have a customer for life."

He had, he explained, a list of more than 3,000 such customers, and Ritter had a similar list. In his career, he added, he had "catered to three generations in one family."

When pressed, Max said he knew the Lansky boys and had taken bets for them. Meyer, he said, was a "small customer," who seldom bet more than $50 on a horse.

Ritter was equally bland when it came to explaining his relationship to Chesler. It seems, he said, that Lou became very angry when he learned that George Sadlo had been "brought out of retirement" to recruit personnel for the new casino. Refusing to accept Ritter's assurance that the eighty-year-old Sadlo was still able and active, Chesler arranged a meet at the Fontainebleau to consult Lansky. Meyer told him he was "very lucky" to have Sadlo, Ritter continued, and the conference ended.

Ritter managed to keep a straight face when assuring the Royal Commission of Inquiry that he had been "in opposition" to Lansky in Cuba. He explained that he had worked for the Habana-Hilton, in competition with Lansky at the Riviera. It was his first experience with casino work, he admitted, and his job was that of "a goodwill man sending customers." The people running the Habana-Hilton "were told about our background, and that is how we were contacted. These things happen by reputation."

The fact that the gambling concession at the Habana-Hilton had gone to Cliff Jones, that old associate of Lansky in Las Vegas, was not mentioned. Nor was anything said about the Thunderbird Hotel scandal, which had shaken Las Vegas in 1955. In that affair the Nevada Tax Commission ordered the hotel's casino license suspended when it discovered that Jones and Marion B. Hicks actually represented hidden interests—Jake Lansky and the elderly Mr. Sadlo. That Sadlo really represented Meyer Lansky no one doubted. When the Nevada Supreme Court, by some tortuous reasoning, refused to uphold the suspension, state officials were able to get new legislation designed to control gambling and prevent future scandals. Nevertheless, the couriers continued to carry cash to Lansky in Florida, and Jones moved on to Caribbean casinos and the Bank of World Commerce.

When asked if "there is some form of criminal syndicate operating in the U.S." Ritter was very emphatic. It was all "a very dramatic myth," he said, and doubly unfortunate because all the nice young men Dino Cellini recruited in western Europe to work in the casino had been smeared.

"These boys never knew how to handle a check, how to handle cards, didn't know the value of American money, and they come and work in the Bahamas. Now, they are coming under the guise of gamblers. My experience is how will these very young boys who are under the gambling stigma now . . . that is what we call it . . . they have to raise families. I know I have gone to more then twenty or thirty christenings already in Freeport. I have attended fifteen or twenty weddings in Freeport. These boys are going to be in the gambling business as long as they live. Are they going to have the same stigma as in Vegas?"

Despite the "stigma as in Vegas," Ritter admitted his "contacts with Las Vegas" were "very valuable." About those contacts, he explained: "It is like everything else. We know a lot of these boys (in Vegas) from business. These boys know about us and our reputation. I think we are known all over the United States."

Some insight into the business activities and reputations of Ritter, Courtney and Brudner is provided by this confidential memo from the files of a federal agency's Miami office, under the date March 20, 1957: "Conf. Informer #59 phoned and alleged that Charles Brudner rode to Tropical Park every day with Saul Silberman.

"The informer believed that the activity was 'come back' money. Frank Reed (Ritter) and Max Courtney allegedly had an account at the track for that purpose. This was allegedly to avoid the necessity of having a large cover bankroll for 'lay offs' at the track. Allegedly Reed and Courtney lost $750,000 in a burglary of a safe box in the Boulevard Hotel, Miami, Florida, about 10 or 12 years ago.

"This telephone activity at the track disclosed in the newspapers came to the attention of the Racing Commission investigators right after Tropical Park had closed for the 1956–57 meeting. They went to ——— with it, with advice that they wait until next year and catch it in action. ——— allegedly went to Reed and Courtney demanding $20,000 in return for his blowing the situation without making a case. Reed and Courtney allegedly returned to their New York office without paying the bribe, but ——— nevertheless launched the public investigation contrary to the advice of the Florida Racing Commission."

Saul Silberman was President of Tropical Race Track in southwest Miami. The track had a long and colorful history of mob control. Among its owners had been a bootlegging associate of Lansky—Owney (the Killer) Madden. Another hidden owner had been John Patton, the notorious "Boy Mayor of Burnham, Illinois," and lieutenant of Al Capone.[1]

The newspaper publicity referred to in the memo concerned

[1] See *The Silent Syndicate*.

reports bookies were using telephones in Silberman's office. Among those temporarily barred from the track as a result was Trigger Mike Coppola, who sometimes handled bets for Lou Chesler. As usual, however, nothing concrete was achieved by the investigation, and the publicity was soon forgotten.

Not so easily forgotten was a raid by special agents of the Internal Revenue Service on February 3, 1956. A Ritter-Courtney-Brudner bookie operation in an apartment on Miami Beach was hit. Among those arrested were Brudner, Sam Kobrin, Abe Schwartz, Hymie Siegel, Bernard Katz, and Herman Stark. Ten years of litigation passed before a federal court judge ruled the defendants had to pay $356,788 in back taxes plus accrued interest and costs.

Following the raid, Brudner joined Ritter in Havana for a taste of the casino business. Among others who found employment there were Stark and Dino Cellini.

An elderly veteran, Stark learned the casino business at the old Cotton Club in the days when it was operated in New York by Owney (the Killer) Madden. It was there during Prohibition days that he first met Meyer Lansky. Later, Madden went to prison and was exiled by the Combination upon his release to Hot Springs, Arkansas, where he built a tightly controlled gambling empire and a repuation as an elder statesman of crime.

Stark said he first met Chesler in 1956, following his arrest. At the time, he explained, he was working for Ritter and arranging theatrical acts. He continued doing this, he said, at the Habana-Hilton. When the operation on Grand Bahama began he become a courier, carrying cash and checks from Grand Bahama to Max Orovitz on Miami Beach.

Dino Cellini apparently was one of the few casino experts per se. Unlike such men as Stark and Ritter, he always specialized in on-the-premises action as opposed to bookies who took bets on races, fights, or games in faraway places. A native of Steubenville, Ohio—a tough and dingy breeding place of gamblers with Italian names—Cellini and his brothers cut their teeth on the pitted cube. Newport, Kentucky, across the Ohio from Cincinnati, served as their training school. Eddie Cellini, Dino's younger brother, stayed behind to work at the Tropicana Club, a bustout joint in Newport, while Dino roamed far and wide in the services of Meyer Lansky.

In Operation Havana, Dino served Lansky well and remained when Meyer fled behind Batista. Ultimately, Castro put him in jail for awhile, but Cellini was released in time to work briefly at the casino in Haiti, which Cliff Jones had been unable to operate. Came time for new adventure in the Bahamas, and Cellini was given the task of organizing the school in London where all those "fine young men" from Sicily were to be taught the meaning of "seven come eleven" and "Mama needs a new dress."

As a direct result of that second meeting in Orovitz's office in the spring of 1963, Courtney and Cellini were posted to London to organize the school. A suitable location was found and a lease signed. The necessary instructional "tools" were ordered from Las Vegas. Nevertheless, there was a little hitch in obtaining the necessary permits from British authorities. Perhaps Cellini as headmaster of the school lacked the usual educational qualifications. In any case, a minor crisis arose.

Just by luck, Stafford Sands was in London attending the constitutional convention that was to give the Bahamas a new government in 1964. Courtney got in touch with Stafford, identified himself as representing Lou Chesler, and asked for help in obtaining the important permits. Sands, who knew his way around, "referred him to a leading firm of London solicitors who as far as I know handled the legal matters."

The firm was Simmons & Simmons. According to Courtney, they were able "to get us permission from the Home Office to open the school."

With the school facilities ready, the "solicitation" of students began. Courtney stayed in London from May until August "when I left for a vacation." Cellini remained behind, hurrying to get the first batch of dealers ready by the time the casino opened at the end of the year.

News that Grand Bahama Island was to become—in Tex McCrary's phrase—"the New World Riviera," interested gangsters everywhere. Those not already in Lansky's confidence began looking for an angle. Top Mafia leaders, who recalled the fate of Anastasia when he tried to muscle in on Lansky in Havana, cautioned their underlings to be careful.

Those faithful observers of what in their official reports they called "LCN" (for La Cosa Nostra), the FBI, noted the sudden interest in things Caribbean, and immediately began trying to fit known facts into their rather rigid and restricted concept of organized crime. If something big was going on on Grand Bahama Island, it just had to be the work of LCN. The only problem was to discover which "family" was running the show.

Typical is a report dated November 7, 1963, out of the Buffalo, New York, office. It begins by quoting a reliable source, the Buffalo *Evening News,* as saying in its June 29 edition:

> Legalized gambling is being proposed for the British held Bahama Islands to finance a massive improvement program and incidentally to attract tourists. Leaders of the ranking Bahamian Party are behind the move which they believe will spur development of hotels and resorts as well as provide direct tax revenue. The plan for legalized gambling reportedly stems from failure to secure financial aid for public improvements from the U.S. or British Governments.

This journalistic gem is interesting as an example of planted propaganda bearing little resemblance to the truth. It is frightening enough to assume that on the basis of such information Americans form opinions and vote accordingly as opportunity offers. It is even more shocking to realize that official investigators display no greater understanding or insight than newspaper reporters or editors responsible for such stories.

The report continued: "In connection with the above gambling casino in which Louis H. Chesler and Jack E. Gellman are reported to have an interest, Samuel G. Rangatore, Jr., of Niagara Falls, New York, returned from Philadelphia, Pennsylvania, on May 26, 1963. While at Philadelphia, Rangatore discussed the gambling casino venture with Angelo Bruno and also met with Felix John De Tullo, Nick Piccolo and Alfredo.

"The meeting on behalf of Steve Magaddino was apparently unsatisfactory for on May 27, 1963, Steve Magaddino and Samuel G. Rangatore, Jr., were observed departing from Buffalo International Airport aboard United Airlines flight 449, non-stop to Philadelphia International Airport. The records of United Airlines reflect Magaddino and Rangatore travelled together under the names Mr. A. Leone and J. Leone. On May 27, 1963, at Philadelphia, Pa., one Peter Maggio was observed driving Angelo Bruno to the Philadelphia International Airport in Maggio's Lincoln Continental automobile.

"An unknown individual was picked up at the airport, deposited at an unknown location and Bruno alone returned to the airport and picked up Magaddino and Rangatore, driving them to the residence of Peter Maggio at 3411 West Coulter Street, Philadelphia. While Bruno, Magaddino, and Rangatore were known to be in the residence of Peter Maggio at 3411 West Coulter Street on May 27, 1963, Bruno's lieutentant, Philip Testa, entered."

The report gives more details of the travels of Magaddino, allegedly the Mafia boss of Pittsburgh. The implication is that his travels are concerned with the casino, but no evidence is cited. However, Magaddino is identified as, "reportedly," a political supporter of Gellman on occasion.

Gellman is identified as an attorney and principal stockholder in Consolidated Bowling Corporation. Louis H. Chesler is said to be a "principal" in the promotion of Consolidated Bowling. The report then solemnly notes: "The files of the New York State Liquor Authority at Buffalo as they relate to Consolidated Bowling Corporation and its subsidiaries do not indicate that Steve Magaddino has a financial interest in Consolidated Bowling Corporation."

Additional information is cited which makes it clear the investigators had the wrong Chesler—Louis H. instead of Louis A. This is not admitted, however, and a report dated May 5, 1964, continues doggedly to pursue the effort to link Magaddino (and Bruno) to the casino: "As previously reported, information was received that Steve Magaddino and possibly Angelo Bruno of Philadelphia were interested in investing funds in a large gambling casino being built on the Grand Bahama Island for which Louis A. Chesler had obtained a license to operate, and that Jack E. Gellman, an attorney in Niagra Falls, New York, had discussed the possibility of members of the 'Magaddino family' furnishing funds needed to operate the gambling casino on Grand Bahama Island.

"Investigation regarding this aspect of Magaddino's interest indicated that in August, 1963, the Governor of the Bahama Islands warned the United States underworld not to attempt to cut in on the 'action' when legalized gambling made its debut on December 1, 1963.

"An article in the Buffalo *Courier-Express,* a daily newspaper of Buffalo, New York, in August, 1963, which reported the above, added that Crown officials were cognizant of reports that Sam Giancana allegedly had been given control of the Caribbean by the underworld syndicate."

The report continued with some background of the right Louis Chesler. It noted he was a Canadian with "extensive interests in major corporations, real estate, nightclubs, ranches, moving pictures and various other enterprises including racing horses." It also disclosed that Chesler "had gross income of approximately $277,000 in 1960 and approximately $592,000 in 1961."

There was this item in conclusion: "In June of 1963 it was reported by the New York office that Meyer Lansky is to be associated in some way with the gambling casino in the Lucayan Hotel, Grand Bahama Island."

Despite the acknowledgment in the final paragraph that Lansky was to be "associated in some way" with the casino, the legend that Magaddino and Bruno had somehow cut themselves in continued to flourish. Years later, respectable publications repeated the story as fact, never realizing, apparently, that it all began when some enterprising agent in Buffalo connected the wrong Louis Chesler with an attorney who "reportedly" was supported by Magaddino, when that attorney was active in politics. Once Magaddino was involved, it was easy to assume that any conversations with colleagues such as Bruno had to concern the casino. And soon an error became converted into fact.

The mention of Giancana reinforced the theory that the LCN was running the show on Grand Bahama. Yet "Mooney" had no more to do with the operation than Al Capone. The use of his name was but a reflection of the "Chicago legend," which boosters of the Windy City have managed to keep alive. If anything of importance happened in Las Vegas, Hot Springs, or Miami, someone was sure to blame it on a Chicago hood. Giancana, an aging playboy who enjoyed getting his name in the papers as he cavorted around with Phyllis McGuire and Frank Sinatra, had replaced Tony Accardo as the Chicago bogeyman. It was inevitable someone would credit the Bahamas venture to him as soon as it became public knowledge.

Meyer Lansky, being a modest man, found it very amusing—and useful.

In addition to equipment and casino personnel, there was yet another matter that had to be settled before the dice could start rolling in the yet-to-be-built hotel on Grand Bahama. A support bank was essentials to handle the flow of cash from the casino and to perform other banking services.

There were several candidates available, but the choice went to the Bank of Miami Beach. It had performed sterling service for Lansky's old allies, the Cleveland Syndicate, in Havana.

The bank opened for business on January 7, 1955, even as the Cleveland boys—with Lansky's blessing—prepared to move into Lansky's old Havana casino, the Nacional. Organizer was Ben Danbaum, former Omaha detective, who turned over his armored car service to Ben Gaines. Gaines was later a partner with Sam Tucker of Cleveland in the Miami Skyways Motel and with Tucker and Joe Linsey of Boston in the Sahara Motel on Miami Beach.

The Casino Internacional was organized on August 25, 1955, with such old rum-runners as Tucker, Moe Dalitz, Morris Kleinman, and Tommy McGinty as equal partners. On January 14, 1956, Danbaum announced the election of four new bank directors: Charles Danton, whose son Daniel was later a partner of Al Malnik in that second-mortgage business; Irving Feldman, a local contractor who even then was building the Havana Riviera for Lansky, and who paid Lansky $25,000 as a "finder's fee"; Samuel Rabin, vice-mayor of Surfside, where many of the top hoods lived; and Charles M. Volk, vice-president and cashier of the bank.

Five days after the new directors were named, the Casino Internacional opened in Havana. Some three months later all stock in the casino company was transferred to Mohawk Securities Corporation, a Panamanian company. On June 12, 1956, the board of directors of Mohawk, meeting at the Nacional, adopted this resolution: "Resolved, that the officers of this corporation be and they are hereby authorized and directed to deposit the funds of this corporation from time to time in the Bank of Miami Beach, at Miami Beach, Florida, and until further order of the Board of Directors to withdraw the same from time to time upon check or other order of the corporation signed in the name of the corporation by any two officers jointly."

The resolution, written on a form supplied by the Bank of Miami Beach, was signed by Sam Tucker as secretary and Thomas J. McGinty as president.

Thereafter, into the Mohawk Securities account at the Bank of Miami Beach came skimmed funds from the syndicate's Las Vegas holdings and cash from Havana. As a foreign corporation, Mohawk's account was not subject to audit. On one occasion Jake Lansky arrived from Cuba and was searched. Customs officials discovered he was carrying $200,000 in cash and more than $50,000 in checks for deposit in the Bank of Miami Beach. Yet, if the money flowed in, it also flowed out, and where it went there was no way to discover. In the three years of the Cleveland boys' operation in Havana, a total of $1,530,000 in checks was drawn against Mohawk Securities' account at the bank. Allegedly the money was used to pay winners in Havana in cash, but evidence mounted that the operation was a device for laundering "black money" and distributing it to syndicate members.[2]

The Cleveland Syndicate unloaded the Nacional on Mike McLaney, a friend and associate of Lou Chesler, in 1958—just

[2] For details, see *The Silent Syndicate*.

136

three months before Castro took over—and the account in the Bank of Miami Beach was closed. The machinery was still there, however, ready and tested. Lansky saw no reason not to use it in 1963.

In 1957 the bank changed hands. A group headed by Martin von Zamft and Harold Thurman took over. A close relationship was formed with the Miami National Bank at 8101 Biscayne Boulevard. The two institutions enjoyed—and the word is used advisedly—some of the same stockholders. Von Zamft at one point was chairman of both banks.

A major stockholder in the 1957 takeover of the Bank of Miami Beach, and president of the Miami National Bank, was Lou Poller. A former owner of radio stations in three states, Poller in 1957 was an investor in a plan to bring one of Miami's favorite sports, jai alai, to mobster-infested Anne Arundel County, Maryland. A license was issued less than twenty-four hours after the county legalized pari-mutuel betting on the sport, but the plan was canceled. Later the county legalized slot machines, and one-armed bandits were installed by the thousands within a few minutes of Washington, D.C.

Backed by Teamsters union funds, Poller won a proxy fight and forced Thurman out of the Miami National Bank. The union at one point invested $1,269,000 in the bank's stock in its own name. The bank also handled disbursements for such other Teamsters' loans as several made to the First Berkley Corporation of Los Angeles. President of First Berkley was George Burris, who in 1959 admitted to the McClellan Committee that he acted as a front for Benjamin Dranow in an attempt to rescue a Florida land scheme involving Jimmy Hoffa. Both Dranow and Hoffa were later convicted on charges growing out of the land deal. Poller was indicted in 1962 on perjury charges in connection with a 1959 meeting in his office which Burris attended. Later Poller "purged" himself by testifying truthfully, and the charge was dismissed.

The trail of Teamsters funds was a dark thread across much of the business life of the nation, and it tied together many underworld deals.

Meyer Lansky, the recognized mastermind of finance and chair-man of the board, was well acquainted with the potential for scandal yet untapped in the tangled affairs of the Bank of Miami Beach. Some housekeeping was in order.

On February 8, 1963, the bank was sold to William B. McDonald. Known locally as a "sportsman," McDonald was co-owner of Tropical Park and won fame later as a promoter of the speedy Cassius Clay-Sonny Liston heavyweight championship "fights." Not so well known is this little drama on October 25, 1963, at the Beverly Rodeo Hotel in Hollywood, California.

Seated at a table with some associates was Moe Dalitz, veteran rum-runner, gambler, and long-time friend of Meyer Lansky. In came Liston, the much-feared heavyweight champion. Liston was drunk. He exchanged words with the white-haired Dalitz and drew back his fist as if to strike him.

Dalitz didn't move. "If you hit me, nigger, you'd better kill me," said the boss of the Desert Inn, "because if you don't kill me, I'll make just one phone call, and you'll be dead within twenty-four hours."

The champion dropped his fist and walked away. Hotel records show he checked out the same night. His family remained at the hotel for two more days.

In July 1963, as plans moved ahead on Grand Bahama, the bank was sold again. Holding a majority of stock in the new arrangement were two New Yorkers: Philip E. Simon and Benjamin Cohen. The latter should not be confused with the Ben Cohen of Miami Beach, a well-known syndicate attorney and political fixer since the days of the S & G Syndicate.

The New York Cohen operated a bar and grill in his home town. Testimony in a district attorney's probe of liquor licenses later revealed that the bar was often the target of vice raids while under Cohen's management. An officer commented: "There have been thirty-four complaints alleging prostitution . . . thirteen arrests for prostitution" at the bar.

Some insight into Simon is supplied by an FBI memo dated in Boston on July 29, 1964:

"Investigation by this office and information received from confidential informants disclosed that Gennaro J. Angiulo has been making trips to Miami, Florida, in an attempt to obtain what he calls 'show money.' Angiulo is bringing down large sums of money to the Bank of Miami Beach in Miami, Florida. He turns this money over to Phil Simon, President of this bank, who is reportedly a connection for the hoodlum element in the Miami area and also backed by the hoodlum element in New York.

"As best the informants can ascertain, Angiulo turns the money over to Simon. Simon then holds this money for a few days and subsequently returns it to Angiulo. After the transaction is completed, it is made to appear that Angiulo has borrowed the same amount of cash that he has brought down with him from banks in the Bahamas and Nova Scotia, which are under the control of the United States. They apparently also obtain a receipt which reflects that the amount of the loan has been repaid; however, the books of these banks indicate the loan has not been paid.

"Informants are not clear on the exact workings of these transactions but are attempting to ascertain more details.

"The Miami office of the FBI is attempting to develop additional information in regard to the aforegoing through, and with, the Internal Revenue Service and the Federal Deposit Insurance Corporation at Miami, Florida.

"Recent information received by this office indicates that Salvatore Iaconi of Worcester, Massachusetts, and Pasquale Erra, well-known Miami hoodlum, have also used this method of obtaining 'show money.' "

Jerry Angiulo was the boss of the numbers racket in the north side of Boston and, presumably, had plenty of cash in need of laundering. As a lieutenant of Raymond L. S. Patriarca, Mafia boss of New England, Angiulo was part of the broad combination that had kept alive the tradition of corruption in Boston.

The "new look" at the Bank of Miami Beach was soon tarnished somewhat when Cohen and Simon began borrowing from the newly organized Five Points National Bank. Von Zamft, former head of the Bank of Miami Beach, formed the new bank in 1963. Miami National, which he also had headed, held controlling interest in Five Points National.

Five Points had a short but exciting life. Von Zamft, aided by other bank officials, began systematically to milk the bank's assets in a long series of phony loans. Financial transactions so complex as to baffle the average man were the order of the day, but the officials were too hungry—they bled the bank to death. Early in January 1966 the weight of the bad loans put it out of business. Even before the bank died, von Zamft and ten colleagues were under investigation. Ultimately they were charged with defrauding the bank of $600,000 and were convicted in 1968. Von Zamft drew a five-year sentence and a heavy fine. An associate, William Marmorstein, got four years, and the others drew lesser terms. Marmorstein was the brother of Max Marmorstein, an old-time member of the Cleveland Syndicate and one of its many real estate dealers.

While no one could feel very sorry for von Zamft and company, there was one aspect of the case that held tragic implications for the innocent.

A stockholder in the 1957 takeover of the Bank of Miami Beach was Aaron Goldman. He continued to play a part in the tangled affairs of the three banks and, reportedly, became disgusted. As the probe deepened into the fake loans of the Five Points National Bank, word passed that Goldman might "blow the whistle."

On March 28, 1966, the Goldman's eighteen-year-old son was kidnapped at gun point from his home on Miami Beach. For weeks the distraught parents waited for a ransom demand, and millions of Americans waited with them. No call came. The FBI, specialists in kidnap cases, remained baffled. Danny Goldman had apparently vanished.

Insight into the strange case came from another agency investigating the bank fraud. Investigators said they learned that Danny was kidnapped to keep his father quiet. As long as he kept silent, the youth would live. Shortly after von Zamft and the others were convicted, the second anniversary of the kidnapping was marked. "Of course we're hopeful," said Goldman. "Nothing has been discovered."

The wait continued. The outcome of the trial raised the possibility Danny—if still alive—might be returned.

Citizens who see nothing wrong with making money so long as armed robbery isn't involved, might well study the further history of the Bank of Miami Beach and its owners. The lesson that men in pursuit of the fast buck sometimes cut corners too closely is well illustrated.

In August 1965 control of the bank passed to Jules Sokoloff of Toronto, Canada. Something of a mystery figure, he had interests in Nassau and lived in a plush home on Star Island in Biscayne Bay. He had made news of a sort some months earlier when he held a party at his home to celebrate his purchase of a cruise ship company.

On November 13, 1965, the cruise ship *Yarmouth Castle* was 131 miles east of Miami off Great Stirrup Cay enroute to Nassau. Suddenly it caught fire. The crew of a nearby freighter sounded the alarm and at Opa-locka Airport, in north Dade County, Coast Guard planes took to the air. Aboard the *Yarmouth Castle* were 376 passengers and a crew of 174.

Complete confusion existed on board the burning ship. Less than half the fourteen lifeboats were launched. The freighter first to spot the fire was first on the scene. The first lifeboat to reach the freighter contained about twenty crewmen and four passengers. The second lifeboat was left unattended as the crew climbed to safety. The captain assigned some of his own men to it and sent it back for passengers.

An utter lack of safety devices and training contributed to the disaster. Only seventy-four days before, a Congressional committee heard testimony that the *Yarmouth Castle* ran short of fuel and water, ran fifteen hours late, leaked in the main lounge when it rained, and broke down completely when a chief engineer added salt water to the boilers. After listening to the testimony, Congressman William S. Mailliard said the *Yarmouth Castle* was "a shining example of a ship that was not in proper condition to engage in cruise trade."

Yet it had sailed from Miami as Canadian-owned, under a

Panamanian flag, financed by United States dollars, and captained by a Greek with a Liberian license.

Before the sun rose over the waters of the Bahamas that morning, eighty-nine persons were dead or dying. Many were burned, others suffocated, still others were hurt in desperate efforts to jump to safety. Gene Miller, Pulitzer prize-winning reporter of the Miami *Herald* who circled above the dying ship in an airplane, described the end:

> Before dawn a strange moan began to come from the fiery Yarmouth Castle, white with heat.
> The captains of both rescue ships listened. Passengers heard it. The crews heard. Survivors heard.
> "It was a wailing sound," said Capt. Brown. "Almost like a coyote."
> The Finnish captain thought it might be steam escaping the Yarmouth Castle's whistle. "It is a noise I want to forget," he said.
> At 6:03 A.M., abruptly and suddenly, the Yarmouth Castle sank within seconds. The flat ocean boiled and vomited debris.
> Then there was stillness and the red fire of the sun arose from the ocean far away.

The owner of the *Yarmouth Castle* was Jules Sokoloff—boss of the Bank of Miami Beach.

Investigation following the ship's loss disclosed that Sokoloff's home in Biscayne Bay was owned by Ed Curd, a former Kentucky gambler who had served as Frank Costello's personal bookmaker. As far back as 1936 Curd had been indicted at the Lookout House near Covington along with two other famous Kentucky names— James Brink and Sleepout Louie Levinson. Kefauver "heat" caused Curd to be indicted on income tax evasion charges in 1952, and he fled to Canada where he worked with Gil (the Brain) Beckley, another refugee from the Bluegrass State. Pressure from the Royal Mounted sent Curd ultimately to Nassau. Scenting the new opportunities, he returned to Kentucky, served his sentence, and moved to Miami. Much of his time was spent at the Cumberland House in Nassau, and it was there he renewed acquaintance with the Canadian Sokoloff. Curd formed the L & W Company, Ltd., in Nassau at the same time Sokoloff was forming three Bahamanian companies. Officers of record in Curd's company were also listed for Sokoloff's firms.

On the morning of the sinking, crowds gathered at the cruise line office in Miami. A police officer was assigned to keep order. The officer spotted Sam Kobrin in the crowd and remembered his reputation as a bookie. Kobrin had been one of those arrested with Charles Brudner and Herman Stark back in 1956. Intrigued, the cop asked Sam what he was doing at the cruise line office. Kobrin replied he worked for Sokoloff at the bank and was there to protect him. The officer reported he got the impression that Kobrin was there to keep Sokoloff from talking.

The Canadian was sick to his stomach. A doctor had to be called. But he didn't talk.

The probe following the tragedy didn't stop with the cruise ship. Investigators learned that Sokoloff had no banking experience when he bought control of the bank and had twice been involved in business bankruptcies. Under tremendous pressure from state and federal authorities he sold his interest in the Bank of Miami Beach in 1966.

One last deal before he relinquished control is worthy of mention. The bank loaned money to promoter John Mancini to buy seven hundred acres of industrial land west of Miami from the Ridgeway Corporation for $3.1 million. Ridgeway, it will be remembered, was one of those "shell" companies first used by Lou Chesler when he invaded the American market.

Mancini defaulted on the mortgage payments, and Sokoloff's successor at the bank had a considerable problem on his hand. Ultimately, it was all straightened out, and trustees of Ridgeway— the shell had been discarded—sold the same land for $3.8 million in 1968. Among the trustees of Ridgeway was Max Orovitz— sportsman, philanthropist, and civic leader. Long before the *Yarmouth Castle* sinking, he had moved to protect the casino's interest by shifting its bank account to a bank where he was trustee. No developing scandals there, Mr. Lansky.

7

Canadian Capers

IT BEGAN AS a drinking bout in Nassau, and it ended in what *The New York Times* called "one of the biggest speculative crashes in history—the collapse of the Atlantic Acceptance Corporation."

The newspaper noted that "the extent of losses incurred by prestigious institutions in the United States" when the 135 million dollars Canadian enterprise went into receivership "is shrouded in secrecy, but estimates run from $50 million to $75 million, and the total could be even higher."

Meyer Lansky certainly didn't plan for C. Powell Morgan and Atlantic Acceptance to become involved in the Bahamas campaign, so he can hardly be blamed for the financial disaster that, as *The Times* put it, "caused the slaughter of the know-it-alls." Yet, able general that he was, Lansky was not only able to survive the shock but managed to use its consequences to good advantage.

Morgan was born in 1910 in Petersborough, Canada, and attended college in Michigan before becoming a chartered accountant in 1935. For twelve years he worked in various Toronto financial institutions, becoming controller of International Silver Company of Canada, Ltd., in 1947 and vice president in 1948. The position gave him many contacts and an opportunity to look for promising ventures. Atlantic Acceptance, formed in 1953 to finance the door-to-door sale of silverware, seemed to be such a venture. Morgan called the company to the attention of one of his contacts: Lambert & Company.

Jean Lambert was founder of Lambert & Company, a new but highly successful investment firm. Born and educated in France, Lambert moved up in the world in 1949 when he married Phyllis Bronfman. Phyllis was the daughter of Samuel Bronfman, who, with his brothers, made millions during Prohibition by supplying Lansky and other New York bootleggers with Canadian booze. Without the liquor shipped by the Bronfmans and their allies in the Reinfeld Syndicate, there would have been no Rum Row off New York and Boston.

Bronfman invested in his son-in-law's company and left the money in the firm after the marriage ended in divorce. Lambert cultivated an air of "elegance and mystery" that impressed many members of Wall Street's upper echelon. More down to earth was his partner, Canadian-born Alan T. Christie. It was Christie who introduced Morgan to Lambert in 1954 and persuaded him to invest $300,000 in Atlantic Acceptance. One of the conditions attached required Morgan to devote full time to Atlantic.

With Lambert & Company as sponsors, Atlantic's stock began to soar in more ways than one. Harvey Mole, head of the giant U.S. Steel pension fund—the Teamsters are not the only union members with money to invest—put an undisclosed part of the $1.66 billion at his disposal into Atlantic.

Encouraged, the Lambert firm next approached the Ford Foundation, which made its own investigation of Atlantic and liked what it saw. Some years later the Ford Foundation gave the author $50,000 in grants to investigate organized crime, and the resulting book[1] disclosed, among other things, the Bronfmans' role in bootlegging. Had the grants been made earlier, the foundation might have saved itself millions.

Having the Ford Foundation and the U.S. Steel pension fund as investors made Atlantic a desirable enterprise. As one invest-

[1] *The Silent Syndicate.*

ment adviser put it to *The Times:* "We were all sheep. What was good for Harvey Mole and Ford made you feel you have a sure thing."

Atlantic began to grow at an ever-increasing rate. Sales went from $24.6 million in 1960 to $45.6 million in 1961 to $81 million in 1962 to $113 million in 1963 to $176 million in 1964. Principal business continued to be automobile and personal loans, but a chain of subsidiaries to make commerical and industrial loans was formed.

One of the nation's most reputable investment banking houses, Kuhn, Loeb & Co., took a look at Atlantic's books and "came away convinced that it was a sound situation." The company placed more than $20 million in Atlantic securities with investment institutions, mostly insurance companies. Attracted by Atlantic's high yields and the Kuhn, Loeb imprimatur, portfolio managers were happy to buy them.

Atlantic was growing so fast, it was learned later, only because it had such good credit. To maintain its "image," it had to make more and more loans, and to do that, it had to keep borrowing. Morgan was continually forced to take greater and greater risks, aware always that if any of his debtors defaulted he would be unable to meet the demands of his creditors.

The Lambert firm, which had seen its $300,000 stake grow into $7.5 million, became uneasy when it heard reports Morgan was becoming involved in other projects and was using Atlantic to finance them. Money suddenly became harder to borrow, although no one realized how completely the hot Bahamas sun was melting the financial ice upon which Morgan was skating.

A baby-faced Canadian promoter named Allen S. Manus was responsible.

Lou Chesler's dislike of Manus—"I've known him for twenty years and didn't speak to him for seventeen of them"—may have stemmed from the fact that the two men were very much alike. Both were big physically, both were hungry for the main chance, both enjoyed putting on a front and knew the value of so doing.

Head of Molly Corporation, manufacturers of the Molly screw, Manus had achieved a bankroll large enough to justify buying a home in Palm Beach. He invested in such other businesses as Adobe Brick Company of Hollywood, Florida, but still lacked a magic key that would open the wealth-conscious doors of Palm Beach society. When word reached him that a hotel-casino was to be built just across the Gulf Stream, Manus knew instantly that he had to have a piece of it. Gambling in Palm Beach, as in Lexington, Kentucky, was a stylish tradition dating in both cases to the days of Colonel Edward R. Bradley. His Beach Club at Palm Beach had the longest run of any illegal casino in America—from 1898 to 1941—and the colonel was considered a real gentleman.

Manus had already met C. Powell Morgan in Canada and interested him in the Bahamas. Confident Morgan would cooperate in the future, Manus in the spring of 1963 went to Nassau and managed to bump into Chesler. Feeling that with the granting of the Certificate of Exemption, he was riding high, Chesler swallowed his distaste for Manus. The two Canadians settled down to some serious drinking. Both men had well-developed capacities, and the bout lasted through the afternoon and into the night. Early in the evening Manus made his pitch to buy the still unbuilt hotel. Chesler rejected the proposal out of hand, but Manus persisted.

Still talking and still drinking, the promoters flew to Freeport. And around dawn, a weary Chesler let himself be convinced that in selling the casino to Manus he would prove, somehow, to be the better man—or, at least, the sharper.

Chesler hadn't lost his wits. He knew more about Manus and his finances than did Palm Beach society, and he seriously doubted Manus's ability to raise the money. When Manus offered $300,000 for an option to purchase, Lou saw a chance to pick up some small change and have the last laugh later. Perhaps he thought it was Manus who was drunk. In any case, he took Manus's check, and Manus went back to Canada to talk Morgan and Atlantic Acceptance into putting up the full five-million-dollar price on the hotel-to-be.

It still looked like a good deal to Manus, who perhaps wasn't aware of the silent role of Meyer Lansky.

Morgan died of leukemia in 1966, his version of events still untold. Information comes, however, from a Morgan aide—a man so "sinister" he was deported after the crash of Atlantic from the kingdom of Wallace Groves.

Nathan Saunders, a short, stocky moon-faced man, was born in Toronto in 1919. A fast-talker and natural salesman, Saunders found his lack of formal education no handicap in the free and easy world of Canadian business. With luck, he might have become another Chesler.

Uncle Lou was no stranger to the young Saunders. A brother-in-law, Morris Fischman, was a partner of Chesler in the horse-racing business. Saunders, however, found a living selling auto parts on both sides of the border and from coast to coast. For many years a bachelor, he enjoyed staying loose.

In 1949 he became acquainted with Morgan, another man with an eye for the Big Opportunity. Morgan had nothing to offer the younger Saunders at the time, but he remembered him several years later, when the rapid growth of Atlantic made it imperative he find trusted aides. Saunders was put in charge of a motor products company, which Morgan had picked up cheap. Within two years Saunders had rebuilt the company, enlarged it by merging with several other small outfits, and made it the number two in its field in Canada. Much impressed, Morgan asked his protégé if he would represent him in Dalite (Canada) Ltd.

Dalite manufactured prefabricated building materials—a field Saunders knew nothing about. Nevertheless, he took the job, becoming sales manager and vice president. The Toronto-based company had potential—and 100,000 square feet of warehouse space near the airport—but it was in default to the tune of $1 million to Commodore Sales Acceptance Corporation, a subsidiary of Atlantic Acceptance. On paper Eugene Last owned 75 percent of the company, but in reality Morgan was boss.

"I took this company, closed it down, reorganized it, and did nothing with it for six months as I tried to put the bits and pieces together," Saunders recalled.

One item he discovered was a huge yacht of prefabricated

materials Last had built in the warehouse at a cost of some $300,-000. Yet Last was something of a genius in the field, and Saunders decided to keep him on the payroll until he could absorb his knowledge.

A friend of Saunders from his auto parts days was Albert Shelman, owner of a large Buick agency in Toronto. Back in the 1940's Shelman had been a partner of Chesler in a large car wash company, and Shelman had followed Chesler's later career with interest. One day Shelman invited Saunders to dinner at his home. He wanted to introduce him to a friend, Allen Manus, who was interested in meeting C. Powell Morgan.

Shelman explained that he had met Manus through his old partner, Lou Chesler. Not too surprisingly, the conversation at dinner concerned Chesler's new ventures in the Bahamas. Shelman explained that one of his companies, in association with Manus, was going to build a marina on Grand Bahama. A great market existed there for prefabricated homes, he added.

"They painted quite a picture," Saunders said, "for me to take back to the board in reference to building homes on Grand Bahama Island."

The following Sunday Saunders had breakfast as usual with Morgan. "I had a long talk with Mr. Morgan in reference to these gentlemen. He knew of Shelman, but he didn't know of Manus. We went over this thing very carefully, and we decided to have a meeting on Wednesday at Mr. Morgan's office and bring in all the chiefs of staff and go over all aspects."

The preliminary session ended with the decision that additional investigation was indicated. Saunders was assigned by Morgan to check out Manus. Complying with the request, Saunders visited Manus's home in Palm Beach and reported: "He had a lovely wife, he had a child, he had a Mum and a brother, and everything looked nice. They had just acquired a company called Adobe Brick. What I saw on the surface, it seemed to me he was a substantial man. He had his own airplane and traveled around the country in it. He had a pilot. He had maids, chauffeurs, butlers in his home, and it seemed to me that with all the nice people that I was entertained with in Palm Beach that even living there he was a substantial businessman."

On a snowy day in Toronto, Morgan gathered lawyers, accountants, and other aides in his office and met with Shelman and Manus. The session lasted five hours. Manus wanted to buy a huge block of Commodore Business Machine Company stock—another subsidiary of Atlantic. In return he wanted Atlantic to take stock in a company he owned with Shelman—Five Wheels, Ltd., a car-leasing firm. The exchange was complicated, but Saunders learned that it provided for Morgan to give Manus a certified check for $200,000 to compensate for the difference in stock values.

Saunders said he took Morgan into the next room and protested the speed with which the deal was arranged. But Morgan apparently had a vision of white sand beaches and blue waters, and for once his usual caution was forgotten. He did authorize Saunders to fly down to Grand Bahama for a firsthand look, however.

Next morning Saunders left for Florida. "I got in with a coat and a fur hat, and I was whisked directly to Adobe Brick." It was a very impressive sight, he said, and strengthened his conviction that Manus was a man of means. On to Palm Beach they went, and the Canadian took advantage of a break over the weekend to buy himself some lightweight clothing.

"On Wednesday I came back to Miami," Saunders continued, "and went up to the International Airport Hotel, and there's where I met Mr. Wallace Groves and Lou Chesler, upstairs in a private room back of the dining room, which they set up just for this meeting."

Lansky, it will be remembered, was a big stockholder in the International Airport Hotel.

"Chesler made a comment—'I know this boy when he was a baby'—which was true. In fact his children used to come over to the house, but years had gone by, and I had put on weight. My target was to go over to the Bahamas, and we all went on separate planes."

Arriving in Freeport, Saunders was stunned at his reception. "I got the red carpet treatment that morning. I was taken to Mr. Groves' multimillion-dollar estate and had coffee and met his wife and talked to his children, and the horses, and I met the bankers. They all knew I was coming to town, and it was just like King Farouk entering Arabia. Of course, later on I couldn't visit their toilet, but at this point they were waiting on me, for the island was at a standstill."

Saunders, although recognizing that the deference shown him was really meant for Morgan, couldn't fail to be impressed. He returned to Toronto full of excitement, and in short order Atlantic decided to buy a million dollars worth of Groves's kingdom. It was decided to move Dalite to Grand Bahama, taking advantage of all those tax breaks Groves had arranged years before, and start building prefabricated houses to serve the growing bureaucracy of Groves's court.

Dalite (Grand Bahama) Ltd., was formed with Saunders as vice-president, representing Morgan. Manus had an interest in the company, but he was concentrating at that point on developing a marina next to the site of the Lucayan Beach Hotel, which Chesler was building. Five Wheels, Ltd., into which Morgan had bought, was assigned the project.

The International Airport Hotel in Miami became the staging ground for the Bahamas project. The entire seventh floor was turned over to the men who were building Grand Bahama. Private planes flitted back and forth to Freeport, taking the men to work at 6 A.M. and returning them after dark. Saunders said he lived at the hotel for more than a year, only occasionally spending the night on Grand Bahama at Chesler's seldom-used apartment.

Eugene Last was still active in Dalite affairs, but Morgan made sure his man had control of the purse strings. Hundreds of thousands of dollars were placed in Saunder's bank account. He, in turn, passed the money on to the company as needed. Most of the millions Morgan invested in Grand Bahama came from Atlantic's subsidiary, Commodore Sales Acceptance. It went to Dalite (Canada) Ltd., and from there, through Saunders, to Dalite (Grand Bahama) Ltd. Investigators later discovered the

Canadian Dalite invoiced the Bahamas Dalite a total of $12 million, but the accounting system was so confused, it was impossible to be sure how much was actually invested or where it went. Some of the figures were bewildering.

The engineering estimate for the marina, its boat repair yards and shops, was $1,091,027. The actual cost, according to records, was $2,416,000. A 150-room motel, complete with swimming pool and service buildings, was estimated to cost $841,704. Bills sent out by Dalite of Canada showed the cost at $3,348,000. Yet the motel was sold to the Lucayan Beach Hotel for only $1,350,-000. A sewage treatment plant, costing $200,000, was bought by the hotel for $160,000. A hydro substation on the books at $118,-000 was sold to the hotel for $15,000. Three other projects costing $4,800,000, were bought by the hotel at $1 million less than cost.

That some funny business was going on all along the line seems obvious. From Canada to Grand Bahama, the boys were cutting themselves in. Morgan became more and more involved, which is what, by now, Manus was seeking to achieve. The original plan to build homes on the $2 million in land Dalite bought was sidetracked. Only one model home was built.

Saunders said that after his years in the snowy wastes of Canada, he found the Bahamas a paradise. Quickly, however, friction developed.

"I started to see things in Manus I had never seen before," Saunders said. "You couldn't talk civilized to this man. He is a very, very excitable man. Go around throwing things, having tantrums. He even told Mr. Groves to go to hell. He didn't care."

Looking backward, Saunders in 1968 couldn't understand why Morgan didn't heed his warnings about Manus. Again and again, he said, he expressed misgivings only to have Morgan tell him: "That's my department, son."

The date for picking up the option arrived, and Manus didn't have the money. Morgan was only up to his waist in the waters. More time would be needed to get him up to his neck. Fortunately, for Manus, hotel construction costs had soared. Estimates now placed the total price tag at $3 million more than originally figured. Chesler—cold sober now—began to wonder if he wasn't overextended personally. Reluctantly, he agreed to extend the option, if Manus would agree to pay the additional costs of construction.

Came the day, and Morgan arrived at Freeport with a check for $1.54 million. Manus was to put up the rest, less a $5 million first mortgage retained by the Grand Bahama Development Company.

"Against my own interests," said Chesler, "I advised him not to advance the money to Mr. Manus. I knew the hotel required very able management, and Mr. Manus had no experience in the hotel business. I didn't think it was a first-class investment for him (Morgan), but he was in it, and he was going through with it."

In taking over the still unfinished hotel, Manus and Morgan were not, of course, getting control of the casino. It was still the exclusive property, thanks to the Certificate of Exemption, of the Bahamas Amusement Co., which, of course, was controlled by Bahamas Development Co., which, needless to say, was the property of Lou Chesler and Mrs. Groves for the Grand Bahama Port Authority.

One of the terms of the sale provided that Bahamas Amusements lease the casino from the hotel for $750,000 a year. Over the ten-year life of the Certificate of Exemption this would mean that Manus would get back the $7.5 million he invested in the first place. Any additional revenue from the rental of rooms would pay operating expenses and provide a margin of profit.

Lansky or any other casino operator could have told Manus at the start, however, that the scheme was impractical. The boys in Vegas learned long ago to operate their huge resort hotels at a loss in order to keep casino patrons coming. The American sucker can blow $1,000 in an evening at craps and still feel satisfied if he has obtained a nice room and dinner at bargain prices. Hotel managers in such joints gave up trying to make a reasonable profit when casino bosses introduced the practice of "compting." The phrase is Morris Kleiman's, until 1967 a co-owner of the Desert Inn with Dalitz and Tucker. It is short for "complimentary" and, in practice, means that any time a high roller or member of the syndicate comes to the hotel, everything from room to bar bill is on the house.

In other words, in Las Vegas or in Freeport, the hotel existed to benefit the casino, and anyone who thought otherwise was in for trouble. Controlled trouble was desired by Meyer Lansky, for whom the opening of the hotel-casino was only the first step.

Under the terms of the Certificate of Exemption, the 250-room Lucayan Beach Hotel had to open its doors by New Year's Eve, 1963. By a vast expenditure of cash, which increased the total costs even more, the requirement was met. The paint was still wet on the walls, and few of the hotel rooms were furnished, but a token opening was celebrated. Chesler and Wallace Groves presided, and only company brass was on hand. Despite the apparent harmony, however, a last-minute disagreement almost ruined everything.

At least $600,000 was needed for the casino bankroll. Who would supply it?

Chesler, who was beginning to feel an economic pinch, wanted Groves to put up the cash. Groves had no intention of changing his policy of letting others supply the money.

Uncle Lou had met his match at last. He put up the cash. Later, he said he raised $350,000 from "friends in Canada" and supplied the rest from personal funds. But Chesler would give no supporting financial records to back up his story, and for a good reason.

The bankroll came from the Syndicate.

Lansky had allowed others to build the hotel, dredge the harbor, build marinas, golf courses, etc. All were necessary, all helped lure the sucker. But the key to everything was the casino. Already he had supplied the important personnel. The bankroll they would spend—or invest—also had to come from him, for it represented power—power exceeding that held by Chesler, by Manus, by Groves, or even, as events were to prove, by Sands and the Bay Street Boys.

In a game where everyone sought to use everyone else and then discard him, Lansky held the trump cards.

And suddenly no one needed Chesler any longer.

Meanwhile the "Grand Opening" was set for January 22, 1964. Allen Manus capitalized on his new status and persuaded Palm Beach society to shift the S. S. *Hope* Charity Ball from Palm Beach to Grand Bahama. In return, of course, he had to agree to fill the hotel with freeloading members of high society. Logically, they could be expected to drop thousands in the casino, but Manus wouldn't benefit from that. In this deal only his ego would be rewarded.

Quite a few of the "Jet Set" showed up for the festivities, and society editors wrote columns about their clothes, their jewels, and their gay abandon. The glittering casino, with its European air, its huge crystal chandelier, and its painting of Queen Elizabeth, was described in breathless prose.

Sir Stafford Sands, resplendent in a brocaded dinner jacket, escorted Mrs. Ulli Lillas, a statuesque blonde of heroic proportions and long the unofficial hostess of the Bahamas. It was quite a bash, and if some of the beautiful young women on hand were professional call girls flown in by helicopter for the occasion, no one really cared.

Jim Buchanan, a veteran Miami *Herald* reporter, was on hand for the grand opening too, but his story didn't go on the society pages. The *Herald* in many respects reflects the amoral society it serves, but occasionally its editors experience an attack of virtue that can be downright embarrassing. Buchanan's story was such a case. The editors played the story in an inconspicuous manner— a small headline and a spot on an inside page. Yet the dynamite it contained caused shock waves from Washington to London.

Buchanan wrote in part:

> The shiny halo of operational purity which was supposed to float over the new legalized gambling casino here had a slight tilt Friday.
>
> What had been promoted as a "strictly high-class European" setup, minus any connection with U.S. gamblers, is far from a fact. The Lucayan Beach Hotel's Monte Carlo Room is in the hands of a dozen or more men long associated with gambling in Las Vegas, Havana, New York, Washington and Miami.
>
> Frank Ritter, better known in Miami and New York as

Frank (Red) Reed, is on the payroll of Bahamas Amusements, Ltd., as "general manager" of the casino. Reed is on the blacklist at Hialeah and other tracks. "Credit Manager" Max Courtney's real name is Morris Schmertzler. He has an old police record from the days he operated a casino at Saratoga. Cashing the checks is Abe Schwartz of Miami Beach, who has his own record of bookmaking arrests. Dino Cellini also knows everybody. He carries the title, "Supervisor." As a resident of North Miami Beach he carries no police record but has a long association with gambling interests in Havana and Washington, D.C., James Baker is "towerman" at the casino. Baker is at liberty on bond from Miami Beach.

Brudner, it should be noted, was busy elsewhere when the casino opened, and thus escaped Buchanan's notice. The role of Sadlo, of Dan (Dusty) Peters, of Herman Stark, of a score of others, didn't become known until much later. Nevertheless, Buchanan's report was bad enough, and it was quickly seized upon by certain eager beavers who—unable or unwilling to see crime conditions at home—are always ready to demand bold action of others elsewhere.

Much later, after the Bahamas had adjusted to the idea, similar cries were greeted with defiance and the challenge: "If Lansky is so bad, why hasn't the great FBI taken care of him?" In 1964, however, the realization that gangsters were running the casino caused consternation on Bay Street.

The Honorable Sir Roland T. Symonette, first Premier of the Bahamas, issued a strong statement promising that "undesirables" would be quickly weeded out. That Symonette was forced by Sands to issue the statement seems obvious from this letter to "Dear Stafford" dated 3rd February, 1964:

Hon. Sir Stafford L. Sands, C.B.E., M.H.A.
Chambers
Nassau, Bahamas
Dear Stafford: GAMBLING AT FREEPORT
I made the statement to the press and apparently it has gone well, but I have no intention of continuously making press statements.
I feel very strongly that the names of employees should have

been submitted to our Police long before the Casino opened so that they could have been vetoed; it should not be the duty or responsibility of our police to run down reports made by the Miami *Herald* on employees at the Casino after they are already there. It was the talk of everyone that these people were being employed (It was told to me on Xmas day). I am not convinced that the management did not know about it.

If any undesirables are found to be in the lot, I agree not to issue deportation orders on your promise that they will leave the Colony within twenty-four hours after so requested by an officer of our Government, but I shall request that they be placed on the prohibitive list and not be allowed to legally re-enter the Colony.

Sincerely,
Sir Roland T. Symonette

Sir Roland could bluff and bluster all he pleased, but Sands was boss. In an obvious effort to gain a measure of freedom, the Premier on February 22, 1964, wrote another letter:

Mr. Wallace Groves
P.O. Box 5,
Freeport,
Grand Bahama
Dear Wallace:
In looking at the agreement which I have made with the Grand Bahama Development Company Limited, I find that I am unable to give the time necessary for inspection and recommendations on your roads, harbour, wharves and airstrip and therefore I should give you notice of the termination of this agreement. Before doing so you probably may wish to discuss this with me when you are next in Nassau.
Let me know by telegram when you are coming to Nassau again and we will try to arrange a meeting.

Sincerely,
Sir Roland T. Symonette

Meanwhile Nigel Godfrey Morris, Commissioner of Police since mid-1963, was grappling with the problem of operating a casino without "undesirables."

Morris had experienced a long career in the Colonial Police Service, with much of his time spent in such faraway places as Malaya and Singapore. While he possibly had learned much about

Chinese tongs and opium peddlers, the posts offered little chance to become acquainted with American gangsters and their sly, sophisticated ways.

After some delay, Morris was given a list of American casino personnel by Sands. He convened a meeting with United States officials in Nassau and decided that ten of the twenty-six persons named by Sands were undesirable: Frank Ritter, Max Courtney, Dino Cellini, George Sadlo, James Baker, Roy Bell, David Geiger, Howard Kamm, Al Jacobs, and Anthony Tobasso.

Again Brudner escaped notice. Sadlo, who had gone back to Las Vegas, was dropped from the final version, in which Commissioner Morris recommended the remaining nine men be asked to leave the Colony. The recommendation was in line with Symonette's letter to Sands, but, unhappily, matters were not that simple.

The officers of Amco—the amusement company—"fought hard and strong" to retain the alleged undesirables and succeeded in convincing Morris that it would wreck the casino operation to boot out all the men at once. A "staged withdrawal" would be acceptable, they argued.

Morris agreed. Dino Cellini, Baker, Bell, and Tabasso left the Bahamas by February 18, and Jacobs followed on May 8 after a replacement had been found for him.

The author happened to be present the day Jacobs got his marching orders. It was late afternoon and casino personnel were collecting. Soon a dozen men had gathered around Jacobs. In the excitement, no one noticed the man lounging casually behind a potted palm in the wide corridor outside the casino.

Jacobs was indignant, and his colleagues shared his feelings. Again and again came the advice: "See Meyer in Miami."

It was obvious to the eavesdropper—the author—that the men considered Lansky the ultimate authority. They gave Jacobs explicit information as to where he could find the chairman of the board: the Airport Hotel, a hotel on Miami Beach, or his home in Hallandale.

Upon returning to Miami, the author—then doing research under a Ford Foundation grant—passed the information on to the intelligence division of the Internal Revenue Service. Yet more than two years was to pass before Lansky's role became well enough established to be reported in national publications.

With Jacobs gone, Ritter, Courtney, Geiger, and Kamm remained and were soon joined by Brudner. Morris visited the States in March and returned convinced that with only a few safeguards he could keep the casino clean. Of his four proposals, one provided that the remaining "undesirables" be replaced as soon as experienced substitutes could be found.

There is little evidence anyone looked for replacements.

The futility of Morris' efforts is well illustrated by the "Stop List" that was issued in April. Six names: Cellini, Baker, Bell, Tabasso, Jacobs, and Kamm were on the list, which was addressed to "all immigration officers" and stated: "This is to inform you that the persons named in this order have been placed on the STOP LIST and will not be permitted to enter the colony. . . ."

It was discovered later that Cellini, who had been reassigned to the school in London, continued to visit Grand Bahama at intervals. Kamm left the Colony to visit Jamaica several times and made routine trips to Miami—allegedly to see his dentist. Not once was he stopped on his return.

There was a reason. The notice never reached either the immigration officers or the police on Grand Bahama. Three years later the paper was found in a box in the Chief Immigration Officer's office in Nassau. The official explanation—it had accidently got lost during a change in office accommodations.

Continuing the solemn farce, the Governor signed a deportation order for Cellini and five friends on October 13, 1964. Yet once again, a certain degree of caution was observed. Kamm, who was still working on the island despite the "Stop List," was omitted from the deportation list, and Sadlo—the eighty-year-old veteran who had been gone for months—was substituted. For good measure a final section requiring the arrest of the deported, should he be found, was stricken from the order. No point in overdoing it, don't you know?

Commissioner Morris later admitted he had received "indications" from Amco officials that he might very well become casino overlord on Grand Bahama when he retired from the Police Service. In such a capacity he would presumably be responsible for maintaining a clean operation.

It was such a tempting prospect, Morris admitted, that he began to look for a future home on the island. He found such a site but, alas, eventually discovered that Devco—the development company —had made a regrettable error and sold it to someone else. Naturally, Devco wanted to make amends. Commissioner Morris was permitted to purchase a second site at a price of only $2,500. The deed was signed on August 24, 1964, and Morris had himself quite a bargain. An identical lot on one side had already been sold for $9,400. A little later, the lot on the other side also went for the same price.

Morris also picked up a licence from the Port Authority—which usually received high prices for its licences—to "carry on the business of investing in the Port Area by way of construction of houses." Amco officials explained the license was granted as part of the effort to get Commissioner Morris to retire to Grand Bahama and become a member of the family so to speak.

The cynical might say he had earned the right.

Max Courtney in testimony before the Royal Commission of Inquiry did a good job of putting Commissioner Morris into perspective. He last saw Morris in the casino: "He [Morris] said, 'Good evening, sir.' I don't think he even knew who I was. I knew who he was."

The publicity over American gangsters and the need to seem to take action increased the pressure on Lou Chesler. Bahamian officials could, and did, blame him for their problems. They could also mention his big mouth, his compulsive gambling, and his habit of finding jobs for friends and relatives.

More basic, of course, was Lansky's program. Chesler had served his purpose in attracting nonsyndicate capital to Freeport and in accepting the responsibility for hiring Lansky's men. Now, as an act of insulation, Lou could be loudly separated from the casino, and the world—if it cared—could assume that with him went the syndicate's influence.

Uncle Lou was having troubles enough already. Manus, the apparent owner of the hotel, was conducting a cold war against the casino. Not only did he fill the hotel with cheapskates who might go to the casino for a look, but not to gamble, he even cut off the air conditioning in the casino on occasion. Chesler and his boys, Ritter, Courtney, and Brudner fought back, and Manus accused Chesler of attempting to get the hotel back by foreclosing on the mortgage.

In addition to the feud between the two men, there were troubles with the natives. Nate Saunders, Morgan's man in Freeport, has described four separate "riots" at the hotel. Characteristically, while the syndicate had gone to great trouble to train handsome young dealers for the casino, no one had given much thought to where the maids, porters, waiters, and other personnel needed to run a luxury resort hotel were to come from. Manus, as new owner of the hotel, found himself confronted with the problem, and his answer was to hire natives.

According to Saunders, Manus disliked Negroes and made little effort to hide it. On the other hand, many of the natives had been pushed off land their ancestors had held for decades. They had seen outsiders take over their island and completely change its way of life. Now they were expected to work long hours for low wages in double service to their masters and to the careless rich who came to gamble.

The hotel planners, while carefully plotting every detail of the casino, neglected to provide showers for the hired help. The natives were asked to come in from miles in the country, change into clean uniforms, and provide efficient, good-humored attention to duty.

Under the circumstances, it was too much to expect. Harsh treatment only increased the tensions, which occasionally exploded. Hastily, some improvements were made. An employee's cafeteria was set up. Some close-in housing was provided. Saunders built the "Driver's Club," where the workers could relax and spend their hard-earned money. And King Wallace encouraged the formation of a union to provide self-discipline.

But still the unrest persisted—part of a general dissatisfaction which the Progressive Liberal Party was encouraging in all parts of the island chain. Grand Bahama was proving once more the wide gulf that existed between the haves and the have-nots. The gulf had long been visible in Nassau—now, overnight, it was developing on an "out island."

And Meyer Lansky could not have been more pleased. Things were developing even faster than he had anticipated.

Chesler, meanwhile, was fighting for life. Manus was only one of his problems. Groves and Sands also wanted him out. And so, for that matter, did Lansky.

Fighting back, Lou formed a group of wealthy friends and tried to buy a controlling interest in the development company for $17 million. Groves wasn't interested.

And suddenly, as if somewhere someone had pushed a button, some of Chesler's past victories began to go sour. His financial house of cards began to crumble. Stockholders in Seven Arts revolted. And who should turn up behind the scenes but Serge Semenenko of Boston. Credit supplied by Serge's "bank within a bank" enabled Seven Arts stockholders to buy up Chesler's holdings in the company—more than 150,000 shares of stock and $7 million in convertible debentures. In turn, Seven Arts disposed of its holdings in Grand Bahama Development Company, which, of course, controlled the amusements company. Chesler tried to buy up all the stock, but failed. Wallace Groves obtained enough to give him—or his wife—control.

Exit Lou Chesler.

Lou was living in the piney woods of Duke Forest at Durham, North Carolina, when the blow fell. He was there to undergo the famous "rice diet" developed at Duke University, but he lost more than weight during his stay there.

Far away to the south, a board meeting was held. Keith Gonsalves, a banker, was appointed president and director of Devco to succeed Chesler. Named director and also a member of the executive committee was none other than Chesler's old associate, the very respectable Max Orovitz of Miami Beach.

The shakeup didn't cost Lansky a moment's sleep.

Meanwhile, there was a comical epilogue to the Manus-Chesler feud. A jet setter, Prince Alexis Obolensky, known to Palm Beach as "Obey," conned Manus into underwriting the "first annual international backgammon tournament" at the hotel. The magazine *Sports Illustrated* was persuaded to cover the event, and high society flocked over to freeload as Obey's guests. The tournament lasted three days and nights and was at last won by socialite Charles Whacker.

The real climax came, however, when Emil "Jelly" Wehby started shooting craps. Jelly was a short fat man, about five by five and weighing in the neighborhood of three hundred pounds. For years he had lived and worked in Newport, Kentucky, serving such masters as Frank "Screw" Andrews and Sleepout Louie Levinson. He was Trigger Mike Coppola's chauffeur on a wild night when Coppola beat up his wife and left her in the ditch on River Road near the Greater Cincinnati Airport.[1] When Newport closed in 1961, Jelly drifted south and attached himself to Chesler. During Lou's absence in Durham, he was living in the boss' $175-a-day suite. Under the circumstances, his feeling of loyalty to Chesler can easily be appreciated.

Jelly, dressed in a size 54 tuxedo, was preparing to shoot when Manus wandered in. The portly Manus was in a bad humor—the sight of so many wealthy freeloaders was too much even for his social ambitions to stomach. As he strolled by the crap table, where Jelly was shaking the dice, someone asked about the health of Lou Chesler. Manus blew up.

"Don't mention that bum," he shouted, and added a few even more specific remarks about Lou's ancestry.

Jelly went ahead, made his point, and walked over to Manus, who was still sounding off. With one punch he dropped the taller man to the four-inch-thick gold carpet. And then he sat down upon him.

The light gleamed off the five thousands pieces of crystal in the chandelier, and was reflected from the golden wallpaper. Yet, in

[1] See *Syndicate Wife.*

the middle of such magnificence, Jelly Wehby continued to sit on the belly of Allen Manus.

When the hotel boss was able to get back some breath, he began screaming for Joey Maxim, former lightweight boxing champion and the official casino bouncer, but Joey apparently wanted no part of the incident and couldn't be found.

At last Jelly was hauled to his feet, and Manus—the weight removed—climbed erect. By now his anger was directed at all who had witnessed his humiliation.

"Gentiles, get out," he shouted. "Get out. This hotel is for Jews only."

Shocked faces stared silently as Manus rushed into the lobby, where the last two backgammon contestants were fighting down to the wire for the international championship. The *Sports Illustrated* photographer imported for the occasion saw a chance at a "different" shot, as the angry Manus stormed toward him. He lifted his camera and fired away. Manus swung wildly at him and then grabbed the camera. The startled photographer ran to the men's room with Manus in hot pursuit. A few backgammon players, who had been eliminated earlier, saved the man from *Sports Illustrated* from further harm.

When released from the hospital, Chesler returned to Grand Bahama, and stopped by the front desk to pick up his key. He was informed he had been evicted on Manus' order for nonpayment of his bill.

This was the crowning insult for Uncle Lou, who boasted he lost more than $200,000 gambling in his own casino and paid off the debt with a check to Ritter. Now he had lost both the hotel and the casino.

Yet Manus' revenge was to be short-lived. In faroff Toronto, the empire of C. Powell Morgan was tottering. When Lansky decided the time was ripe, a few strings would be pulled in Nassau, and the whole edifice would come tumbling down.

And in the interim the casino was making millions. The boys were shipping out bundles of cash in used beer cartons without bothering to mark a return address on the package.

8

Hog Island

MAX OROVITZ, that dedicated civic leader and philanthropist of Miami Beach, played a behind-the-scenes role in Grand Bahama affairs from the time plans for the casino were formulated. Lansky and his boys used Orovitz's office as a meeting place. So when the casino opened, who should turn up in the counting room to help tally the action but Orovitz?

Given this background, investigators in 1967 were not overly surprised to find Orovitz's name on several of six checks totaling $525,000. Drawn on the Bank of Miami Beach in favor of the Grand Bahama Amusements Company, Ltd., the checks were cashed in that three-month period before Chesler was deposed and Orovitz emerged as an official of Devco—the development company.

The Royal Commission of Inquiry was intrigued to discover that photostatic copies of the checks made by the bank at the time they were presented for cashing bore only two endorsements—Chesler and either Orovitz or James Maher. At that time Maher was executive vice president of Devco. Yet the original checks, when recovered from the files of Amco, also carried the signature of Herman Stark.

There was one exception. The first check, for $50,000, bore the signatures of Orovitz, Maher, and Max Courtney. The others followed in this fashion: February 11—$50,000, endorsed by Orovitz and Maher; February 16—$25,000, endorsed by Maher and Chesler; February 20—$100,000, endorsed by Maher and Chesler; March 2—$150,000, endorsed by Chesler and Orovitz; and on March 16—$150,000, endorsed by Chesler and Maher.

The question asked by the Royal Commission was when and why—when did Stark's name get on the checks, and why was it put on after the bank had cashed the checks?

White-haired and soft spoken, the elderly Stark was of little help. He explained his job with the casino was to make deposits for Amco and to collect gambling debts. He operated, he said, from his home in Miami Beach.

Each Tuesday and Friday, he said, he went to Freeport to pick up checks. On the other days the pilot of the company plane would fly over and leave with him a sealed envelope containing checks. On "practically every day" he visited the Bank of Miami Beach to make deposits.

When the casino opened in January 1964, the veteran gambler continued, "there was very little cash on hand." (Presumably, the bankroll supplied by Chesler was not on the island.) It became the practice, he continued, to send a check to Max Orovitz by mail or by plane some three or four days before it was needed. Stark would notify the bank that the money would soon be wanted.

Orovitz was identified by Stark as a "big real estate dealer," which was true enough as far as it went. Max would give him the check received earlier, and he would take it to the Bank of Miami Beach and endorse it in the presence of President Philip Simon, and Simon would initial it in the upper left hand corner.

When asked why his signature was missing from some of the checks, Stark said he just couldn't understand it.

When Simon produced the cash, the courier continued, he would take it to Dusty Peters and drive with Dusty to the airport. He would watch, he said, until Dusty and the cash disappeared in the eastern sky toward Freeport. The flight was always on Friday in preparation for the heavy weekend action.

Peters, who disclosed that his real name was Samuel Lepides, was born in 1903 in Rochester, New York, confirmed that he usually flew over to Freeport on Fridays and returned to Miami Beach on Sundays.

Asked his background, Dusty said he worked for Mohawk Realty Company—an obvious reference to Mohawk Securities—and for Wilbur Clark and Sam Tucker. Later he moved to the Havana Riviera (Lansky's personal casino), "and there I worked for Mr. Levinson, Mr. Feldman, and Mr. Jules Rosengarten." When Havana closed, he worked for the Fremont in Las Vegas—the home base of Ed Levinson and Nig Devine—but continued to live in the Miami area.

His job in Havana, Las Vegas, and Freeport was essentially the same, Peters explained. He was in "public relations," and was primarily concerned with steering customers from the joints of Miami Beach to the casinos of other cities. For this he was paid $550 per week, plus expenses that usually totaled $1,000 a week.

To do his duty to the Freeport casino, Peters had printed a handsome gold business card, which listed his title as public relations director of the Grand Bahama Amusement Company, Ltd. He really wasn't a director, he admitted, but the title "gives my job more prestige."

On occasion he would steer as many as 200 customers to Freeport, and then fly over to serve as host. When asked why he took two suitcases for his weekend jaunts, Dusty explained he needed a lot of clothing. "I change two or three times a day, sometimes more," he said.

Yes, he admitted when pressed, during "the first year we were open, I used to take checks to the Bank of Miami Beach, and after that it was stopped."

And it had been eight years since he had seen Meyer Lansky—this despite the fact that he roamed Miami Beach hotels looking for gamblers and—according to Dusty—Meyer lived at the Fontainebleau.

Peters could not explain the mystery of the superfluous signatures on the check any better than did Stark. The Royal Commission of Inquiry could find no records "which would permit the tracing of specific entries in respect of either the issue of these cheques or the receipt of the money into the casino's cash on hand."

In other words, the situation was very similar to the earlier day at the Bank of Miami Beach when Sam Tucker would cash checks on the Mohawk Securities account and walk away with the money. He claimed it was being returned to Havana, just as Stark claimed the $525,000 went back to Freeport, but there was no way to prove it.

For that matter, it was only Stark's word that gambling debts he allegedly collected in the Greater Miami area ever got to the Bahamas. The casino under Ritter, Courtney, and Brudner had a very liberal policy on credit, and much of the action was based on the motto "Play now; pay later." Those that paid later did so in the States, and where the money went only the syndicate could be sure. The Royal Commission of Inquiry put it this way:

> The inadequacy of the accounts maintained by the Amusements Company and our inability to determine the existence and effectiveness of controls during its early years of operation precluded the Commission from establishing that all revenue arising from the operation of casinos by that Company was properly reflected in its accounts.

As to the adequacy of the Amusement Company's bookkeeping system, the Royal Commission said this:

> The Amusements Company did not maintain formal books of account at all from the commencement of casino operations in January, 1964 to September, 1964. Furthermore, the accounts were not properly maintained through the first half of the Company's financial year ended 31st October, 1965. Due to the inadequacy of the records, accounting procedures and controls, the auditors declined to express an opinion on the financial statements of the Company for the first financial year ended 31st October, 1964, and could only express a heavily qualified opinion on these statements for the following year ended 31st October, 1965. Documentation to explain the nature and propriety of transactions or to substantiate the authenticity

of entries in the books of account of the Amusement Company and the Development Company were in many instances not available.

In the absence of records, the Royal Commission could only accept the assurances of Lansky's men that Lansky got no part of the profits. The probe revealed a nationwide organization devoted to steering suckers to Grand Bahama. In New York, Ernie Braca headed a staff of "ropers." Braca, like some others in the organization, had connections with the fight racket. He had managed the incomparable Sugar Ray Robinson.

New England was under the jurisdiction of Eddie Brudner, son of Charles. Regular junkets were organized in Boston by the active younger Brudner, who had no difficulty finding friends in Lansky's old home town. Hymen Lazar had the Midwest, with headquarters in Chicago, and—according to Max Courtney—was even better than Dusty Peters at digging up "new business."

The Royal Commission of Inquiry in its final report had this to say about the work of these free-wheeling agents: "The Commission regards junkets, the personal collection of debts in discharge of I.O.U.s, and the carrying of cheques into the United States as undesirable features of casino operations, open to abuse, and recommends that junkets be discontinued forthwith."

Allen Manus put a lot of things into perspective when in May 1966 he told the Securities & Exchange Commission: "You are getting the American suckers coming down on junkets, and American suckers buying the swamp land down there that will never be developed for big money. You can't run a hotel with these people in it. It is just impossible. It wouldn't matter if you lined up Hilton, Sheraton, every hotel man of any great importance—they couldn't run that hotel because of the people that are behind that island."

Obviously, Max Orovitz didn't share Manus's sentiments. With Chesler out, he was now "boss" of the casino. Apparently the Grand Bahama Development Company decided Max needed an operating title to explain his activity. On November 1, 1964, he went on the payroll as—what else—a consultant.

The pay was modest when compared to the requirements of Sir Stafford Sands—only $20,000 a year. But every little bit helps.

That Bahamas history was also the family history of Sir Stafford Sands has already been noted. The fact that history repeats itself is also generally accepted. Thus no one should be surprised to learn that in 1964 the old tradition of wrecking ships was revived in the Kingdom of Wallace Groves.

The old wreckers used moving lights to lure a passing ship to its doom. Sands and Groves used more modern methods.

Henry and Dan Dubbin, two smooth-talking promoters from Miami Beach, were persuaded to buy the 26,000-ton cruise ship *Italia.* The Dubbin brothers earlier had parlayed some surplus barges into a business called Canaveral International Corporation and won some government contracts to haul supplies to Cape Canaveral. The brothers also operated a cruise ship, the *Calypso Liner,* which carried swingers between Miami and Bimini in the Bahamas. So the new venture seemed logical.

The *Italia* had for thirty years plowed the transatlantic run. Now it was to be moored in the harbor at Grand Bahama—the harbor Groves had arranged to have built for free—and be converted into a five hundred-room floating hotel.

Etienne Dupuch, Jr.'s, 1964 *Bahama Handbook* gurgled proudly about "the $2 million investment." It noted: "The 608-foot vessel, which will be renamed Imperial Bahama Hotel, has 32,000 feet of deck space, three night clubs, two dining rooms, four swimming pools, a cinemascope movie theatre, gymnasium, children's playrooms, bars and other facilities."

When the ship arrived in harbor, an intricate sewer system was attached to it to avoid fouling the precious waters. Another must was air conditioning. In fact, the ship had everything needed for success save one—a casino.

Sources close to the situation have stated that a casino was promised the Dubbin boys by none other than that old rumrunner Sir Roland T. Symonette. Indeed, the ship was bought with money borrowed from Barclay's Bank on the strength of the "understanding" that gambling would be permitted.

Promises instead of moving lights, as in the past.

After refitting at Dodge Island in Miami, the once proud ship sailed to its doom. The Dubbins had counted on a flood of tourists, but the tourists never came. The few that did show up complained of cramped quarters and an all-Italian crew that spoke little English. Warnings were given that if gambling began, the ship would be confiscated. What about the "understanding" with Sir Roland? After all, he is Premier. Yes, but this is Grand Bahama, where Wallace Groves is king. No dice.

Desperate efforts to salvage the situation were made. A taxi service from the ship to the casino was organized, but the road was bad, the cabbies worse, and the price outrageous. Soon the homesick Italian crew mutinied when they didn't get their pay. Not even an attempt to turn the ship into a floating brothel worked. The girls from Miami Beach found more profit in working the hotels—on Miami Beach and Grand Bahama—and the customers found it more convenient.

The experiment lasted just six months. In January 1964 Dan Dubbin announced the Imperial Bahama Hotel was being closed. He said the company had lost $1 million in the venture. In the settlement that followed, who should end up with the *Calypso Liner?* Why Wallace Groves, of course.

Barnacles took over the ex-*Italia*.

Long before the *Italia* foundered, the Bullies of Bay Street were wrestling with another salvage problem. In mid-1964 a group of four skin divers began probing the waters off Freeport and stumbled on to the biggest find of sunken treasure since 1687. From all appearances, the ship had once been part of the fleet of Piet Heyn, the Dutch privateer, who in 1628 captured the Spanish Silver Fleet and made the stockholders of the Netherlands West Indies Company rich.

The skin divers found thousands of coins and other valuable artifacts. Preliminary estimates placed the worth of the find at much more than $2 million. Immediately the vultures began circling. Hastily thumbing through their law books, the Bay Street Boys could find nothing covering the situation. Sir Stafford, as

Minister of Finance and Tourism, had jurisdiction, and he rammed through the "Abandoned Wreck Act." Among other thing, applied retroactively, it gave the government 25 percent of the treasure. In return, the skin divers were allowed to form a company, Sosco, Ltd., which was granted exclusive prospecting rights to an area two thousand yards in all directions from the sunken ship.

A noble gesture, under the circumstances. Sir Stafford's luck was running hot. But, as Chesler could have told him, a hot streak can end abruptly when the dealer is Meyer Lansky.

In Canada, C. Powell Morgan learned the hard way.

Allen Manus, who rejoiced when Chesler was ousted, discovered he still had problems. He explained to the Securities & Exchange Commision: "I had a man by the name of Mr. Last who was running around saying *I* was an employee of Morgan, and anybody who needed to know anything or wanted anything with the hotel had to see him because *he* was Morgan's man. He was saying that I would be off the island in two weeks, that the hotel would never meet their payroll."

When asked why Eugene Last would act like that, Manus had a quick reply and a lot of details: "Because he wanted to take over the hotel. He wanted Dalite of Grand Bahama, to take over the hotel. We had terrible problems with the help, terrible problems with the Port Authority, terrible problems with the casino. It was tough getting anything done. Last was running around making all kinds of deals with the Grand Bahama Development Company and the Port Authority, buying land at all-time high prices for Dalite, and getting various exclusive licenses.

"And when I wanted to sue the Grand Bahama Development Company and the Port Authority, Morgan and Last said that they would make up the loss. There was a loss of $250,000 and Last negotiated for the hotel company without the directors' approval, without our knowledge or consent."

Manus said Devco officials "just drove over me with a truck and presented me with this Chinese bill of $310,000." He looked at it, he said, laughed, and said: 'We don't owe them three ten; they owe us about seven hundred thousand, and I'm going to sue them for a million."

Asked why he didn't sue, Manus gave a revealing answer: "The truth was I couldn't get a lawyer to sue the Port Authority down there. They had them all tied up. I would have to go to England to bring in a counsel."

The suit would have been based on a loss of revenue due to a faulty air-conditioning system, strikes, and "all kind of things." He added: "I'm sure I wouldn't have collected a million dollars, but the three ten would have been a standoff, you see."

Apparently Last had a better understanding of business methods in Wallace Groves's kingdom. Trying to "be the big hero," Last settled the development company's bill for $250,000, and paid it out of Dalite funds.

Some conception of the lack of control that Morgan—at this point trying to keep up with thirty-five financial groups running 286 companies in six different countries—exerted on Grand Bahama is apparent here. Three men—Manus, Last, and Nate Saunders—were vying with one another to be known as "Morgan's man." Each had a degree or area of responsibility, but each constantly interfered with the other.

Manus outlined other troubles in his year of operation.

"They had their land salesmen," he continued. "As our guests would register—legitimate people with their families on a Christmas vacation—they would have our front desk clerks bought off, and the next thing the guests would get a phone call from some land hustler touting them on land, and the three-week stay ended up as a two-day stay.

"Another headache that we have—a thieving Port Authority that ought to be in jail. Our first utility bill was $60,000, and they threatened to turn off the lights."

Exactly how intelligent was Manus's understanding of electricity isn't known, but his next remark is a matter of record: "We found openings that went into the Atlantic Ocean where the power went on purpose—trying to break the hotel."

Manus had harsh words for Ritter, Courtney, and Brudner. He called them "the three mongrels" and said "there is no living with them. They are impossible."

Asked why, if he owned the hotel, he didn't keep them out,

Manus said: "We couldn't keep them out. The casino is part of the hotel."

Becoming impatient with his client, Manus' attorney tried to clarify the matter. Milton E. Mermelstein of New York explained that the casino lease contained special clauses, which required the casino operators to conduct themselves properly. The special clauses could have been invoked, "but the next thing you know, if they had gone out, and there had been litigation, the rent would have stopped."

Obviously, without the rent, Manus & Company could not hold the hotel. To have thrown out Lansky's men would, as Mermelstein put it, "have accomplished the very thing they were trying to do—put on the squeeze and have the hotel fall right back into their hands."

The attorney continued: "I was one for cracking down on them, and then I was informed, well, you are not going to beat these fellows. And that is the first time I learned of the background of these three men and the people."

The moment of truth had arrived for Manus and Morgan.

Mermelstein—who found the role of counsel to his client too confining—volunteered that Manus went to the United States Attorney in New York Robert Morgenthau, and offered to sell the hotel to the Justice Department. He quoted Manus as saying: "You want to break it. Here is the opportunity to break it."

As part of the plot, Manus volunteered to accept federal agents "as captains, as waiters, as busboys—in whatever capacity you want to send them." But apparently the efficient Morgenthau had no desire to go into the hotel business on Grand Bahama.

And so May 1965 arrived. Atlantic Acceptance Company, although vastly overextended, was still keeping up a good front. Kuhn, Loeb & Company began trying to arrange a "financial bridge"—a short term loan, which would tide Atlantic over while a new long-term stock issue was being readied for sale. The First National City Bank of New York agreed to purchase a $3 million Atlantic note. And at the beginning of June the Madison Fund—a $200 million mutual fund, bought a $1 million Atlantic note with a one-month maturity date.

Just two weeks later Atlantic paid out checks for $5 million in notes that had matured. On June 14 the Toronto Dominion Bank refused to honor Atlantic's checks.

Why?

On the same Monday morning, 41 New York brokerage houses received orders on the letterhead of Sassoon's Far Eastern Trust, Ltd., for two Atlantic-controlled companies.

Accompanying the orders were forged certified checks drawn on the Nassau branch of the Royal Bank of Canada.

While there was a Sassoon Banking Company, Ltd., in Nassau, not even on Sir Stafford Sands's office could anyone find a Sassoon's Far Eastern Trust, Ltd.

"I was sitting," said Manus, "at Sassoon's Bank, doing my own business, when the phone rang, and there were lots of phone calls from lots of brokers. The director excused himself and went into his own office. He just said there is something crazy going on in New York."

The orders from a nonexistent company, together with the forged checks, were seen in financial circles as the last effort of a desperate man to gain breathing space. Kuhn, Loeb & Company sent Thomas E. Dewey, Jr.—son of the man who chased Lansky from New York to Florida and the Caribbean in the 1930's—to Toronto to determine if Atlantic could be saved. It couldn't.

On Thursday, June 17, before any money could be raised to support the crumbling empire, the Montreal Trust Company, trustee of Atlantic, threw Morgan's company into receivership.

And around the world, scores of bankruptcies and lawsuits bloomed as company after company went busted. A Royal Commission was appointed by the Ontario government to begin digging into the complex corporate remains. Its hearings lasted 93 days. A total of 148 witnesses supplied 3,650 exhibits and more than two million words of testimony. According to *The New York Times,* the hearings "disclosed incredible blunders as well as fraud, bribery, corruption and conspiracy in Atlantic's tangled business deals."

But one question remained officially unanswered: Who pulled the plug out of the bottom of the boat down in sunny Nassau? The unofficial answer, however, was easy. The chairman of the board had sacrificed another pawn in a game that was now six years old.

The Lucayan Beach Hotel went down the drain. Manus sold his interest to Montreal Trust, receiver for Atlantic, and apparently received enough cash to salve his many wounds. His rival, and the man who introduced him to Morgan, was not so fortunate. Nate Saunders stayed on Grand Bahama after the collapse and operated a nightclub for the natives. Apparently he became a little too popular. With natives, you know, one must be careful. It wouldn't do to let a white man get too friendly with them—especially when they are in such a majority. He might give them ideas.

So Saunders was declared an "undesirable" and booted off the island. Ironically, he found work at Adobe Brick and Tile Company in Hollywood—the same company that had so impressed him on his first visit to Manus in Florida. His opinion of Manus had changed, however, and as soon as he could find another job, he went to the Internal Revenue Service with his facts and theories.

Just to be on the safe side, he also applied for the informer's reward of 10 percent of all back taxes the IRS might collect from Manus.

Shortly after Atlantic collapsed, Meyer Lansky sailed for Europe. Such trips abroad were not uncommon for Meyer. They got him away from the summer heat of the Gold Coast and allowed him to meet with colleagues under better conditions of privacy. Of course, his travels were marked by federal agents and the police of every country he visited, but that was so familiar as to be routine.

That international courier John Pullman met his boss in Switzerland. Meyer, according to one official wag, visited his money in a Swiss bank. Earlier in the year, the courier had been on an extended trip. Starting in the Bahamas, he had gone in January to Bogota, Colombia, and then to the Eden Roc Hotel in Miami Beach. In mid-February he moved on to the Sands in Las Vegas, where Lansky's old bootlegging buddy from Boston, Hy Abrams, was boss. Early in March he was conferring with Mike Singer in Los Angeles, and from March 18 to March 29 he was in Honolulu.

Next stop in April was the Peninsular Hotel in Hong Kong. After a stop in the Middle East he got back to Switzerland by June.

So there was much to talk about.

From Pullman, Lansky went next to the Gold Coast of France to check the action and perhaps determine if Grand Bahama could properly be called the "New World Riviera." Who should turn up at Cannes but Frank Ritter?

Just a coincidence, Ritter said later. Meyer was ill and had his wife with him. They just talked about the good old days.

Perhaps it was just another coincidence, but shortly after Lansky left southern France, the largest shipment of heroin ever confiscated in the United States left too. It got all the way to Georgia, and the men most directly involved were arrested all along the East Coast. Frankie Dio, a neighbor of Lansky in Hallandale, where he operated a garish neighclub, was one of the men convicted.

Oh well, you can't win them all.

Back on Grand Bahama, Groves was looking forward to the construction of a second gambling joint in his kingdom. El Casino would be its name, and it would look like something out of Araby and put to shame those exotic castles in Vegas and Miami Beach. How the suckers would love it.

Bigger things than El Casino were in the works, however. From the beginning, Meyer Lansky had aimed at Nassau. Victory in his campaign required more than one or a dozen casinos on an Out Island. To achieve his purpose, gambling Las Vegas style had to conquer Bay Street. Thanks in part to Sir Stafford Sands, the opportunity existed. The dreams of other men would be used once more.

This time Huntington Hartford would be the pawn in the game. And Paradise Island would be the immediate prize.

Plunk in the middle of Nassau's bay was a long, narrow sand dune covered with mangrove bushes and scrub pine and known unflatteringly for decades as Hog Island. Over the years many men had seen the potential of Hog Island, and a few had tried to do something about it. The only person to make any money out of it, however, had been Harold Christie—the real estate dealer who said he slept through the complicated murder of his good friend, Sir Harry Oakes, back in 1943.

One of the first men to give Christie a commission was the mysterious Axel Wenner-Gren, Swedish industrialist and buddy of Nazi Hermann Göring. During World War II, at the "request" of another friend, the Duke of Windsor, Wenner-Gren provided employment for a lot of natives. Exactly what he was constructing on Hog Island, no one could be sure. Whatever it was looked a lot like submarine pens, when, after the war, the public got a look at it. Fortunately for the Duke, then Governor of the Bahamas, the British and American governments blacklisted the multimillionaire, and he wasn't permitted to return to the Bahamas until the war ended.

All doubts and suspicions were forgotten when Wenner-Gren returned. Why? He had money to spend and a reputation as a "philanthropist" to establish. On Hog Island he built a fabulous mansion known as "Shangri-la." He also invested in Andros Island, until his holdings there were valued at $14 million.

Nothing much was done for Hog Island, although Wenner-Gren still talked of a gigantic resort and residential development. In 1959, however, he permitted the ever-ready Christie to sell his property on Hog Island to George Huntington Hartford II. The price tag was $11 million but Hartford, grandson of the founder of the Great Atlantic and Pacific Tea Company—better known as A&P—had money to burn. He named his new possession "Paradise Island."

As Chesler maintained, you have to spend money to make money, and Hartford started spending it. A small but swank hotel, the Ocean Club, was built. A very expensive nightclub, the Cafe Martinique, was opened. An eighteen-hole golf course was developed. Finally, just to prove he was democratic, Hartford made Paradise Beach public. Of course it was pretty hard for the public to reach, unless they were good swimmers. Recognizing the problem, Hartford established a ferry service. To do this, he had to build a terminal on the Nassau side of the bay and equip it with a restaurant, bar, and lounge facilities. If, after enjoying these comforts, anyone still wanted to go to Paradise—there was a fleet of large passenger ferries available, and few of them were ever crowded.

There was some discussion with officials about building a bridge across the bay to make access to Paradise more convenient, but Hartford didn't push the matter. He wanted his new project to be exclusive and hard-to-reach in a literal as well as a financial sense. Only one development would cause him to change his mind —the introduction of big-time gambling. Officials reassured him that nothing of the kind was contemplated. He could continue to concentrate on attracting millionaires on a selective basis and quit worrying about suckers in masses.

The development opened with a flourish in 1962 and lost a cool $1 million in its first year of operation.

Hartford had made two major mistakes. In the first place, he selected a Nassau law firm to represent his interest. This was a violation of the unwritten law that required Stafford Sands to be consulted about any big project. A partner in the law firm had successfully defended Alfred de Marigny in 1943. Sands had washed his hands of de Marigny, charged with murdering his father-in-law, Sir Harry Oakes, and Sands had never forgiven the lawyer for proving de Marigny innocent.

The second mistake came in the critical election of 1962. Something of an idealist, Hartford had been moved enough by the plight of the Negro majority to donate $15,000 to the Progressive Liberal Party. This, in the eyes of Bay Street, almost amounted to treason. Any hope Hartford had for favorable consideration of any project died then and there. Furthermore, there was considerable sentiment that the "grocer" should be taught a lesson despite his millions.

Largely unaware of the true state of affairs, but sensing that where there was a will to spend money there was a way, Hartford began looking for someone with influence. Connections in New York arranged in the summer of 1962 for him to meet Sam Golub of Miami Beach. Golub had a reputation for having good connections with Sands, and in this situation connections as well as money were essential. He was an old associate of Chesler and a stock manipulator to boot.

Golub arranged for Hartford to meet his "connections." An appointment was set up for early fall at the Fontainebleau Hotel. The multimillionaire was introduced by Golub—to Alvin Malnik.

A very busy man was the founder of the Bank of World Commerce. The attempt to capture Ewa Plantation in Hawaii was in full swing, and young Alvin was up to his neck in a hundred other deals. But he had time to listen to Huntington Hartford, as several years before he had taken time to investigate the claims of Fortman and Krevitt to property on Grand Bahama. Just as the two land speculators couldn't have been permitted to establish a valid claim, neither could Hartford be allowed to work out a deal with Sands.

On October 15, 1962, Hartford signed a contract with Golub, which provided for the payment of what Hartford called "a substantial fee" to Golub and Malnik if they could get a Certificate of Exemption for a casino on Paradise Island. Hartford had decided that a casino was his only chance to recover his investment in the Bahamas. He was still naïve enough to believe that such men as Sands and Symonette could be influenced by public opinion.

In an effort to influence them, he announced that if granted an exemption and permitted to operate a casino, he would guarantee that one-half of the profit would be given the government for such public welfare projects as schools, sewers, and paved streets. Once again, without being aware of it, Hartford was branding himself a dangerous revolutionary. Encouraged by Malnik, who certainly knew how foolish the proposal would sound to Sands, Hartford buried himself a little deeper.

By the time the contract with Golub and Malnik expired, any faint chance Hartford might have had to make a deal with the Bay Street Boys had gone aglimmering. Lansky was free to proceed at his own pace without worrying about an outsider beating him to Paradise.

Malnik continued to be very busy, as some of the telegrams

charged to his Miami Beach office in 1963 show: On January 17 this cryptic message was sent by Malnik to Senator Floyd Lamb at Cliff Jones's new casino on the Caribbean island of Aruba: HE DECIDED TO KEEP DEAL HIMSELF.

An "N. Simpson" at Ocean View Hotel, Barbados, British West Indies, got a message on February 21: CANNOT AUTHORIZE YOU TO PROCEED.

Things were still going badly, apparently, six months later, when Jack Dietz in Rome got this message: CLOSING DELAYED AGAIN ARRIVING 9/3 LONDON HILTON WILL ADVISE.

On the same day, August 22, Dino Cellini at the London Hilton, where he lived while conducting the school for dealers, received a two-word message: TRIP CANCELED.

Five days later Malnik sent this coded telegram to the International Credit Bank in Geneva, Switzerland: CODE PETERSON THIRD AND FOURTH EDITIONS ATTN SYLVAIN FERDMAN ARRIVING LONDON HILTON 9/3 REGARDS.

Come September, and Malnik was in London receiving telegrams from that nephew of Bookie Al Mones. Young Danny, who was never particular about last names, signed them "Danny Malnik." The first one on September 4 was longish: JOE STAMPS WANTS ALL STOCKS AND CONTACTED JAY RELATION THERETO DO NOT WANT TO RELEASE ANYTHING WITHOUT YOUR APPROVAL PLEASE WIRE ME YOUR APARTMENT AS TO DISPOSITION WAITING.

A week later Danny was even more wordy: RECEIVED LETTER RE BANK OF W COMMERCE FROM LAWYER SILVER RE 28,000 DR. LEON BLOOM CALLED AND SPOKE TOLD THAT YOU WERE IN EUROPE SEEMED IMPORTANT CALL OR CABLE AND I WILL SEND ORIGINAL LETTER SCOPITONE IS ON WAY TO MIAMI BEACH SPOKE TO BEN COHEN RE INVESTIGATION OF HIM HE SAID HOT AND HEAVY.

Scopitone was a French device that featured music and appropriate moving pictures in color. Malnik bought the American rights and, with the help of such friends of Lansky as Jimmy Blue Eyes, promoted it into a multimillion-dollar stock deal. How much of the cash remained with Alvin was questionable, but the venture got him a writeup in *Time* magazine and a reputation as a young man on the move.

The Ben Cohen referred to was not the Ben Cohen of the Bank of Miami Beach but the political boss of Miami Beach and attorney of such gangsters as Chesler's friend Trigger Mike Coppola. Cohen was later convicted of income tax fraud in connection with some Teamsters pension fund loans he had handled, and despite his advanced age he was sent to federal prison.

On October 11 Malnik had returned to Florida and was apparently still trying to nail down the Scopitone deal. A telegram to Stas Radio, Paris, France, says: SORRY FOR DELAY EVERYTHING FINE SHALL FORWARD COMPLETE FILE WITHIN THE WEEK REGARDS.

Eleven days later the complicated Syndicate financing was completed, and Malnik sent a jubilant message to Philip Mero—the old friend who formed the Bank of the Western Hemisphere—at Bush House, London: DEAL CLOSED FUNDS REC'D WILL FWD THIS DAY HALLELUJAH REGARDS.

But apparently there was still a loose end left. On November 2 this message went winging its way to Ferdman at the International Credit Bank in Geneva: ARRANGE $5,000 90 DAY LOAN CABLE FUNDS TO ZUCKERMAN & SMITH NYC IMPORTANT YOU CABLE ON RECEIPT THIS WIRE."

Whatever the problem, it was soon straightened out, and Scopitone became a great success. Involved were such assorted people as Alfred Miniaci, who had been host to Frank Costello on that 1957 night when Costello was shot; Maurice Uchiel, formerly a director of Garfinkel's American News Company; Aaron Weisberg, owner of a piece of the Sands in Las Vegas; Hyman Fischback, one of Jimmy Hoffa's attorneys; and Jay Weiss, that close friend of Dade State Attorney Richard Gerstein. When the stock of Scopitone started soaring, Gerstein bought and sold at the right time.

Meanwhile, left to his own devices, Huntington Hartford pondered his next move. Were the Bay Street Boys trying to tell him something?

The lesson began to sink in on that April day in 1963 when Hartford picked up his newspaper and read that a Certificate of Exemption had been issued for a new gambling casino on Grand Bahama island. Even so, the full implications escaped him for the moment. Despite the lies that had been told him in the past, Hartford was still ready to believe most men were honest—well, fairly honest—and honorable. He called his lawyer.

On April 17 G. A. D. Johnstone, Minister for Road Traffic and Records, who also happened to be a law partner of Higgs, made formal application for a Certificate of Exemption on behalf of Hartford. He asked for permission to operate a casino at the Ocean Club on Paradise Island.

In due time, the Governor in Council informed the applicant that the Grand Bahama exemption was "purely an experiment" and his application could not be considered.

Still unconvinced, Hartford ordered his attorneys to try again. Four days later Johnstone officially inquired if the government would be prepared to consider his client's application after the government had an opportunity to evaluate the results of the Grand Bahama "experiment."

The applicant was solemnly informed in reply that the application would be considered "in the light of the results of the experiment at Grand Bahama at an indefinite date in the future."

Encouraged for some reason, the naïve Hartford decided he could swing the deal if he increased the stakes a bit. On June 21 Johnstone filed a supplementary request with the Governor in Council. It proposed that Hartford be permitted to purchase the old and honorable Bahamian Club and transfer the Certificate of Exemption already issued to a new home on Paradise Island. In addition, Hartford promised he would expand the Ocean Club from fifty to at least five hundred rooms within four years.

It sounded like an attractive package—an increase in tourist facilities for Nassau and, at the same time, no increase in the number of gambling casinos. Surely the Bay Street Boys could accept such a plan.

No dice.

The applicant was informed that the Executive Council—the Governor passed the buck—advised that there "should be no change in the policy previously laid down and that no further exemption would be issued until the expiration of the trial period for the casino at Freeport, Grand Bahama."

Hartford abandoned his effort for awhile. Yet the situation was becoming annoying—even for a millionaire accustomed to losing money in far-out ventures. He began talking to other wealthy men, who he thought might be interested in investing in his beautiful white elephant. All refused. Some mentioned that they might be interested if there was a bridge connecting Paradise Island with New Providence and Nassau. Always optimistic, Hartford proposed a bridge be built. Back came the official word—a bridge would destroy the beauty of the waters on which Nassau depended. Unthinkable!

Months went by, and with the coming of 1964, the casino opened on Grand Bahama. Hartford waited three months. Surely that was long enough for the Governor in Council to evaluate the "experiment" at Freeport. Despite all the publicity about American gangsters, it seemed to be surviving.

This time he would shoot the works. On April 16 the patient Johnstone filed yet another "supplementary" application. This time the millionaire promised to construct immediately a hotel with at least five hundred bedrooms. Within five years an additional one thousand bedrooms would be added. And the whole shebang could be operated by Hilton Hotels International in conjunction with the casino. An exemption for ten years was requested.

Routinely, the applicant was informed "that government could not approve the grant of an exemption since it considered that the experiment in having a casino on Grand Bahama had not been working long enough for a decision regarding additional permits for casino licenses."

The Royal Commission of Inquiry in 1967 noted dryly:

> It is clear that the Government had no intention of issuing a casino licence to either Mr. Huntington Hartford, or to the Company, despite the fact, as mentioned in this last attempt,

that there was a continuing yearly loss in substantial figures for operating the existing facilities at Paradise Island. There was evidently no will on the part of the authorities to reinforce Mr. Huntington Hartford in his losing battle.

At last Hartford learned his lesson. He retained Attorney Sidney Pine, an American specializing in Bahamian law. Pine was very friendly with Premier Sir Roland Symonette, and, through Pine and Symonette, Hartford made his peace at last with Sir Stafford. He was given a "piece" of the action-to-come.

The breakout of the Grand Bahama beachhead began on June 8, 1965, when Sands made an application "substantially similar to the last proposal of Mr. Huntington Hartford," as the Royal Commission put it. "This application was successful."

An immensely complicated scheme was proposed, which, among other things, called for construction of a five hundred-room hotel on Paradise Island to be opened by December 31, 1967, and the erection of a bridge across the gin-clear waters by March 31, 1967. The Certificate of Exemption would be transferred—as Hartford had proposed two years earlier—from the Bahamian Club to Paradise Island.

The breakout was not completed until 1968. Much happened in the interval. Hartford gained a measure of revenge as the chairman of the board moved against the last obstacle to his goal—the Bay Street Boys.

His weapon was Black Power.

PART IV BREAKOUT

9

The Ugly Bahamians

ALLAN H. WITWER tried his hand at a lot of things before he decided to write a book about the Bahamas.

A native of New Jersey, he attended the University of Southern California back in the distant days before World War II, and worked as a reporter for the Los Angeles *Times.* Other jobs included stints as a writer for RKO, Warner Brothers, and Columbia Pictures; some experience as an oil driller; and a post with Douglas Aircraft.

Following the war he became a writer for the now defunct *Liberty* magazine and, while at *Liberty,* became a close friend of syndicated columnist Jim Bishop. When *Liberty* folded, he went to work for the Music Corporation of America and then entered the hotel business. While managing the La Jolla Townhouse in La Jolla, California, he became personally acquainted with FBI Director J. Edgar Hoover.

This varied background was useful when in 1963, on recommendation of his friend Jim Bishop, he went to work for the Grand Bahama Development Company as a public relations man.

Immediate boss of Witwer was Ken Beirne, who was later to be indicted by the United State Justice Department in connection with the publication of a book recommending the use of safflower oil in dieting.

Beirne told his new man that a lot of funny business was going on and suggested he do a book about it. Bishop, who had written several best-sellers, offered encouragement, and in February 1964 Witwer began his "research."

The material was at hand—in those confusing days after the first casino opened and Chesler was being pushed out, security was lax. Confidential documents were scattered about in plain view. Witwer began making copies of all he found. Among other things he discovered were the "consultant's contracts" of various Bahamian officials.

By December the supply of data on Grand Bahama had been exhausted. Witwer resigned to accept a position with Hill & Knowlton, a New York public relations firm which had a contract with the Bahamas Ministry of Tourism as headed by Sir Stafford Sands. As he expected, Witwer was assigned as press officer for the Ministry of Tourism in Nassau. This opened up a vast new field of research, and the agile Witwer continued to collect material for his book from the files in Sands' official offices.

The research was handicapped by his duties as press officer, which consisted largely of getting visiting journalists drunk. Witwer already had a drinking problem and began to fear he would develop into a confirmed alcoholic of which there were several around. Nevertheless, he achieved a few coups of a public relations nature. His friend Bishop came over and wrote several columns about Sir Stafford and the wonderful development on Grand Bahama.

The columns were well received. Max Courtney, Lansky's old bookie, had high praise for Bishop when he testified in 1967 before the Royal Commission. He contrasted Bishop's work to that of reporters "who wrote what they pleased from files in newspapers years apart."

Gangsters have a strange aversion for writers who dig up associations in the past to explain relationships in the present. They don't object to someone writing two and again two, but, somehow, it is un-American if you add it up and get four.

Bishop, who lived in Hollywood, Florida, once came to the defense of a cop who later admitted he made a habit of stealing valuables from dead bodies.[1] Witwer made good use of him in Nassau and managed to hang on to his job until he finished his research.

In April 1965 the would-be author was about ready to write. He resigned from Hill & Knowlton, explaining very clearly to everyone interested that he was going to Miami to write a book. Wanting to make certain the message was understood, Witwer personally notified Ed Dougherty, vice president in charge of Bahamas publicity, that he planned to write "an explosive book" entitled *The Ugly Bahamians*.

Dougherty, not too surprisingly, was not happy about the project and asked Witwer for the privilege of a "first look" when the book was completed. He followed up that request with a meeting on April 8 at the Columbus Hotel in Miami and, according to Witwer, was "quite worried" about what documentation the author would have for the book.

On June 3, after completing some seventy-five pages, Witwer got "collaborator" in the person of James Maher. A Chesler man, Maher had been a key official until Uncle Lou was booted out. As of September 1, 1964, Maher was also given the gate, but Groves tried to soften the blow by paying him an additional year's salary. Nevertheless, Maher said he was sore. According to an official Justice Department memo, Witwer credited Maher with supplying much documentation. According to the memo: "Witwer states that Maher provided documentation consisting of tab sheets from the accounting firm of Peat, Marwick and Mitchell showing debts owed to the casino by Trigger Mike Coppola of Miami and Carroll Rosenbloom of Baltimore. Maher also had documents showing counting room procedures where 'either a Lansky or a Norris man had to be present at all counts'; proof that the Certificate of Exemption had been broken by the gamblers before it was issued and continually after such issuance; proof that a pre-organization meeting had been held in Miami in the office of Max Orovitz with Meyer Lansky and Lou Chesler being present; proofs

[1] See *Syndicate in the Sun*.

of payoffs of over $1,000,000 to Sir Stafford Sands in order to get the gambling exemption; proof of a bank account controlled by Sir Stafford Sands in New York where $10,000 per month was deposited by the casino; proof of a bankroll put up by Courtney and Ritter of $600,000 in order to start the casino with the indication that such $600,000 bankroll came from Meyer Lansky; and proof of a collection account in the Bank of Miami Beach with Max Orovitz taking millions of dollars out of the account for the benefit of Lansky and Chesler."

The documentation supplemented the material Witwer had secured on his own and gave him a vision of the completed book. He asked Maher his price for the material and was told the ousted official wanted only the satisfaction of hurting Groves.

With some people, revenge can take priority over money—especially if they have plenty of the latter already. Witwer was not one of these. Was Maher?

Utilizing the new material, Witwer abandoned the actual writing of the book and concentrated on putting together a very detailed outline, by chapter, of what it would contain. With that done, he let word out that he was ready to talk business.

In September, Dougherty, of Hill & Knowlton, contacted Witwer and offered to buy the book. A meeting was arranged at the offices of Exposition Press—known to the book trade as a "vanity press" where frustrated would-be authors pay to have their work published. President Edward Uhlan sat in on the meeting in New York, as did a mysterious attorney.

The author of the still unfinished book said he was asked a blunt question: "Would you like to go through life looking over your shoulder?"

While he pondered the question, a $10,000 offer for all rights to the book was made by the attorney. Witwer refused and started to walk out. The attorney called him back and raised the bid to $30,000. Again Witwer refused.

A few days later, on October 1, Witwer met with the president of Exposition Press in Uhlan's room in the Dupont Plaza Hotel in Miami. When he entered, the publisher put his finger to his mouth and handed Witwer a note which said the room was bugged. Many hotel rooms in Miami were bugged in those days. In fact, State Attorney Gerstein told a Senate subcommittee headed by the ubiquitous Ed Long that 10,000 wire taps were in operation in the Miami area. Long, however, was only interested in the four the Internal Revenue Service had installed on gangsters' phones.

To escape the bug, Witwer and Uhlan went down to the coffee shop, where the publisher informed the writer that private detectives were on his tail. Stating that he represented Dougherty, he offered Witwer $50,000 and expenses for the book. Witwer accepted the offer.

A few days later the parties met in a hotel room in New York, and the contract was signed. It was surely one of the most unique contracts in publishing history, containing such clauses as these:

> The Author represents and warrants that he has delivered to the Publishers all existing copies of the manuscript of the Book, together with all outlines, work papers, research material, supporting data or other documents or materials relating or pertaining to the Book, and that he has retained nothing in connection with the foregoing.
>
> The Author agrees that he will not without the written consent of the Publishers directly or indirectly write, print, or publish, or cause to be written, printed or published, any revised, corrected, enlarged, or abridged version of the Book, or in any wise assist or be financially interested directly or indirectly in any such version, or in any book of a character in any way directly or indirectly related to or dealing with the subject matter of the Book or the places and persons referred to therein or that might interfere with, or enhance or reduce the sales of, the Book without the written consent of the Publishers; nor shall the Author without the written consent of the Publishers discuss or comment upon the Book with any person, firm or corporation, or government authority or otherwise.
>
> The Author further agrees that he will not without the written consent of the publishers directly or indirectly communicate in any form or through any medium of written, oral or visual communication or in any way relating to or dealing with the the subject matter of the Book or the places or persons referred to therein.

The Publishers shall be under no obligation to publish the Book, apply for or obtain the United States or any foreign copyright for the Book or take any action whatsoever in connection with the Book. The Author shall not possess any rights whatsoever in and to the Book after the date of this Agreement.

The contract provided that the author would receive $53,050 in full payment. It was signed on October 8, 1965, by Uhlan for Exposition Press and Witwer as author, and duly witnessed and notarized. Witwer turned over to the attorney—who also served as notary—three copies of the book and all supporting documents. Taking the check, he headed south for Miami, leaving Exposition to make its own deal.

The book, of course, was never published.

Some five months later Witwer was back in New York. United States Attorney Robert Morgenthau subpoenaed him. On three separate occasions he was questioned about the book and the supporting documents. He learned later that Tex McCrary, that public relations genius who had helped Bernard Goldfine and Lou Chesler, tipped the United States Attorney.

Witwer said he told Morgenthau he no longer had a copy of the book and the documentation. He lied. In violation of his contract he had kept copies of everything as a form of insurance. The lie didn't stop Morgenthau—he subpoenaed the material from Hill & Knowlton, who had "bought" it from Exposition Press for $13,363.

The copies retained by Witwer came into the possession of this author in November 1966, while he was a contract writer for the Miami *Herald*. Using the material, he wrote a long article for the *Herald*. Executive Editor John McMullen—for reasons he didn't bother to explain—didn't publish it.

Other writers for other publications were more fortunate.

Meyer Lansky could not have planned for such a person as Allan Witwer to come along and rifle the confidential files of Wallace Groves and Sir Stafford Sands, but he was assuredly capable of using the incident for his own purposes.

So it was that although Sands, moving swiftly and realistically, bought off Witwer and prevented the publication of *The Ugly Bahamians,* he was unable to prevent the material Witwer had collected from reaching federal officials and the press.

The chairman of the board had reached a comfortable position as far as Sands and the Bay Street Boys were concerned. For more than three years reports of his involvement in the casino on Grand Bahama had been circulating. Additional publicity could not hurt him in any way, but it could ruin Sands and the Bay Street Boys.

And that is exactly what Lansky wanted.

To complete his program, a revolution was necessary—an upheaval that would bring a completely new order with which he would have no obvious connection and which would find in gambling the economic salvation the political realities demanded.

So it was that men who had served his purpose in the past leaked information. Morgenthau, who months before had secured indictments of Ritter, Courtney, and Brudner on gambling-related charges, was interested in pushing "the three mongrels" out of the Bahamas where he could secure their arrest. He was also interested in Lansky, recognizing full well his role in organized crime.

As part of his effort, Morgenthau in March 1966 had been quoted in the press as saying he believed the casino on Grand Bahama was controlled by Lansky's men. Immediately the new Governor of the Bahamas—Sir Robert Stapledon had been replaced by Sir Ralph Grey—wrote a formal demand for a retraction. The Department of State, after some hurried conferences, replied that while "press accounts of his [Morgenthau's] views on the Lucayan Beach Casino in essence reflect his opinion on that establishment," his remarks "should not be construed as any denigration of Bahamas law enforcement."

Governor Grey, who considered Ritter, Courtney, and Brudner to be "small fry," was unsatisfied with this statement, but Morgenthau pushed ahead. Inevitably, however, there came a time when law enforcement could do no more, and the power of the press was required to continue the battle.

Some of the same sources who leaked information about Witwer and his book to Morgenthau now began talking to representatives of various publications, and something of a race began. For reasons that aren't important here, the *Wall Street Journal* got the post position and reached the wire first.

On October 5, 1966, a long story bearing the bylines of Monroe W. Karmin and Stanley Penn appeared under these headlines:

LAS VEGAS EAST

U.S. GAMBLERS PROSPER IN BAHAMAS WITH HELP FROM ISLAND OFFICIALS

TOP POLITICAL LEADERS GRANT CASINO LICENSE, ALSO RECEIVE CONSULTANTS' FEES

IS THERE LINK TO U.S. CRIME?

The story began with Ritter, Courtney, and Brudner, moved on to describe Wallace Groves as an ex-convict, and turned to the Bay Street Boys. For the first time the story of Sands's huge payoffs and the consultants fees to his colleagues became public knowledge. The connections with Lansky were bared, and the suppression of *The Ugly Bahamians* was briefly sketched.

Airmail copies of the newspaper quickly vanished from the stands in Nassau and Freeport, but the impact of the article was not lost, and that impact was something very little short of an atomic bomb.

The Bahamian *Times,* organ of the Progressive Liberal party, devoted much of its October 8 issue to the *Journal's* article. Various sections of the *Las Vegas East* story were used as the basis of separate stories, and for anyone able to read the entire story was thus repeated.

Along with the stories was a strong editorial. It began with these words:

> From the very beginning this newspaper has been warning the Bahamian people about the terrible consequences that would follow the introduction of Las Vegas-style gambling in Freeport, Grand Bahama. While other sections of the press defended the gambling deal or pretended not to know what was going on,

Bahamian *Times* presented the situation with all its implica-
cations for the consideration of the public.

It was clear from the outset that the intentions of the UBP
Government toward the Bahamian people in this matter were
less than honorable. It was clear that the public good was being
trampled in the dust under the feet of greedy politicians scram-
bling for their cut of the pieces of silver which was the price
of a nation's honor.

The editorial continued to develop this theme for sixteen more
paragraphs, and then came the punch lines:

> And now the future spreads before us. It might have been
> a bright and happy future but it will not be unless drastic
> changes are made now. The country is already getting a reputa-
> tion as a rotten little hole and it will be only a matter of time
> before the whole place is corrupted and Freeport and Nassau
> become the twin sin cities of the Caribbean.
>
> The education of the people will mean nothing. As it was
> in Havana, so it will be here. Prostitution and dope and the
> other assorted evils of the mob will drag this country down
> into the depths of degradation.
>
> On some future day of wrath, those who now sleep will hang
> their heads and cry blood. But it will be to no avail. We will
> have allowed ourselves and our children to be sold, and all for
> the profit of a privileged few.

The editor wrote with more insight than perhaps he realized.
Implicit in the editorial was the hope that "drastic changes" were
coming and would remedy the situation. Yet, as he made clear,
the damage had been done. The virus had been introduced into
the bloodstream, and for Lansky the rest was but a matter of
detail.

No such understanding of problems present and future could
be found in the pages of *The Tribune,* the Honorable Sir Etienne
Dupuch, O.B.E., K.C.S.G., C.H.M., Editor-Proprietor. On page
one of the edition of October 10, appeared this headline: THE
TRIBUNE TO DEAL WITH ARTICLE IN WALL ST. JOURNAL.

The article began by charging the *Journal* with publishing "a
misleading and, in the opinion of many, irresponsible article on

the Bahamas." It charged the article was "full of half-truths, slurs, innuendos and downright inaccuracies." It quoted a "prominent Bahamian banker" as saying: "The whole article is ill-conceived, ill-timed and ill-willed." It warned gravely that "there may well be legal advice taken on the matter."

It is interesting to compare *The Tribune*'s reaction to statements made over the years in many corrupt cities by advocates of the status quo. The pattern is the same: a charge of inaccurate reporting, a strong implication that malicious forces are at work and, finally, a threat—seldom carried out—of legal action.

Meanwhile, the story announced, *The Tribune* considered it had a "duty to redress the wrong and give our readers the truth." To achieve that goal, it planned "a series of analytical articles." The series that followed sought to confuse the issue. It noted that many of the allegations of consultants' fees had been denied by the officials involved. The *Journal,* it said, printed the denials but refused to accept the official's word. This refusal was sinister, according to *The Tribune*—after all, Sands, Symonette & Company were gentlemen. Why Queen Elizabeth had knighted them.

So went the reasoning. The "analytical articles" may have pleased the Bay Street Boys, but they did nothing to stem the tide of public indignation suddenly rising among the black majority. The natives had long suspected their leaders of being, at the least, amoral. Now they could quote a newspaper which was not only respectable but the "voice" of businessmen everywhere. No wonder the Bay Street Boys felt betrayed and Dupuch kept asking "Why?"

The fact that some few newspapers still have respect for journalistic principles comes as a shock to many people—including some newspaper editors. Persons accustomed to intrigues and conspiracies find it hard to believe that sincere dedication to a moral or professional code is for real. To such people, there has to be an ulterior motive.

It is possible that such astute businessmen as Groves and Sands suspected that somewhere in the background was Meyer Lansky, pulling invisible strings. That Lansky could use legitimate as well as illegitimate tools they recognized, but of course in counterattacking they could not speak of the chairman of the board. Their assault had to fall on the obvious targets, and to such targets had to be attributed the deviousness and Machiavelian cunning of a Lansky. Such attribution didn't make sense, and the attack failed.

More telling than Dupuch's attempt to defend the ruling class was the announcement on October 13, 1966, that Ritter, Courtney, and Brudner would be removed from their jobs at the Lucayan Beach Casino as of January 15. Officials of the Grand Bahama Development Company expressed regret.

The heat was on.

Among those trying to cool down the situation was Governor Grey, a man after Sir Stafford Sands's heart. Early in November he flew to Memphis to address the Executives Club and defend gambling. Criticism was dismissed as "the result of sensational journalism." He suggested the *Wall Street Journal*'s article "was intended to entertain rather than inform."

The speech got big play in *The Tribune,* and Sir Roland Symonette got his picture taken greeting Governor and Lady Grey on their return to Nassau. However, waiting for the Governor was a letter from Lynden O. Pindling, Leader for the Opposition in the House of Assembly.

Pindling, speaking for the PLP, expressed shock "that you regard the said article as 'long on rumour and short on fact' without even bothering to investigate the charge." He noted that Governor Grey's speech in Memphis had been arranged by Kemmons Wilson, head of Holiday Inns of America, Inc., and pointed out that a Holiday Inn on Grand Bahama was subsidized by the casino there.

The PLP had planned, Pindling continued, to give the Governor full facts about the consultants agreements of Bahamian Ministers; instead it was demanding Governor Grey resign.

"We feel that you can no longer honourably hold the high position of Governor," Pindling wrote. "Consequently, we are making a direct request to the Secretary of State for Commonwealth Affairs for an early interview to demand your immediate withdrawal and to lay before him all facts in our possession as the basis of our demand for the oppointment of a Royal Commission to investigate the allegations."

Pindling was a thirty-six-year-old native of Nassau who had emerged as leader of the PLP after a dispute with Cyril Stevenson, a cofounder of the party. The son of a grocer, Pindling was an intelligent and intensely ambitious man. He wore a thin black mustache in the style of Dr. Martin Luther King, but King's concept of nonviolence was not part of his political philosophy. Indeed, the hard line adopted by Pindling and such allies as Milo Butler caused a group led by Paul L. Adderly, former deputy leader of the PLP, to break away and form a splinter group, the National Democratic Party.

The shadow of impending events was recognized by Pindling months before the *Journal*'s bombshell. In Miami and in New York, Pindling was briefed by such men as Allan Witwer, Tex McCrary, and James Maher. Forewarned, Butler and Pindling staged a dramatic scene in the House of Assembly. The official Mace, symbol of authority, was tossed out the window as UBP members gaped in consternation. Adderly, a member of a Negro family long important, was also frightened. "We thought they were generating some sort of activity leading to insurrection," Adderly explained later.

Not an insurrection but an election was the goal. Under law, the UBP could have waited a year, but the threat of a Royal Commission of Inquiry forced its hand. Better to call the election now. Hopefully, the UBP could be returned to power for another five years before the Commission could begin hearings. There would be a scandal, yes, but in five years it would blow over.

Such was the reasoning of the Bay Street Boys, who saw no great occasion for alarm. As so often happens in an amoral society, the leaders of the UBP had lost the capacity for measuring the impact of the *Journal*'s disclosures or, for that matter, the extent of the discontent arising from decades of neglect and contempt. Confidently, Sir Stafford predicted victory, and no one within the party disagreed. Governor Grey, as a mark of continuing confidence, was guest speaker at the annual banquet of the Freeport Chamber of Commerce on November 22. The dinner was held at that same Holiday Inn Pindling had noted was subsidized by the casino.

The election was set for January 10, 1967.

Early in December, Pindling and Butler flew to London to ask for Governor Grey's removal and for an investigation. Grey beat them to the punch. His request for a Royal Commission of Inquiry took some of the wind out of the PLP's sails and, in the minds of many, raised the possibility of a whitewash. The suspicion, which ultimately proved unfounded, handicapped the work of the commission in its early stages. Some people were unwilling to talk—in public.

The chairman of the board was confident as the election approached. Unlike the Bay Street Boys he had no illusions about their popularity—or lack of it. Any victory the UBP might win would be of short duration. The words of the Bahamian *Times* expressed that possibility: "On some future day of wrath, those who now sleep will hang their heads and cry blood."

Yet Lansky did not expect the PLP to lose. One reason for his confidence was a busy little man named Michael Julius McLaney.

Mike McLaney was born February 1, 1915, in New Orleans. Graduating from high school in 1931, he become locally famous as a tennis player. In 1935 he entered Louisiana State University and continued to play tennis. In short order he graduated to golf. Along the way he was making many connections in the sports field. While still officially in college, he became a deputy sheriff in 1938 and was employed in a clerical capacity until 1938, when he quit classes and began serving on criminal cases.

New Orleans in those days was a completely corrupt city. Huey Long had opened the doors to the National Syndicate, and Costello, Dandy Phil Kastel, and Meyer and Jake Lansky had accepted. Slot machines provided one source of income, and the plush Beverly Club—as elaborate a "rug joint" as any built later in Las Vegas—was a gold mine. Other casinos operated just across the river in Jefferson Parish and continued to run years after Kefauver heat closed the Beverly.

Prostitution and other forms of vice were rampant all those years in the so-called "French Quarter," and a system of graft collection known as "The Big Payroll" was in force. All graft was turned into a central pool, and officers drew regular amounts according to rank. The scale ranged from $20 weekly for sergeants to $100 for captains of the police force. There was also another system in wide use—rape by rank. When an attractive woman, white or Negro, was arrested, all men with nothing better to do assembled. According to a victim: "They would line up and take their turns. First would be the ones with the white caps, and then it would be the ones with stripes on their arms, and then the lower ones."

These and other conditions were exposed by Aaron Kohn, who headed a special citizen's committee to investigate the police department. Kohn later became head of the New Orleans Crime Commission. In those days, however, no one bothered to investigate the sheriff's department.

In 1942 McLaney quit as a deputy and served four years with the Air Force, being discharged with the rank of staff sergeant. Upon getting out, he became a liquor salesman and tried his hand at building houseboats. The business failed, and McLaney was left with his skill at golf and his friends to help him. Golf paid off first. McLaney won half interest in a Miami drug store and moved to Miami Beach in 1950. The decision was made easier by the troubles of Larry Getz. McLaney had been partners in the construction business with Getz, and his brother, William J. McLaney, hired Getz as a horse trainer at Mike's request. The McLaney brothers owned a stable of race horses. On July 16, 1949, Getz was barred by the Michigan Racing Association for doping a horse, "Lucky M."

Golf continued to pay off as McLaney won a luxury houseboat, *Sleepy Carolina,* and lived on it for several years. The houseboat was kept moored at a small but plush spa then known as the Isle d' Capri off the 79th Street causeway. The joint was owned by the Cleveland Syndicate and became a key cog in the complicated machinery known as Mohawk Securities, which the syndicate set up to operate the Casino Internacional in Havana. McLaney eventually took over the casino, when the Cleveland boys pulled out just ahead of Castro.

During the 1950's Mike continued to play golf and make friends. He formed several companies, arranged loans through the Bank of Miami Beach, and worked for Lou Chesler at the L'Aiglon Club on Miami Beach. They didn't make much money, but according to Mike they had a lot of fun. Among the friends Mike could count Saul Silberman, co-owner of Tropical Park. When Silberman got into trouble with the Thoroughbred Racing Association, Mike came to his rescue. All those phone calls from Silberman's home and office, which the TRA suspected were gambling transactions, were really made by McLaney—or so Mike testified. Another friend was "sportsman" William McDonald, interim owner of the Bank of Miami Beach. And then, of course, there was Carroll Rosenbloom, owner of professional football's Baltimore Colts.

Came 1958 and the Cleveland Syndicate decided to pull out of Havana. Officially, they were forced to sell the Casino Internacional because Nevada authorities decided their casinos shouldn't be linked—on record, anyway, with Havana. Cliff Jones over at the Riviera was similarly embarrassed, but Jones was also running a casino in Haiti.

Lansky still bossed Havana gambling in 1958, and any sale of an existing property had to have his blessing. McLaney got his blessings. The casino sold for $800,000. Chesler and Rosenbloom put up the balance of the money with Chesler's share coming from the sale of General Development stock. McLaney said he also sold some General Development stock as his share of the investment.

In any case, McLaney became the nominal boss of the casino. Less than three months later, Castro took over, and Lansky and his friend Batista flew off into the night. McLaney remained behind, striving desperately to win the confidence of the new dictator and seeking—in Lansky's absence—to become the gambling czar of Cuba. He was also doing a big business buying property from friends of Batista who were willing to sell dirt cheap in the expectation of having it confiscated if they didn't. When the casinos were allowed to reopen, Mike tried hard to operate, but, as the tourist flow dwindled to nothing, he learned the wisdom of Lansky's remark ten years before to the Kefauver Committee: "You can't live off the Cuban people."

There were some light moments, however. McLaney once boasted of how he brought his mother to Havana and rigged the roulette wheels so she could gamble and win. A man of sentiment was Mike.

Why did Rosenbloom invest in the Havana casino on behalf of McLaney? The answer became apparent early in 1960. Facing failure in Cuba, Mike suddenly filed a $4,250,000 suit against Rosenbloom claiming he had been cheated in a complicated Chesler-Rosenbloom stock deal involving the takeover of the American Totalizator Company.

In connection with the suit McLaney charged Rosenbloom had engaged in gambling with him—even to the point of betting against his own football team. In a deposition taken on October 4, 1960, he said:

> One of the other transactions was my betting knowledge and background, and a business relationship was formed for the purpose of betting large sums of money on football games. It was Mr. Rosenbloom and myself usually in partnership. These bets were made on professional and college games and were for large sums of money. On some occasions we would not be equal partners because Mr. Rosenbloom had much more money than I and was able to bet higher. On one occasion, for instance, he bet as high as $55,000 against his own team, the Baltimore Colts, against the Pittsburgh Steelers.

McLaney went on to say the Colts won the game and the partners lost the bet. He added that he placed the bet from Miami, where he was moored at the syndicate-owned joint now called the Harbor Island Spa. Later Mike claimed he meant the San

Francisco 49ers instead of the Steelers, and that the Colts did lose the game.

There was also testimony about golf matches. Rosenbloom described Mike as "a man who played golf for money," and admitted helping McLaney cash a $25,000 check he had won from a golfing partner. Rosenbloom's lawyer called the charges and the suit an "utter shakedown . . . worse than blackmail."

After hearings in federal court in Miami and New York, the case was dismissed in 1961. Rosenbloom renewed the charges in 1963 and the National Football League investigated. Again Rosenbloom was officially cleared, but rumors of a compromise circulated when some of Mike's witnesses recanted their sworn testimony. And suddenly Mike was in the chips again.

In 1961 McLaney tried to operate a dog track in the Dominican Republic, but, like so many of his ventures, it was a failure. He returned to Miami and waited for his good friends to produce another opportunity. Interestingly, the next chance came in the Bahamas.

Back in 1939, when Stafford Sands set up the legal machinery for gambling that was to make him rich three decades later, the excuse was the necessity to legalize existing operations—the Bahamian Club in downtown Nassau and a semiprivate operation on tiny Cat Cay. The island was controlled by virtue of a 99-year lease to Louis Wasey, a founder of the Barbasol Corporation. Only two miles long, it is located on the edge of the Gulf Stream and was for many years the site of the International Tuna Match.

Wasey died in 1961 and left the island and its small casino in charge of his daughter. Two Canadian gamblers had operated the casino on a seasonal basis since 1946, but in 1962 they had some tax trouble in Canada and pulled out. Roland McCann, manager of the Cat Cay Club, where the casino was located, needed a new operator fast. In April 1962 McCann happened to be in an isolated restaurant in South Dade County—a joint which sometimes featured gambling as well as food. He was introduced to McLaney and promptly offered him the casino.

It was as if, in a casual way, Mike was being groomed for the same role he had tried to play in Havana, but this time he would be assured of a better reception in Nassau.

McLaney got over to Cat Cay, some sixty miles from Miami, in time for the Tuna Tournament, which runs from mid-May to mid-June. The casino opened at 1 P.M. and continued until the players had enough. Under the deal with McCann, Mike was supposed to split the profits 50–50 with Jane Wasey, but he kept no books or records of any kind. Observers noted Mike had no trouble finding a casino bankroll.

Until McLaney took over, the club had been semiexclusive, catering only to a very restricted group of millionaires. Mike changed the rules and began trying to develop a big-scale operation by flying in suckers of all kinds. Despite the fact that many of them later admitted to heavy losses, the casino was closed at the end of the 1964 season. The Wasey Estate felt it wasn't making enough money to justify continuing the operation.

It was a good deal while it lasted, however—for McLaney. And later he was able to present himself in Nassau as a man who had experience in Bahamian gambling. He could even point to M & M, Ltd., a Bahamian company he had formed to operate the casino in the style of Mohawk Securities.

McLaney made an effort to secure the gambling exemption for Cat Cay by buying the island, but he abandoned the attempt when informed the price was $3 million. Another man with more money at his disposal put in his bid. But of that more later.

Las Vegas was next to get Mike's eye. His many friends arranged for him to install his brother, then in the horse feed business in New Orleans, as nominal owner of record of the Carousel. The financial arrangements were involved and also widespread. In Providence, Rhode Island, the FBI was listening one day to Raymond Patriarca's bugged telephone and heard a conversation about a new Las Vegas venture. The official FBI summary of the conversation left some unanswered questions: "Mike (LNU) ascertained from JOE LINSEY, noted Boston Philanthropist, that he, LINSEY, was not interested in obtaining the points. Informant was of the opinion that the points were worth $10,000, but was unable to determine what corporation the points were being sold for. LINSEY was of the opinion the points were not worth $10,000 and, therefore, declined to purchase same."

Comprehension was not aided by the fact the FBI tried to disguise the source of its information by referring to an "informant," but later admitted in a court action to bugging the so-called Mafia boss of New England's phone. Joe Linsey was, of course, the ex-bootlegger who over the years had remained a close friend of Lansky. And Mike was later identified as McLaney.

In 1967, when McLaney was involved in the Bahamas, the Las Vegas casino was officially sold. Principal owner of record became Salvatore A. Rizzio—who along with Patriarca had been connected with the scandal-ridden Berkshire Downs Race Track at Hancock, Massachusetts. The "points" were worth $2,500. Rizzio took 96 points, and the remaining four points—worth $10,000—were bought by two local Las Vegas men.

A somewhat detailed history of McLaney has been given only because he was to have an important role in post-election Nassau. In normal times, gamblers traditionally play both sides of the political fence so that regardless of the outcome of an election they will have friends among the victors. In the 1967 election, with plans eight years old getting their final test, Lansky had even more reason than usual to be careful.

Leaders of the PLP began visiting Miami and New York early in 1966 to make plans for the next election. On one occasion they met with Angus Stevens, a former aide to State Attorney Gerstein, who, it will be remembered, was an associate of Alvin Malnik. They also talked to Allan Witwer, author of the suppressed book he was pledged not to discuss with anyone. In New York, Tex McCrary took them in tow, furnishing information and unwanted advice on how to run gambling after they won office. On another visit to Miami as the campaign neared, they were lodged at the Holiday Inn in Coral Gables. The owner was Ben Gaines, partner with Cleveland Syndicate boss Sam Tucker in the Skyways Motel in Miami, and with Tucker and Joe Linsey of Boston in a Miami Beach hotel.

McLaney offered more than advice and information. He provided a helicopter, which was used by Pindling to tour the Out Islands during the campaign. A single-engined plane was also supplied for the same purpose. A DC-3 was made available for several days to Pindling as well as another plane supplied by Lewis Colasurdo of the Crescent Corporation. For good measure, a power boat was furnished, but it proved to be faulty and saw only limited service.

McLaney later estimated the cost of the services he provided at about $60,000. In return he asked for nothing, but admitted he expected "kindness to bring back kindness." He also made it clear he expected to be put in charge of regulating gambling when and if the PLP won the election—the same position he had failed to win from Castro. At one point he even left a draft of a bill to regulate gambling for Pindling to study.

That Pindling was more deeply involved with McLaney than anyone suspected didn't become known until after the election. A Securities & Exchange Commission investigation, centering around a blueberry plantation, uncovered a fantastic story.

In 1960 the same Lewis Colasurdo who provided a plane for Pindling, sold a family-owned blueberry plantation to a newly formed company he controlled. The company, Pakco, held the plantation for five years and then sold it to Caletta Blueberry, a new company controlled by McLaney. Caletta promptly sold the plantation to a newly formed Bahamian company known as Makepeace. President of Makepeace was Anthony Cipo, a veteran employee of Pakco. Meanwhile, Colasurdo bought controlling interest of the Crescent Corporation on the basis of a short-term loan. Crescent then bought the plantation from Makepeace—which had held it only two weeks. Makepeace promptly invested $1.9 million of the money it received in the convertible debentures of a company known as Six M. It was organized in Nassau on October 1, 1965, the very day Crescent paid the $1.9 million to Makepeace. President of Six M was Pindling.

The complicated transaction was completed when Colasurdo met with Pindling and borrowed $2 million from Six M. He used the money to pay off the short-term loan with which he had purchased Crescent in the first place.

Colasurdo later disclosed that he considered buying the Desert Inn from the Cleveland Syndicate prior to the 1967 sale of the club to Howard Hughes. McLaney arranged for him to meet Moe Dalitz, Sam Tucker, and other owners in New York, he said, but the deal fell through.

Despite the aid of McLaney and Colasurdo, and the advice of Tex McCrary, the odds seemed to favor the UBP as the election approached. The scandals had hurt the Bay Street Boys, but they could still count on their unique system of gerrymandering, which over the years had kept the majority party ineffective at the polls. As to the scandals, they had this to say in their official platform: "The party rejects the false and untrue accusations of dishonesty and conflict of interest leveled by the opposition parties and the foreign press against its ministers, and seeks from the voters of the Bahama islands a vindication of its past conduct of public affairs and a mandate to continue the government of the colony, for it is the voters alone, and not outside newspaper bodies who have the right to determine who shall govern these Bahama islands."

Spokesmen for the PLP had a simple answer: "We don't get schools, we don't get sewers, we don't get medical facilities, because the men who control the government are more interested in taking care of themselves."

Tension grew on the islands as election day approached. Sir Stafford Sands, long a client of The Wackenhut Corporation of Coral Gables, called on the private detective agency for a variety of services. As of January 3, 1967, the agency had been the official crime-fighting arm of newly elected Republican Governor Claude Kirk, but some of the investigators were too tied up with Sands in the islands to begin fighting crime immediately in Florida. Head of the company was George Wackenhut, a professional ex-FBI agent and a friend of that special-agent-in-charge of the Miami FBI office who found Sands to be so charming.

Came election day and across the Bahamas voters turned out in record numbers. By late afternoon it was obvious the PLP had scored gains, and the control of the government was in doubt. It was still in doubt when the votes were counted—the PLP had increased its representation from 4 to 18 seats. The UPB dropped to 18. An opposition splinter group led by Negro Paul Adderly lost the three seats it had won in 1962. The Labor party elected its leader, Randol Fawkes—the man who called the general strike back in 1958. One independent was elected.

Governor Grey hesitated, and reports circulated that he might call for another election. Meanwhile, the natives took to the streets of Nassau to celebrate victory. Cowbells and bongo drums resounded down Bay Street as black men danced and sang in joy. Governor Grey got the message.

Fawkes, holding the balance of power, agreed to work with his old party and became Minister of Labor in the new government. With a one-vote margin, Pindling was asked by Governor Grey to become Premier.

The "Quiet Revolution" was an accomplished fact.

Almost unnoticed in the confusion of the election was the opening on Grand Bahama of the glittering El Casino. At the moment few people would have bet it had a promising future. There was even some doubt if plans for Paradise Island would be developed.

The doubts were not well founded. The Bay Street Boys had been defeated, but that was according to plan. Meyer Lansky had every reason to feel encouraged.

In May 1967 Stanley Penn and Monroe Karmin of the *Wall Street Journal* won a Pulitzer Prize for their reporting "of the connection between American crime and gambling in the Bahamas."

Al Witwer was not asked for comment.

10

Paradise

SHORTLY AFTER the election two national magazines featured the sordid story of Grand Bahama in major feature articles. They came too late to influence the voters but just in time to capitalize on the sudden interest aroused by the election of a black government. Whether they would have been printed had the UBP won is a question only the editors can answer.

On February 6 a high-ranking official of the Justice Department's Organized Crime Section visited Governor Grey in Nassau. A copy of *Life*'s article by Bill Lambert lay open on the governor's desk. According to a memo of the interview: "The governor immediately accused the Department of Justice of having caused the loss of control of the Bahamas by the UBP [Sir Stafford Sands, Bay Street Boys' party] and allowing 'this bunch of baboons' to take control of the government. Grey was very abusive in his remarks directed at the Negro PLP party, stating that most of them cannot read or write. Grey further stated that by the Department of Justice's activities we have probably opened the door for bigger crooks to take over in the Bahamas. The governor was obviously angry over the allegations made in the *Life* magazine article."

Later that same afternoon, the American official met with

Premier Pindling and received a more cordial reception. According to the memo these points were discussed: "As to insurance, Pindling stated that he would take prompt action in controlling insurance companies in the Bahamas by making such companies have a stated amount of assets deposited within the Bahamas and annual certified publication of the business done by such companies.

"As to the gambling situation, a suggestion was made to Pindling that he might consider taxing the gambling casinos on a percentage basis rather than the present system of a flat annual fee per casino. By taxing on a percentage basis the Bahamas government would gain the right to control the counting rooms and the issuance of credit in order to make sure they gained their proper tax. . . .

"Pindling stated that he recognized that just about every 'leech' in the United States would be trying to latch onto him and his government and asked what aid we could give him as to identifying such persons."

The two men worked out a system for checking out suspect persons after the Justice man made it clear his department "would never be in a position to 'clear' anybody." Pindling then said he intended to hold an inquiry into the racketeer influence and would like to defer deporting Ritter, Courtney, and Brudner until after the inquiry.

Some idea of the "Department of Justice's activities" that Governor Grey resented and Premier Pindling welcomed is supplied by another saga of Cat Cay.

Mike McLaney was not the only man to dream of expanding the tiny casino so close to Miami into a major operation. Ben Novack, the owner of record of Miami Beach's finest, the Fontainebleau, conceived the idea of building an annex to his hotel on Cat Cay to be known as the Cat Cay Fontainebleau. He had planned to do the same thing in Havana much earlier, but Castro spoiled the deal.

On June 22, 1965, Novack and others made application for transfer of the existing gambling exemption to Cat Cay Fontainebleau, Ltd. Advising him was Sir Harold Christie, who presumably had the ear of Sands. A check for $100,000 by way of a deposit on a 120-day option to buy Cat Cay for $3,750,000 was sent to the representatives of the Wasey Estate. But for reasons not clear to Novack, he could not gain approval despite assurance from his attorney that a deal had been made which provided "that Sir Stafford Sands was to get Paradise Island and we will get Cat Cay."

Revealed here for the first time is the reason the deal fell through. Extracts from two Department of Justice memos tell the story: "On July 29, 1965, I received a telephone call from Robert Tepper, Chief, Bahamas area desk, Department of State. Tepper stated that the State Department had been contacted by the British Government with the information that subject Novack had applied for a license to operate a gambling casino at Cat Cay, Bahamas.

"The British informed Tepper that it is anticipated that the Bahamian government will grant the license on August 12, 1965. Since the Bahamian government has ceded the right to conduct its foreign affairs to the United Kingdom, the governor of the Bahamas has the power to veto such license grant. Tepper stated that the Bahamas police have some information that was supplied to it by the FBI. Tepper requested that we supply him with information concerning Novack which could be passed in confidence to the United Kingdom for use by the Governor in his considerations.

"Attached is a memorandum which I recommend be forwarded to State. Even though the information is to be supplied in confidence, there is a danger that such information might become known through the Governor's staff. All information in the memorandum is taken from FBI and IRS sources deemed to be reliable."

The accompanying memorandum *was* passed on to the State Department, which sent it to the British government, which sent it to the Governor of the Bahamas with instructions to deny the application. Dated August 4, 1965, the memo entitled "Ben Novack" is as follows: "Pursuant to our conversation of 29 July, 1965, the following is submitted concerning Novack for possible

use by the Governor of the Bahamas in determining whether subject should be granted an exception to operate a gambling casino in
the Bahamas.

"Novack is the principal owner of record of the Fontainebleau
Hotel, Miami Beach, Florida. Informants who have given reliable
information in the past state that Novack is the front man in the
Fontainebleau for notorius United States racketeers, including
Sam Giancana, Thomas Luchese (Three-fingered Brown), Michael
Coppola (Trigger Mike), Max Eder (Maxie Raymond) and
Joseph Fischetti.

"Novack has closely associated himself socially with leading
members of the Cosa Nostra. On May 18, 1965, Novack attended
a meeting of the top racketeers of the Eastern Syndicate in Suite
2003 of the St. Moritz Hotel, New York City, with Vincent Alo,
Michael Coppola, Joey Rao, Benny Levine, Tommy Milo and
Meyer Lansky. During 1958, Novack entered into a business
relationship with Joe Adonis and Frank Costello in the purchase
of Cuban property. During 1960, while on a trip to Italy, Novack
in company with Charles Tourine (Charlie the Blade), lunched at
the Excelsior Hotel, Naples, with Charles Luciano (Lucky
Luciano). During August, 1962, Novack spent two days in Atlantic
City, New Jersey, with Sam Giancana of Chicago, Illinois, and
Joseph Bonnano of Tuscon, Arizona. Leaders of the Cosa Nostra
in the United States such as Giancana are given complimentary ac-
comodations at the Fontainebleau during the winter vacation
season.

"On March 1, 1961, Novack paid $5,000 by check to Allen
Smiley (Aaron Smehoff), a notorious West Coast racketeer and
extortionist, who is a former member of Murder, Incorporated.
Novack utilizes the services of Joe Fischetti, brother of the notorious Rocco Fischetti of the Al Capone gang, to book name entertainers such as Frank Sinatra at the Fontainebleau.

"Max Eder has been closely associated with Novack for a
period of years in the operation of the Fontainebleau. Eder, a
notorious racketeer, is alleged to represent the Cosa Nostra interest
in the hotel. He has been observed giving orders to Novack as to

hotel operations and on the day following publicity of an Internal Revenue Service demand for certain financial records of the hotel, was in extended conference with Novack, Sam Giancana, and the hotel's attorney.

"Information has been received from reliable sources that major racketeers utilize the services of Novack and the hotel in cashing 'hot' checks for which no records are maintained."

Frustrated when the deal fell through, Novack kept trying. Sam (Radio) Winer, operator of a notorious Miami-Area nightclub known as the "Bonfire," introduced Novack to George Thompson, a member of the UBP. Winer, it should be mentioned in passing, made a habit of sending Christmas turkeys to Chesler's old friend Trigger Mike Coppola. He was happy to help an important man like Novack, and Thompson was assured of a $100,000 reward if he could secure an exemption certificate.

Thompson tried and failed. Not even Sands could veto the Governor's orders from London. Angry, Thompson switched over to the PLP and defeated a UBP man in the 1967 election. But that's all he achieved.

Another example of Justice Department "activity" is supplied in the case of Sir Roland Symonette. On April 1, 1966, a department official met with Sir Roland "and asked his advice as to what could be done to effect the deportation of Ritter, Courtney, and Brudner. A memo of the discussion says in part:

"Sir Roland stated that there is a split in the United Bahamian Party between himself and Sir Stafford Sands over the question of gambling in general and the three American racketeers in particular. Sir Roland expressed the opinion that Sands at the present moment is in a more powerful position party-wise than himself.

"Sir Roland warned that due to his position as the party leader in the Bahamas, he might possibly be required to publicly attack the United States State Department and Justice Department for pressuring the Bahamian government. However, unofficially he desires that we keep the pressure up as this will give him a stronger hand in effecting the deportation.

"Sir Roland was very frank in his appraisal of Sir Stafford

Sands as being a man of extremely high talent, but one who seems to have a blind spot as far as honesty is concerned."

That the ex-rum-runner's friendship was considered worth cultivating was demonstrated in October 1966, when—according to a memorandum—the Justice Department was told by State:

"Sir Roland Symonette, Premier of the Bahamas, owns a small inter-island shipping company whose ships on occasion put into the Port of Miami. Several years ago the United States Maritime Commission issued a regulation requiring the filing of schedules of tariffs with the Commission by any line using the ports of the United States. The regulation called for a penalty of $1,000 per day after a certain date if the tariffs were not so filed.

"By the time Sir Roland heard of the regulation his fines had amounted to $700,000. The Maritime Commission has referred the case to the Civil Division of Justice and the Civil Division is attempting to compromise the case for $5,000.

"——— expressed the opinion that in the day to day operations of the State Department vis a vis the Government of the Bahamas, it would inure to the benefit of the United States to drop the matter. ——— is of the opinion that if we can get Civil Division to drop the case and let it be known through State that we did same, we would greatly benefit in our continuing Bahamas inquiry."

But presumably this type of "activity" was not what Governor Grey had in mind when he accused Justice of allowing "this bunch of baboons" to take control of the government. Just before they took over, Lansky's men managed one final coup.

Whether "the three mongrels," as Allen Manus called Ritter, Courtney, and Brudner, would have indeed been ejected from the casinos on Grand Bahama had the UBP won the election is a question that can't be answered. There can be no doubt, however, that the trio made plans for any eventuality.

On January 10, 1967—election day—an article of agreement was drawn up and signed on Grand Bahama. Signing as "lessee" was the Grand Bahama Amusements, Ltd., and as "Lessors" were

Ritter, Courtney, and Brudner. The agreement declared in part: "For the past three years the Lessors have been employed in supervisory capacities by the Lessee to operate and manage the aforesaid casinos and pursuant to said employment have allowed the Lessee to utilize their personal files and records containing the names of clients located throughout the United States including the credit ratings and addresses thereof.

"The Lessors are terminating their employment with the Lessee on 15th January A.D. 1967 and the said Lessee believes that its continued use and custody of the said files and records is absolutely essential to the proper conduct of its business in the future."

The Agreement continued with provision for the Lessors to "lease and rent" the files for ten years. Basically, the files were those lists of suckers compiled by the three gamblers over the years—each name complete with a code number which indicated how much credit the sucker could be safely granted. Payment for this data was provided in the following clause: "The Lessee for the said use and possession of said files and records agrees to pay to the Lessors by way of rental the sum of Two million One hundred thousand United States dollars ($2,100,000 U.S.) payable in Ten (10) annual installments of Two hundred and Ten thousand United States dollars ($210,000 U.S.) commencing 1st February, A.D. 1968 and terminating 1st November, A.D. 1977 and further agree that the said annual rental will be paid in the following manner: each installment shall be divided into three (3) equal parts and each of the said Lessors shall be paid Seventy thousand United States dollars ($70,000 U.S.) a year in Four (4) equal payments of Seventeen thousand Five hundred United States dollars ($17,500 U.S.) payable on the First day of February, May, August and November during each year of the term hereby created in such manner and place as will be designated by each lessor simultaneously with the executing of this agreement."

Other provisions of the Agreement provided promissory notes totaling the full $2,100,000 should be executed and delivered to the Lessors with the execution of the agreement. The Lessee agreed to "establish and maintain a separate bank account of Two hundred and Ten thousand United States dollars ($210,000 U.S.) equivalent to the amount to be paid annually to the Lessors."

The boys were making certain a future government could not cancel the deal. The Royal Commission of Inquiry later called the agreement "one of the tightest contracts ever drawn by lessors." It added this pertinent comment: "The Agreement was designed to permit the real masters in this casino enterprise to depart without hard feelings, for who could feel aggrieved at an income of $70,000 a year from an asset that was worth virtually nothing to the owners?"

Of course Lansky's automatic cut of 25 percent reduced each man's income by $17,500 (U.S.) a year. Still, it was good retirement income for three veteran gamblers who had grown old in Lansky's service. Now if only they could stay out of United States Attorney Robert Morgenthau's clutches, all would be well.

They tried.

Permitted to remain in the islands pending the Royal Commission investigation—primarily because they were wanted as witnesses—the boys hired Edward Bennett Williams, the famed criminal lawyer, to make a deal with Morgenthau. They paid Williams $50,000 for the task, but he failed. However, he did draft that air-tight Agreement.

Late in July, Courtney decided to take off. Lack of a passport didn't bother him. Back in 1965, with help from Police Commissioner Nigel Morris, he visited London to help Dino Cellini "recruit" more students for that well-known educational institution he was operating there. On that occasion his nationality was listed as stateless on a special certification of identification provided by the helpful Morris.

On July 24, 1967, Courtney—using his real name of Morris Schmertzler—boarded a jet at Nassau and took off for Israel via London. Five weeks passed before his departure became public knowledge. Nassau officials could only speculate that the trip had been arranged with the government of Israel. United States officials, noting that Max Orovitz had many investments in Israel, assumed he had done the arranging.

Shortly thereafter, Frank Ritter also landed in Israel. Brudner, who had long claimed to be in poor health, waited awhile and then surrendered in New York. Entering a plea of not guilty to gambling charges contained in four indictments, he was released on $100,000 bond.

Apparently new word was passed to officials in Israel, for suddenly Ritter and Courtney appeared in New York and surrendered. They too posted bail and were released. Morgenthau's long fight had paid off. The three gamblers could say with equal justice, however, that their long flight had paid off too.

Meanwhile, the "heat" caused a comic-strip hero trouble. The Nassau *Guardian* noted on August 19 that it was dropping a strip featuring "Davy Jones." The editor explained that Davy "started out apparently to deal with dope and gambling in the Bahamas. The first caption, which made my hair stand on end was one which read, 'The mob owns a gambling casino in the Bahamas and the weekly take is a couple of million.'

"For legal reasons," continued the editor, "the *Guardian* has discontinued the strip. Watch for something new on the comic page."

The effort as noted earlier to break out of Grand Bahama and establish gambling on heavily populated New Providence Island began on June 8, 1965, when Sands made application for a Certificate of Exemption to permit a casino on Paradise Island in Nassau Bay. Although the Governor in Council had earlier rejected a very similar proposal from Huntington Hartford, it now approved Sands's request. Apparently, according to the Justice Department memorandum, Ben Novack's plea for Cat Cay was scheduled to be approved in August, but the deal failed—at least temporarily.

Unaware of the plans Lansky had for him, Sands moved ahead with Paradise Island. He notified the Secretary to the Cabinet that he represented: Mary Carter Paint Company; Paradise Island Limited; Bahama Hotel Company Limited; Paradise Island Realty Limited; Paradise Island Enterprises Limited; and C & R Limited.

According to the plan worked out with Hartford, the frustrated grocery store heir would convey everything he owned on Paradise Island to his own company, Beach Head Limited. The Mary Carter Paint Company, after incorporating Paradise Island Limited as a development company, would buy Hartford's properties for $10,475,000.

The next step in the complicated program called for Geoffrey Russell, a hotel man in Nassau, to incorporate Bahama Hotel Company Limited and buy ten acres of land from Paradise Island Limited. On the land would be built a five hundred-room hotel to cost more than $10 million. In addition, Paradise Island Limited would build a one hundred-room hotel.

Paradise Island Realty Limited would be jointly formed by Paradise Island Limited and Mrs. Wallace Groves. Her husband, the ex-convict, was still using his wife to front for him. Paradise Island Realty Limited would lease a parcel of land from Paradise Island Limited, and construct a casino building at an estimated cost of $3 million. A similar building on another plot of land would be built for slot machines. After all, some people felt one-armed bandits detracted from the dignity of craps.

Finally Mrs. Groves would incorporate Paradise Island Enterprises Limited and be the owner of all shares. Paradise Island Realty Limited would then sublease the casino buildings to Paradise Enterprises on terms that would ensure that 50 percent of the net profits of Enterprises would be returned through the Realty Company to Paradise Island Limited.

It was a typical Sands-syndicate arrangement, designed to frustrate investigators and permit money to flow in many directions once the casino began operating. The Royal Commission of Inquiry called it "a complex of companies unnecessarily interwoven in their responsibilities, thus providing facilities for inter-company financial manoeuvres as with the complex on Grand Bahama."

Some adjustments were immediately necessary, however. On November 25 Sands gave notice that Russell had dropped out of the picture due to his inability to raise the necessary money to build the hotel. Replacing Bahama Hotel Company Limited in the scheme of things was Island Hotel Limited—a wholly owned subsidiary of the Mary Carter Paint Company. It took over the task of building the hotel.

Sands announced that a bridge connecting New Providence with Paradise Island would be constructed by March 31, 1967. The hotel was to be open by December 31, 1967, in time to catch the suckers in a New Year's Eve mood.

C & R Limited was created as a precautionary measure to protect its owners, the Mary Carter Paint Company. A "deferred" Certificate of Exemption was awarded C & R—officially, at least, to be used only if the complicated arrangements involving Mrs. Groves and Hartford failed. In view of later developments, the creation of C & R is rather intriguing.

The certificate awarded Paradise Enterprises covered more than the island in the bay. The company was given exclusive casino rights on all of New Providence "and all other adjacent islands and cays within ten miles." The venerable Bahamian Club was purchased as part of the deal, and was to be closed as soon as the new casino was ready.

Quite explicit was the certificate in detailing the type of entertainment to be furnished casino patrons. Item eleven provided: "The Company shall procure that from the New Casino Opening Date and for so long thereafter as this Certificate shall continue in force on at least Six (6) days a week during at least Forty-four (44) weeks in every calendar year there shall be presented at the New Casino twice nightly a lavish and spectacular entertainment of no less than Seventy-five (75) minutes duration and so that such entertainment shall employ the services of not less than Fifty (50) artistes dancers showgirls and musicians provided that during such time as a star performer is engaged at a salary in excess of Five thousand dollars ($5,000) per week the total number of artistes dancers showgirls and musicians need not be more than Twenty-five (25)."

A Justice Department memorandum, dated January 1966, attempted to clarify the Paradise Island corporate haze and fix ultimate responsibility. It noted in part: "During 1964 and 1965 negotiations have been conducted between Hartford and Mary

Carter Paints, Inc., of Tampa, Florida, for the purchase of Paradise Island. These negotiations are to be culminated by the signing of a contract between Hartford and Mary Carter Paints on Friday, January 14, 1966, the principal provisions of which are:

"(1) Hartford is to turn over 80% of his holdings on Paradise Island to Mary Carter Paints, retaining 20% for himself.

"(2) Management control of Paradise Island will be vested in Mary Carter Paints.

"(3) Mary Carter Paints will immediately build a 500-room hotel on the Island with 1,500 more rooms to be added on the Island within the next twelve years.

"(4) A gambling casino will be built on the Island adjacent to the hotel. The gambling exemption for such casino has already been granted by the Bahamian Government.

"(5) A motel will be constructed adjacent to Paradise Beach. The motel rates will be moderate.

"(6) A bridge will be constructed from Nassau to Paradise Island. The Bahamian Government has approved same.

"Hartford states that the casino is to be owned as follows:

"(1) $\frac{5}{9}$ of all shares by Mary Carter Paints.

"(2) $\frac{4}{9}$ of all shares by Grand Bahamas Amusements.

"(3) An unknown percentage "off the top" as an inducement to the casino operators.

"(4) Hartford to own 20% of Mary Carter Paints' share or $\frac{1}{9}$.

"Mary Carter Paints will be in control of Paradise Island with the exception of the Casino which Groves will control.

"The atmosphere seems ripe for a Lansky skim."

Based on what had happened on Grand Bahama, the Justice Department official who wrote that memorandum and made that judgment was justified. However, he greatly underestimated the chairman of the board's ambitions and abilities. Still ahead was the election of 1967. The victory of the PLP, although limited in scope, was decisive to Lansky's plans.

The UBP had gambled in calling for a Royal Commission to investigate the gambling scandal—and it had lost. With the Bay

Street Boys out of office, any chance of restricting the probe was lost. Furthermore, the findings of the Commission would help keep the UBP from regaining power.

So it was that on March 4, 1967, the formation of a Royal Commission of Inquiry headed by Sir Ranulph Bacon was announced. Other members included Robin E. Auld, an attorney, and John E. O'Connell, detective superintendent of Scotland Yard. Later Joseph A. Wharton, a Queen's Counsel, and Vernon Turley, an accountant, were added.

The Commission assembled in Nassau and was sworn in on March 13, 1967. Three days later the first hearing began.

It was then that Sir Stafford Sands announced that Mrs. Groves and the Bahamas Amusements Company had relinquished their whole interest in the Paradise Island venture to the Mary Carter Paint Company.

Chesler had been forced out first. The financial force represented by Manus-Morgan had followed. Then came Ritter-Courtney-Brudner, the last obvious link to Meyer Lansky. Sands and the Bay Street Boys had been next. And now Groves, the man who, with Sands, had started it all in conversations off Little Whale Cay, had been shut out of Nassau and left to wither on Grand Bahama.

A year later, in 1968, Groves and the president of Benguet Consolidated, Inc., announced that an agreement had been reached for Benguet to acquire about 66⅔ percent of the Port Authority's outstanding shares in a transaction amounting to $80 million in cash or common stock.

Observers first assumed Groves had abdicated as King of Grand Bahama, but upon closer examination concluded the deal was but a "paper" transaction which permitted Benguet to control the Port Authority while leaving Groves in command of Benguet. Records proved that Allen and Company of New York had been active in Benguet for many years and Allen had held a minority interest in the Port Authority since shortly after its formation.

The new Premier issued a press release welcoming the proposed sale. Later, however, after it was noted that under the terms of the Hawksbill Creek Act the shift—even if it was only a paper transaction—had to be approved by the government, Pindling changed his tune. Some of his ministers began pressing for a new look at the Hawksbill Creek Act and the Premier decided to issue a new press release stating the sale to Benguet had not been approved.

In the weeks prior to the announcement of the deal with Benguet, there had been what one business writer called "an almost unbelievable demand for Benguet stock." After Pindling's first press release, the stock rose by approximately $2.00 per share. After the second press release, it dropped back where it had been.

Exactly what was going on, few people knew. It seemed obvious, however, that Groves was attempting to arrange for his kingdom to be annexed by that mysterious empire of international finance where Meyer Lansky had so long been powerful. Benguet was an international company, based in the Philippines, and active in gold and copper mining. It also owned controlling interests in other enterprises.

Regardless of the outcome, Groves had made a remarkable comeback since his release from prison and would, no doubt, be permitted to retain his title if not his authority. In that respect he was better off than Sir Stafford Sands.

With his millions stashed away in Swiss and Canadian banks, Sands began liquidating his Bahamas holdings shortly after the January 10, 1967, election. The grocery chain, the family mainstay for many years with near-monopoly status in the islands, was sold in May to the Winn-Dixie Stores. After many trips to Europe and other islands around the Caribbean, Sands resigned his seat in the House of Assembly and left the Bahamas. Spain became his new home, permitting him to exchange notes with Bastista, who now lived there as well. Paul Adderly, the intelligent if cautious critic who broke with the PLP when he feared it was too revolutionary, commented in the Bahamas *Observer*: "The effective leader of the UBP silently stole away and put an end to the end of an era. Nobody seemed to be sorry, nobody seemed to care, least of all the UBP. It has been a strange but not entirely unexpected end in the best tradition of a deposed dictator."

Meyer Lansky, reading those words, surely recalled the night eight years earlier when he fled on the heels of a deposed dictator. The lessons of Cuba had been well applied in the Bahamas. This time the flight of a dictator meant not defeat for the chairman of the board but ultimate and complete victory.

The process that began when bootleggers alone had cash and credit was approaching its sophisticated climax. Lansky, his empire self-sustaining, could now afford to be invisible in a country where gambling had become an economic necessity to maintain achieved political power.

To win victory the PLP had not promised to abolish gambling but to use the government's share for public good rather than private profit. It had also promised to see that the government got a bigger cut of the pie. Indeed, an increase was essential if the PLP's goals in education and public works were to be met. Should anyone object on moral grounds, the PLP could always blame the UBP for introducing gambling on a ten-year basis.

By thus allowing gambling to become a source of public funds, a substitute for other forms of taxation, stability for the gambling industry could be accomplished in the backward Bahamas as it had been achieved in barren Nevada. With stability a fact, direct control no longer was necessary on even the political level. A retreat into the shadows of international high finance was not only possible but desirable. The chairman of the board had every reason to feel pleased as on Paradise Island the Mary Carter Paint Company took over. Mary Carter was such an innocent-sounding name, it was a shame to change it.

The Mary Carter Paint Company was no stranger to the Bahamas. In 1963 the company bought 1,300 acres along Little Hawksbill Creek, about three miles from the center of Freeport. Another 2,200 adjacent acres were under option. Work had begun on the development of Queen's Cove and 1,729 building sites had been platted. Some of the lots had been sold to corrupt sheriff's deputies who protected the syndicate's varied assortment of rackets in Dade County, Florida. A citizen's revolt in 1966 caused Dade

County to abolish its system of elective sheriffs, and some of the deputies had need of a second home.[1]

Mary Carter took over the project in July 1963, and expanded it. Why Wallace Groves and Lou Chesler were willing to permit a rival company to enter the lot-selling field on their home island is a bit of a mystery. It will be remembered that the General Development Company, engaged in the same business in Florida, refused to permit Chesler to use its funds to create Devco.

The land already under option was purchased by Mary Carter from the Port Authority and $1,300,000 was spent in developing it. A 100,000-gallon water system, a landscaped recreation area, and a hard-surfaced road from Queen's Cove to the airport were among the items constructed. Prices for the lots ranged from $3,195 to $27,995, depending upon size and location. So successful was the project in the kingdom of Wallace Groves that Mary Carter bought an additional 2,900 acres and announced that King's Cove would be developed as well.

At the same time Mary Carter was negotiating to buy land on Grand Bahama, it was loaning $100,000 to an outfit known as LPF, Inc. The letters stood for Leo F. Popell, and the company owned warehouses and office buildings in Miami, which it leased to Leo F. Popell, Inc. And therein hangs a tale which some observers have advanced as a possible reason why Mary Carter was so welcome on Grand Bahama.

The story begins in 1961 when Jay Weiss, that friend of Alvin Malnik, formed a company to obtain American rights to a Swedish toothpaste known as Vademecum. Weiss had just been forced by federal and state pressure to sell a liquor empire. He had cash to spare. Among the stockholders of his new company was State Attorney Richard E. Gerstein, who, during the liquor probe, had investigated charges that the liquor empire had been linked to a "protection system."

Weiss and his friends sold the rights to the toothpaste, in June 1962, to the Leo F. Popell company for 60,000 shares of stock, which was then transferred to the newly formed Jayedwall Corpora-

[1] See *Syndicate in the Sun.*

tion. A Popell auditor later estimated the 60,000 shares were worth $861,000 more than the value of the assets acquired by Popell. Yet to come was an aggressive promotion campaign which featured, among other things, a "hospitality house" staffed with beautiful girls. The stock of the Popell company suddenly started climbing from its base price of $3.00 per share. When the stock reached $40 a share, there was a three-for-one stock split—and suddenly the bottom fell out.

Weiss and two of his associates turned their shares over to none other than that young genius Alvin Malnik. He disposed of it at exactly the right time and collected a neat $54,000 commission. Gerstein, who had received 2,400 shares, also made a comfortable if not gaudy profit.

Down, down went the Popell stock. The loan of $100,000 by Mary Carter was not enough to halt the fall. Later the Securities & Exchange Commission charged that fraud had been employed in the rapid rise of the stock. When Popell was unable to make the first payment on the loan, Mary Carter threw the company into bankruptcy—an inevitable development under the circumstances. Mary Carter treated Popell very gently. At a public auction on November 1, 1963, the physical property of Popell's company was bought by Mary Carter for $25,000. Generously, Mary Carter allowed Popell to use the premises after reorganization of his company—a gesture that Malnik, who had friends on Grand Bahama, surely appreciated. After all, Popell and his company had been used as a vehicle for a stock promotion from which Malnik and Weiss profitted. It was only fair that his fall should be cushioned.

Weiss and Malnik, with Gerstein picking up some crumbs, went on (as has been previously mentioned) to promote Scopitone. It was a deal in which many top hoods were involved, including Lansky's old friend Jimmy Blue Eyes. Profits were large but the interest of United States Attorney Robert Morgenthau was aroused and Malnik decided to curtail his international activity. With Weiss, he concentrated upon the Penthouse Lounge atop a Teamster Union-financed apartment building on Miami's infamous 79th

Street Causeway. The place became home and social headquarters for top gangsters such as Tommy (the Enforcer) Altumura. When Tommy was murdered in 1967, State Attorney Gerstein was once more forced to investigate the Weiss-Malnik business interests. A public hearing conducted by State Senator Robert Shevin caused more pressure on Malnik than Gerstein's probe.

Meanwhile, Mary Carter, which had money to loan in 1963, needed cash in 1966 when the deal with Huntington Hartford was consummated. According to the company:

> On July 13, 1966, the board of directors authorized the sale of $2,000,000 of its 6½% Series A convertible subordinated notes and $1,000,000 of its 6½% Series B convertible subordinated notes, which by their terms were convertible into Class A common stock at the initial rate of $5000 per share. All the Series A notes and $150,000 of the Series B notes were thereupon purchased by five persons. . . . At the time of the sales of the Series A notes, the company granted an option to purchase 25,000 shares of Class A common stock at $5.00 per share to Kleiner, Bell & Co., in payment for services rendered in connection with the placement of the Series A notes. The latter firm purchased $100,000 face amount of Series B notes, which it has agreed to convert into 20,000 shares of Class A stock.

Buying $1,750,000 of the Series A notes was the American National Insurance Company of Galveston, Texas. It is a company with a history as interesting as Galveston itself.

Jean Lafitte, a pirate as famous as any of those based in Nassau, founded Galveston after the War of 1812 made him a legend at New Orleans. It was a corrupt city then and it has continued the tradition to modern times. American National, an insurance company, was chartered in 1905 by William L. Moody, Jr. When he died in 1954, he owned half of the wealth of the city and vice was the principal industry of the city. Upon Moody's death, much of his fortune was left to the Moody Foundation and it continued to control American National as well as several other large financial institutions of the Southwest. A grandson, Robert L. Moody, took charge of the family interests.

In June 1966, Robert Moody almost became controlling stockholder of the syndicate's favorite south Florida bank—the Bank of Miami Beach. Jules Sokoloff, that friend of gambler Ed Curd, was trying to get out of the bank after the Yarmouth Castle disaster put him on the spot. Moody agreed to buy 65,541 of the bank's 120,000 outstanding shares at $8.86 a share. He filed an application with the Florida Banking Commissioner for the necessary approval. The sale was blocked when former owner Ben Cohen of New York filed suit to stop it. Cohen claimed that the controlling stock he earlier had sold to Sokoloff had been pledged back to him pending payment of a series of $5,000 notes the Canadian had given him as part of the purchase price, and only eight of the total twenty-two notes were paid.

Another example of private enterprise in an amoral society:

Moody made yet another effort to get control of a Miami-area bank and was temporarily successful. The Curtiss National Bank of Miami Springs—to the west of Miami—was the new target and Moody got operating control long enough to make a loan from the bank to Martin Von Zamft, former president of the Bank of Miami Beach and the equally unhappy Five Points National Bank.

Von Zamft needed the loan from Moody's bank to buy the Bankers & Telephone Employees Insurance Company of Pennsylvania. As collateral for the loan, he offered a million dollars in assorted stocks, which was refused. He then produced some blue chips—IBM stock—but he requested that if it was ever offered for sale he would be permitted to substitute other stock in its place.

A sharp-eyed investigator for the Securities & Exchange Commission, who had helped convict such stock manipulators as Louis Wolfson, became suspicious. He asked the FBI for serial numbers of some stolen IBM stock and discovered the numbers matched the serial numbers of Von Zamft's collateral. The ex-banker, already awaiting trial for looting for Five Points bank, was again indicted along with several colleagues. Included was Richard Gladwell, former captain in the Dade County sheriff's office. Gladwell resigned during the 1966 reform drive and complained about being forced to live "in a goldfish bowl." Some of his colleagues owned lots in Queen's Cove.

The Moody-controlled American National had, at the time it

helped Mary Carter buy Paradise Island, large investments in Las Vegas casinos and other Nevada projects. Invested in the Sahara Tahoe Corporation was $1,940,466, and in Sands, Inc., $2,460,517. Other investments in Clark County, Nevada, totaled $33,814,000 and elsewhere in Nevada the total was $19,808,000.

In March 1968, after the casino on Paradise Island opened, it was announced that Continental Connector Corporation had agreed in principle to buy the Dunes Hotel and Casino in Las Vegas. The announcement came just three months after Continental Connectors came under the control of a "western banking group." Spokesman of the group was E. Perry Thomas, chairman of the Bank of Las Vegas. Associated with him were William I. Vogler and R. A. Furbush, chairman and president respectively of the American National Life Insurance Company of Galveston.

Meanwhile, couriers continued to deliver cash from Las Vegas casinos to Meyer Lansky at his headquarters in the Singapore Hotel on Miami Beach.

A final note about Mary Carter's financing of the Paradise Island venture concerns Kleiner, Bell & Co., the underwriter who was rewarded with 25,000 shares of Class A common stock for helping make the deal with American National. Stylon Corporation of Milford, Massachusetts, utilized the services of Kleiner, Bell to sell $3 million in convertible debentures in 1967 and paid the company a 6 percent commission. Purpose of the sale was to enable Stylon to buy Adobe Brick and Tile Company of Hollywood, Florida, from Allen Manus—former owner of the Lucayan Beach Hotel on Grand Bahama.

A coincidence, perhaps.

The Royal Commission of Inquiry conducted a series of hearings in March and April and in August and September 1967. Despite earlier fears of a whitewash, the commission did a good job within its limitations of time and jurisdiction. The United States Justice Department cooperated unofficially but declined to provide a witness who could put much of its information on the record. While the UBP came in for the most caustic criticism, the commission cast curious eyes at Mike McLaney and his efforts to help the PLP. McLaney testified at length, but apparently was unable to convince the commission of the rightness of his cause. In its final report, the commission stated:

> The Premier, while admitting the indebtedness of his Party, told us that, subsequent to the election, he had made a number of enquiries about Mr. McLaney which had convinced him, with hindsight, that he and his Party would be ill-advised to continue their association with him. On the evidence of his past activities, which we heard in detail from the Commissioner of Police, we formed the opinion that Mr. McLaney was an unscrupulous individual who was playing on the worldly inexperience of the Premier and the PLP with the aim of manoeuvring them into a position whereby they would feel obliged to "do a deal." There is little doubt that the deal would have involved some sort of gambling concession. We regard Mr. McLaney as a thoroughly dangerous person who is likely to do nothing but harm to the Bahamas.

Despite the report, and various unflattering magazine articles in the United States, McLaney refused to leave Nassau. Nor did Premier Pindling do anything to discourage his remaining there. McLaney fought back, filing huge libel suits against all who, he said, had defamed him. Not content, his attorney wrote to Attorney General Ramsey Clark charging that Internal Revenue Service Special Agent Paul Mahan had been offered a job by one of the magazines. Mahan, noted the lawyer, had conducted "an interminable tax investigation" of McLaney. He asked Clark to "advise Mr. Mahan of our intention to take any steps necessary to protect Mr. McLaney from any further disclosures of information taken from Government records that could be misconstrued and misused in a manner which would cause Mr. McLaney damage."

The attorney signing the letter to Clark was Ronald S. Golub. He proved to be the son of Sam Golub, the man who steered Huntington Hartford to Alvin Malnik back when Hartford was trying to get a certificate of exemption for a casino on Paradise Island.

"Just one big happy family," commented the unflappable Mahan.

McLaney, meanwhile, bought an old hotel, the Cumberland House, located on the hill just northwest of stately Government House, and converted it into a place for steaks. The move made it necessary for Ed Curd, the old Kentucky gambler who had been bookie for Frank Costello and friend of Jules Sokoloff, to move. Curd bought a huge mansion just east of Government House and connected to it by a private drive. Governor Grey was becoming encircled.

McLaney had remained when Lansky fled Havana behind Batista. As the months passed in Nassau, it became apparent that Pindling did not intend to follow Castro's example and toss him out.

Another straw in the wind was the presence of Eddie Cellini, Dino's brother. Dino had been deported from Grand Bahama and, later, from London, where he had worked at the casino known as the Colony Club with George Raft. Returning to Miami, Dino took charge of organizing gambling junkets to the Colony Club and to a new casino which opened in 1968 outside Lisbon, Portugal. Suckers signing up for the junket at $1,500 a head were promised roundtrip jet service, hotels, restaurants, and $1,500 in chips at the Casino Estoril. After four nights in Portugal, they would go to London, where, if their credit was still good, they could try their luck at the Colony Club for four more nights before jetting home.

While Dino was thus applying his talents to the syndicate's world-wide gambling empire, his brother, Eddie, was managing the Paradise Island casino at Nassau. Like his brother, Eddie was a graduate of the gambling dens of Steubenville, Ohio, and had done postgraduate work in the bust-out joints of Newport, Kentucky, before moving on to Havana. When Castro stopped the Big Crap Game there, Eddie returned to Newport to become a "collector" for the Tropicana Club. It was at the Tropicana in May 1961 that reform candidate for sheriff, George Ratterman, was arrested in bed with a stripper after being drugged in a Cincinnati hotel.[2] Ratterman proved his innocence and won elec-

[2] See *Syndicate Wife*.

tion. Newport's casinos closed. Eddie Cellini was one of hundreds of gamblers suddenly in need of a job. The opening of action in the Bahamas was a welcome opportunity for Dino's younger brother.

So it was that when Sands arranged for Groves and Mary Carter to buy the old Bahamian Club as a first step in transferring the certificate of exemption to Paradise, Eddie became casino manager. He continued to manage after Groves pulled out, and he moved with the certificate across the bridge to Paradise Island. Mary Carter officials were warned of Eddie's background but they were apparently powerless to remove him. The old days of bust-out gambling seemed very far away in the jet age. Yet Eddie Cellini was still a young man.

The official opening of the new casino in December 1967 amounted to little more then the unlocking of doors. Premier Pindling, taking note of the Christmas season, said he hoped the casino would provide great "gifts" for the Bahamian people.

Early in January 1968 came the gala opening, and it bore no small resemblance to the scene four years earlier at the Lucayan Beach on Grand Bahama. Once again, Serge Obolensky gathered a collection of freeloaders seldom equaled. Suzy Knickerbocker, the syndicated society columnist, was agog for weeks. Here's how she described the upcoming event:

> The junket of international swells that good Col. Serge Obolensky has gathered together to make Paradise Island (Nassau) casino opening scene in early January boggles De-brett's, the Almanch de Gotha and maybe even the Social Register.
>
> If the whole thing turns out as gala as it sounds, some of them might just stay over there for good and never go back to their palaces and their yachts, do you suppose? No, I guess not.
>
> All the gilded guests from Spain, Italy and France will meet the gilded guests from England in London and fly off to Nassau.
>
> The just completed casino, decorated by Le Tulle White of New York, is situated on the grounds of the Paradise Island Hotel. The ground floor of the casino contains a theater lounge, the Bahamian Club restaurant, and a private gaming room in case you wish to gamble in semi-solitary splendor.

The Bahamian Club restaurant is done in charcoal, white, silver and taupe, with charcoal velvet banquettes and arm chairs upholstered in flower print.

Candlelight and chandeliers are reflected in large mirrors to achieve the utmost romantic atmosphere. Oh, kiss me quick!

Shortly after the new casino opened, Premier. Pindling called for new elections. For more than a year he had been content with his narrow margin of control. It provided an excuse for moving slowly on campaign promises and it also discouraged any internal battles for power within the PLP. There were some leaders who looked askance at Pindling's dealings in blueberries and the continued presence in Nassau of Mike McLaney, but loyalty to the party prevented any open break.

The death of a PLP member of the house forced the issue, however, and on March 10, 1968, the black majority of the Bahamas gave Pindling an overwhelming victory at the polls. The PLP took 29 of 38 house seats. The UBP dropped from 18 to 7 seats, winning only in those districts containing white majorities.

Paul Adderly, the Negro moderate who broke with Pindling to form a splinter group, suggested after the election that his party would now become the official opposition to the PLP. He commented, "Nothing stands in our way. The UBP has been removed. The defeat was too final, too complete."

Perhaps Meyer Lansky agreed. For now came the final move in the chess game he had planned nine years earlier as he fled Havana. The Mary Carter Paint Company suddenly sold its paint division, reorganized itself and became Resorts International, Inc.

Control of Resorts International soon passed into the hands of Investors Overseas Services. The Geneva-based company was described by *Fortune* magazine in 1968 as "by far the world's largest financial sales organization and one of the largest privately held financial institutions of any kind, with control of more than $1 billion in investment funds." It was organized by Bernard Cornfeld, a man whose background is as international as the company he founded. Cornfeld was born in 1928 in Instanbul of a Romanian father and a Russian mother, and was brought to the United States in 1932.

Under Cornfeld's direction, IOS grew rapidly into a complex international financial empire with branch offices in fifty countries and scores of subsidiaries from Nassau to Hong Kong. According to *Fortune,* "the administrative headquarters in Geneva, helped by systems-development teams in the Bahamas, coordinates the finances of the entire empire."

The Securities & Exchange Commission has been complaining about IOS for years. *Fortune,* in a long article, explained that the IOS principle of confidentiality was believed by SEC to conceal "hot money" from criminal operations both in the Bahamas and Nevada. The article added the thought that it was possible Cornfeld couldn't reveal names of the owners of numbered accounts because IOS didn't even know who owned them.

The advantages of such an organization to organized crime in general and to the chairman of the board in particular could be immense. Indeed, organizations like IOS could be used as but another sophisticated step to launder gambling profits from Las Vegas and Paradise Island and permit the "clean" money to reappear anywhere on earth in vastly different guise.

In July 1968 plans were announced by IOS in Geneva to build a $40 million luxury apartment and club complex on the beach at Hallandale, Florida. The location was just east of Lansky's home in an area known for years as "Lanskyland."

Was some of Lansky's profit coming home? There was no way to be sure—thanks to the sophistication and secrecy of IOS. Lansky had become invisible.

Meanwhile, demands for additional casinos arose in Nassau. Spokesmen for other hotels insisted they were necessary to compete with Paradise Island. The virus was in the bloodstream to stay.

Organized crime had won its greatest victory. The process that began with the investment of bootleg profits was now complete and the shape of things to come was clear for all with eyes to see.

A PARTIAL CHRONOLOGY
OF EVENTS WITH WHICH
THIS BOOK IS CONCERNED:

1903—Meyer Lansky is born in Poland.

1913—Stafford Sands is born in Nassau; Louis Chesler is born in Canada.

1920—The Prohibition era brings economic boom to Bahamas.

1927—Joe Linsey convicted in New England.

1931—Maranzano is murdered by the Bugs & Meyer Mob.

1933—Prohibition era ends; economic slump in the Bahamas.

1934—National Syndicate formed along NRA lines.

1935—Thomas Dewey appointed special prosecutor in New York.

1937—Lansky operates in Havana.

Max Courtney takes bets from Lou Chesler.

Wallace Groves buys Little Whale Cay in Bahamas.

1938—Groves is indicted on mail fraud charges in New York.

1939—Lepke (Louis Buchalter) surrenders, ending "Big Heat."

World War II begins.

Sands creates legal machinery to permit gambling in Bahamas.

1940—Cleveland Syndicate expands into Newport, Kentucky.

1941—Pearl Harbor ends Lansky's Cuban venture for duration.

Groves sentenced to two years in federal prison.

1943—Operation Underworld features Lansky and Lucky Luciano.

Sir Harry Oakes murdered in Nassau.

1944—Batista loses election, flees Cuba for Florida.

1945—Lansky buys Colonial Inn near Hallandale; has piece of Beverly Club with Costello outside New Orleans; invades Las Vegas with Bugsy Siegel and Clifford Jones.

1946—Lou Chesler visits Miami Beach and makes new friends.

Groves buys Abaco Lumber Company on Grand Bahama Island.

Sands fails to get gambling monopoly for Bahamas.

Flamingo Club opens in Las Vegas with Lansky a silent partner.

1947—Lansky operates Arrowheard Club at Saratoga, N.Y.

1948—Lansky expands in Broward County, Florida; bankrolls Thunderbird with Cliff Jones and George Sadlo in Las Vegas.

1949—Cleveland Syndicate opens Desert Inn at Las Vegas and run joint ventures with Lansky in Miami.

1950—Kefauver Committee heat closes Florida casinos.
Sands appointed chairman of Development Board of Bahama.

1951—Ed Levinson moves to Las Vegas with Irving (Nig) Devine. Reform drives fail in Newport.

1952—Batista regains power in Cuba. Lansky plans his return to Havana.

1953—Groves proposes Grand Bahama development to Sands.
Lansky serves three months in jail for Saratoga gambling.

1954—Ed Levinson revealed as a secret owner of Flamingo in Las Vegas.
Lansky moves to Havana and promotes new laws there.

1955—Cleveland Syndicate takes over Nacional in Havana. Jake Lansky is pit boss.
Hawksbill Creek Act makes Groves King of Grand Bahama.

1957—Albert Anastasia tries to muscle in on Lansky—is murdered.
Lansky's use of Cliff Jones as front in Thunderbird becomes known.

1958—Bernard Goldfine exposed, and Sherman Adams and Maxwell Rabb resign White House jobs.
Mike McLaney "buys" Nacional from Cleveland Syndicate.

1959—Batista and Lansky flee Havana as Fidel Castro wins war.
Chesler buys Seven Arts stock.
Alvin Malnik graduates from law school.

1960—Lansky offers one million dollars for Bahamas gambling, Sands says.

Hawksbill Creek Act amended to encourage "tourism."

Chesler visits Grand Bahama as McLaney quits Havana.

1961—Robert F. Kennedy becomes U.S. Attorney General.

Allied Empire formed.

Bay of Pigs disaster ends Mafia hopes for Cuba.

Grand Bahama Development Company, Ltd., is formed.

George Ratterman survives frame to close Newport gambling.

1963—Lansky holds meetings with associates in Max Orovitz's office.

Sands reappointed to Executive Committee.

Bahamas Amusements Co., Ltd., is formed to run casino. Gets a Certificate of Exemption.

Isle of Man gambling becomes scandal.

Mary Carter Paint Company develops Queen's Cove.

1964—Cabinet system of government begins in Bahamas.

Lucayan Beach Hotel and Casino opens with Lansky men in charge.

Chesler is forced out of Devco and off Grand Bahama.

1965—Lansky visits his money in Switzerland.

Atlantic Acceptance collapses.

Ben Novack foiled in Cat Cay casino bid.

Sands gets okay for Paradise Island gambling casino to be operated by Groves and Mary Carter.

1966—Allan Witwer writes *The Ugly Bahamians* and is bought off.

Wall Street Journal exposes Bay Street Boys. Election is called.

Trigger Mike Coppola dies.

Dade County abolishes elective-sheriff system.

1967—PLP wins control in close election.

Sir Stafford Sands moves to Spain.

El Casino opens in Grand Bahama.

Bahamas Amusements withdraws from Paradise Island.

Royal Commission conducts gambling probe.

1968—Paradise Casino has grand opening.

Mary Carter Paint Company changes name to Resorts International, Inc.

IOS gets control of Resorts International.

Bay Street Boys suffer total defeat in new election.

Robert F. Kennedy, syndicate foe, is murdered.

Meyer Lansky becomes invisible.

Index